Animals, Biopolitics, Law

Lively Legalities

Typically, the legal investigation of nonhuman life, and of animal life in particular, is conducted through the discourse of animal rights. Within this discourse, legal rights are extended to certain nonhuman animals through the same liberal framework that has afforded human rights before it. *Animals, Biopolitics, Law* envisions the possibility of lively legalities that move beyond the humanist perspective. Drawing on an array of expertise—from law, geography, and anthropology, through animal studies and posthumanism, to science and technology studies—this interdisciplinary collection asks what, in legal terms, it means to be human and nonhuman, what it means to govern and to be governed, and what are the ethical and political concerns that emerge in the project of governing not only human but also more-than-human life.

Irus Braverman is Professor of Law and Adjunct Professor of Geography at University at Buffalo, The State University of New York. She is author of *Planted Flags: Trees, Land, and Law in Israel/Palestine* (2009), *Zooland: The Institution of Captivity* (2012), and *Wild Life: The Institution of Nature* (2015), and co-editor of *The Expanding Spaces of Law: A Timely Legal Geography* (2014).

Space, Materiality and the Normative

Series Editors: Andreas Philippopoulos-Mihalopoulos and Christian Borch

Space, Materiality and the Normative presents new ways of thinking about the connections between space and materiality from a normative perspective. At the interface of law, social theory, politics, architecture, geography and urban studies, the series is concerned with addressing the use, regulation and experience of space and materiality, broadly understood, and in particular with exploring their links and the challenges they raise for law, politics and normativity.

Books in this series:

Spatial Justice: Body, Lawscape, Atmosphere
Andreas Philippopoulos-Mihalopoulos

Urban Commons: Rethinking the City
Christian Borch and Martin Kornberger

A Jurisprudence of Movement: Common Law, Walking, Unsettling Place
Olivia Barr

Forthcoming:

Placing International Law: Authority, Jurisdiction, Technique
Fleur Johns, Shaun McVeigh, Sundhya Pahuja, Thomas Skouteris, and Robert Wai

Spacing Law and Politics: The Constitution and Representation of the Juridical
Leif Dahlberg

Animals, Biopolitics, Law

Lively Legalities

Edited by Irus Braverman

Routledge
Taylor & Francis Group
LONDON AND NEW YORK

First published 2016
by Routledge
2 Park Square, Milton Park, Abingdon, Oxfordshire OX14 4RN

and by Routledge
711 Third Avenue, New York, NY 10017

First issued in paperback 2017

Routledge is an imprint of the Taylor & Francis Group, an informa business

British Library Cataloguing in Publication Data
A catalogue record for this book is available from the British Library

Library of Congress Cataloging-in-Publication Data
Animals, biopolitics, law : lively legalities / Edited by
Irus Braverman.
pages cm. — (Space, materiality and the normative)
Includes bibliographical references and index.
ISBN 978-1-138-94311-7 (hbk) — ISBN 978-1-315-67273-1 (ebk) 1. Animal rights—Philosophy. 2. Human-animal relationships—Philosophy. 3. Animal welfare—Law and legislation. 4. Bioethics. I. Braverman, Irus, 1970– editor.
K3620.A97 2016
344.04'9—dc23
2015030106

ISBN 13: 978-1-138-05791-3 (pbk)
ISBN 13: 978-1-138-94311-7 (hbk)

Typeset Baskerville
by Apex CoVantage, LLC

For Gregor

Contents

Acknowledgments

The idea for this book was born during the 2013 Annual Law and Society Association meeting in Boston. Listening to presentation after presentation, it became painfully clear to me that the sociolegal community, at least the hundreds of scholars present in that particular room, seldom paid attention to anything other than human subjects (with the exception of corporations). A quick survey that I conducted then of two central law and society journals, *Law and Society Review* and *Law and Social Inquiry*, backed up my initial intuition: of 265 articles, 165 book reviews, and 63 review essays published between 2008 and 2013, only two were dedicated to questions concerning nonhuman animals. Other nonhuman organisms have typically been even less visible in sociolegal scholarship.

This book is an attempt to engage prominent thinkers from a variety of disciplines, who have been dealing with questions about nonhumans in their work, to consider the role of law in the lives of nonhumans and the potentiality for lively legalities that take such lives into account. The book collection emerged from a two-day workshop in Buffalo, New York on September 11 and 12, 2014. Before, during, and after this workshop the various contributors—anthropologists, geographers, environmental historians, and legal scholars from the United States, Canada, England, Scotland, and Australia—engaged with each other's work and with the difficulties of talking across disciplinary divides. It was particularly challenging to talk about law in this context, for this has largely been an unexplored terrain. The contributors bravely took on this task, working in collaboration to make this unique collection possible.

I have many people to thank without which this collection would have not been possible. First and foremost, I would like to thank the contributors of this collection for their intense involvement in this project, which went far beyond what a typical collection entails. Special thanks to Jamie Lorimer, who helped me come up with this idea and assisted in the invitation stage, and to Andreas Philippopoulos-Mihalopoulos for being there with helpful advice for the more difficult editorial decisions. David Delaney deserves a special thank you for reading through the chapters and offering his thoughts and his afterword. Many thanks also to Jack Schlegel for always lending an ear, to Caitlin McIntire and Laura Muir for their editorial assistance, and to Colin Perrin of Routledge for recognizing the importance of this collection and for being such an enthusiastic supporter from the minute he set eye on the proposal. Finally, I am indebted to the Baldy Center for Law & Social Policy, and to Errol Meidinger and Laura Wirth in particular, for their generous funding and administration of the 2014 workshop and for their overall support of this project.

As always, I am especially grateful to my family: to my daughters Ariel and Tamar for their support throughout the always-too-long process of writing and editing a book. I would like to dedicate this book to Gregor, my life partner, best friend, and most dedicated editor.

Migration by Maria Whiteman, 2014. Used with Permission.

Foreword

"Life" and "the Living," Law and Norm

Cary Wolfe

Has there ever been a more fascinating (and, for some, more frustrating) moment for those of us who are concerned with the relations between that scientific and cultural designation called "life," that branch of philosophy and culture called "ethics," and that social institution called "law?" Hardly a week goes by in the mass media without new discoveries being announced in *The New York Times, National Geographic*, or any number of television programs about the remarkable complexity of the life around us, both as an ecological reality (think of the bracing lessons of global warming and the Anthropocene) and as a phenomenological one (think of everything we have learned about how a wide range of nonhuman creatures are more complex, both biologically and phenomenologically, than we ever imagined). Part of what is so rewarding about the collection of chapters you have before you is that we are provided with ample doses of each. As for the ecological and the biological, think of the "fluid ecologies" of Christopher Bear's essay, and how the blowback from regulating them effects particular creatures, marking them as "polluters" or "pests;" the "rewilding" Jamie Lorimer discusses, and how the ecological paradigm that orients it sits uncomfortably alongside concern by some about the welfare of individual animals involved in this "probiotic" experiment; or the jellyfish discussed by Elizabeth Johnson, whose flourishing serves to index the plight of a planet experiencing warming seas and the consequent loss of biodiversity.

The jellyfish are thriving, for sure, but are they "happy"? To ask that question is to shift to the second register I just mentioned, one taken up in Elan Abrell's examples of Tony, the 14-year-old Siberian-Bengal hybrid tiger, living in a cage at a Louisiana truck stop, or Lolita the orca, also the subject of various legal actions calculated to recognize and alleviate her suffering; in the crows mercilessly beaten to death, as Adam Reed recounts, while trapped inside a state-sponsored cage (an event that is all the more troubling in light of how much we have learned about the intelligence and complexity of corvids over the past decade and more, making it clearer and clearer that "intelligence" and "the human" are often coincident but they are far from coterminous); in the acts of nonhuman animal resistance that Kathryn Gillespie examines in domesticated bovines; and in what Eben Kirksey calls the "bubbles of comfort" experienced by nonhuman (and human) creatures in those multispecies families created by the unpredictable crossing of capital and life forms in post-natural landscapes.

It is on this terrain—and it is, as Johnson points out, usually a terrain—that we confront perhaps the most jarring asynchronicities between law and life, most pointedly, of course, in the dominant legal designation of such creatures (excluding those who live in the wild) not as "persons" but as "property." As various essays in this collection demonstrate, such a designation, counter-intuitive as it may be, may work for good or for ill for the creatures involved. As Gillespie and Abrell show, it may allow those who own animals to engage in abuse, violence, or neglect; or it may, as Kirksey demonstrates, enable a kind of flourishing and even, perhaps, a new path for conservation efforts, predicated precisely on the value of animals as a commodity to those who own and care for them. But one thing is for sure: the "property" status of animals not living in the wild seems completely out of sync with what we know about the mental, emotional, and social lives of many nonhuman beings. Many readers will no doubt ask, "what sense does it make that a highly developed animal such as a tiger or an orca is regarded as 'the same' as a toaster or a pile of bricks, while in US law at least, corporations and ships of state are legally designated as 'persons'?"

For those who expect from our social institutions a convincing modicum of responsiveness to social change, these developments in our understanding and appreciation of the nonhuman lives around us have put an enormous amount of pressure on legal institutions—a pressure that the traditions, habits, and precedents of legal institutions perhaps mitigate against handling effectively (which is perhaps just another way of defining, with Foucault and many others, what an "institution" is). That question is explored in some detail in Richard Janda and Richard Lehun's contribution. For them, the Anthropocene confronts us with the antinomy between human and nonhuman law; human law may be historically and socially contingent, but nonhuman law (as in the laws of physics, chemistry, and the like that determine biogeophysical outcomes such as global warming) sets limits and boundaries of a different sort to what human beings can and cannot legislate. "What is the relevant, proper human law that is governing our collective behavior?" they ask. "It cannot be the law of any specific jurisdiction alone, since the collective impacts of our behavior upon the biosphere are not attributable to any single jurisdiction. Nor can it really be international law, which does not purport to engage in the general governance of collective behavior" (this volume, 179–80).

Adam Reed puts his finger on a different kind of asynchronicity between law and life when he notes that even though crows in their natural habitat have no statutory rights, once they are inside the trap monitored by the trap-setter or game-keeper, they acquire various forms of legal protection, such that decoy birds, for example, must be provided with suitable food, water, and shelter, and captive, caught animals must be "destroyed humanely" (this volume, 111). Here, as with the herbivores involved in the Oostvaardersplassen (OVP) rewilding project in the Netherlands that Jamie Lorimer discusses, legal protections for animals depend upon their being under human control. As Lorimer notes, animal welfarists who are concerned about the starvation of cattle in the OVP reserve have been arguing that they are not truly wild but are instead still domestic and, as such, were subject to the 1976 European Convention for the Protection of Animals Kept for Farming Purposes, which requires that animals under human control be "free from hunger, thirst, discomfort, pain, injury, and disease" (this volume, 44). But here, of course, a rather common-sensical question suggests itself: isn't the crow or cow the moment before entering the biopolitical space in question the same biophysiological being, with the same capacities, needs, and vulnerabilities, as the one now enclosed and protected by law? Why does the law recognize the capacity for suffering and the need for well-being in one context and suddenly ignore them in another, when the animal is no longer in "our" space?

To put it this way is to raise a question central to biopolitical thought, the difference between "*bios*" (or the political form of life within the bounds or "space" of a particular community) and "*zoë*" (or "bare life," life "at large," as it were) made famous by Giorgio Agamben—a distinction, it should be noted, for which the taxonomy of "animal" versus "human" is not constitutive (Agamben 1998). And it is also to raise the question of the relation (or disrelation) between what Jacques Derrida calls Law and law, or law and justice: "Law" in its socially, institutionally, and historically specific form, versus "law" in the sense of the ethical question of justice, against which the operations of the law must always be measured. For Derrida, justice can't simply consist of formulaically applying a set of legal rules, which would then simply be the performance of a mechanical calculation that, in principle, would not even require a living being to carry it out. Such a procedure, in his view, would utterly *avoid* the question of whether the legal judgment in question was just or not, whether it justly applied to this particular instance that is brought before the law. As he puts it in "Force of Law":

> An address is always singular, idiomatic, and justice, as law (*droit*), seems always to suppose the generality of a rule, a norm or a universal imperative. How are we to reconcile the act of justice that must always concern singularity, individuals, irreplaceable groups and lives . . . with rule, norm, value or the imperative of justice which necessarily have a general form, even if this generality prescribes a singular application in each case? (Derrida 1990, 949).

As the essays in this collection amply demonstrate, this relationship of iterability (as Derrida puts it) between Law and law that is conjugated in each individual case is, in fact, a reservoir of complexity for the legal system, in the sense that it ceaselessly confronts it with the fact of its own contingency and immanence, its reach but also its limits. It is, in fact, part of what keeps the legal system "lively." Or as Derrida puts it, the grounds or foundations of the law, because they are by definition historically and socially contingent, "can't by definition rest on anything but themselves, they are themselves a violence without ground," not in the sense of "illegal" but as what he calls a *coup de force* that exceeds the opposition between "legal" and "illegal," "founded," and "unfounded" (941). Or to put it in terms of systems theory, the legal system may be the example *par excellence* of an autopoietic system, but autopoietic systems by definition operate in an environment that is always already far more complex than they are (Luhmann 1995). And hence, the iterative relationship between Law and law that we reconjugate in every particular legal ruling always takes place in culturally, politically, and ecologically saturated contexts, try as the law might to insulate itself from those very factors.

This dynamic is explored in some detail by Janda and Lehun's discussion of possible "conflict of laws" frameworks and how they bear upon the difference between "man-made" and "natural" law, and it is also at work in Kirksey's ethnography of how exotic animals in Florida stand not so much "before the law" as *beside* the law in the multispecies households that are allowed to flourish. In contrast to the picture of the "becoming law of animals" that we find in Bear's chapter—where legislation focused on protecting humans and their hygiene creates newly demonized species of animals as "polluters," making them "visible, legible, and governable"—the "*laissez-faire* policies" of the state of Florida point in the opposite direction, not toward immunological purification along species lines in the name of biosecurity, but rather toward what Kirksey calls the "queering" of the household and the site of the nuclear family as a newly diverse, multispecies space that the state sees no need to purify—a process largely driven by the overdetermined interlacing of bodies (both human and animal) and capital. As one official puts it, "we allow just about anything as a pet as long as the owner obtains a proper license and proper cages. . . . [W]e are simply not going to spend billions to kill everything that escapes" (this volume, 157).

In both of these seemingly opposed cases, it is not a matter of "more" or "less" law being "good" or "bad," but rather of an historically new kind of relationship between what Foucault calls "law" and "norm," one that is key to how biopolitics articulates "life." The state of Florida's permitting system in Kirksey's chapter is a perfect example; it is primarily concerned with codifying a graduated set of standards, in the name of what Foucault calls "governmentality" (Rabinow and Rose 2003, 229–45)—a process for which the particular animals in question assume the legal status that they do only as a kind of after-effect: "we allow just about anything as a pet as long as the owner obtains a proper license." And this is precisely what makes the state of Louisiana's conduct in the case of Tony the Tiger—its granting of a wild animal permit exemption to the animal's owner, who thereafter enjoyed a legal status shared by no one else in the state—seem so egregious; the process of issuing permits is a perfect example of the relationship between law and norm, and yet here, that relationship seems suddenly subject to fiat, as if we had regressed to an earlier and more archaic social logic, where law is conditioned not by norms but by social ties, local fealties, and the like.

To be sure, it is not as if the law in contemporary society recedes in importance—indeed, its reach has become ever more expansive; rather, the law's primary function shifts from a relationship anchored to sovereignty to one that is oriented mainly toward the constitution and perpetuation of norms. Foucault identifies "the growing importance assumed by the action of the norm, at the expense of the juridical system of the law" (Foucault 1980, 135; quoted also in Ewald 1990, 138) as central to the biopolitical, but at the same time, as Francois Ewald points out, "normalization tends to be accompanied by an astonishing proliferation of legislation" (138). And what this means is not the diminution of law (quantitatively speaking, as it were) but a different *role* for law in the constitution of biopolitical societies. As Ewald puts it, "the norm, then, is opposed not to law itself but to what Foucault would call 'the juridical': the institution of law as the expression of a sovereign's power." And it thus becomes "part of a different sort of power that 'has to qualify, measure, appraise, and hierarchize rather than display itself in its murderous splendor'" (138).

The fundamental logic of the norm is thus to regulate what Foucault calls "the entry of life into history" under the biopolitical by means of "positive controls" founded on a logic of standardization, measurement, and statistical analysis, of which both human beings and animals then become examples or (to use bureaucratic language) "outcomes" (Ewald 1990, 141). A couple of points are worth emphasizing here. First, as the chapters by Irus Braverman, Elizabeth Johnson, and Christopher Bear make clear, this relationship between law and norm—and the biopolitical enframing more generally—is not limited to human society or even to domesticated animals. Johnson shows the complexities of actualizing this relationship when it involves a marine environment and international waters, and highlights the rather different form this relationship takes when brought under management in the stem cell laboratory with an eye toward profit. Braverman's chapter give us a wonderfully exacting picture of the relationship between law and norm at work in the IUCN Red List (and the genealogy of such lists in general), which "has evolved," as she puts it, "from a subjective expert-based system lacking standardized criteria to a uniform and global rule-based system" (this volume, 22). As Braverman shows, what Ewald calls the "self-reference" of the norm does not compromise the list's efficacy; it is precisely what gives it power. This is why some countries produce at least two separate lists: as a prominent IUCN official writes, to "prevent blurring the line between extinction risk assessment, which is a scientific endeavor, and conservation priority setting, which is very much a value-based judgment" (Ewald 1990, 154). It is not that either list is pure or uncontaminated in its self-reference—neither is or ever could be a pure typology—but rather that, under modernity understood as what Niklas Luhmann calls "functional differentiation," what gives each list its authority and utility is its specialization in the form of an expertise and a discourse not achieved elsewhere (Luhmann 1995, 53–4). And under biopolitics, the *political* moment occurs at the conjuncture of their articulation, the non-generic and overdetermined binding together of norm and law under quite specific circumstances. As Ewald reminds us, "it is essential to distinguish between the norm itself and the apparatus, institution, or technique of power that brings it into action and functions according to its principles" (1990, 153). The articulation of a norm via the list then becomes part of a larger biopolitical apparatus in which, as Braverman writes, "through their listing as threatened, certain species lives are elevated to a political status, while the rest (initially, at least, the unlisted) remain biological, or mere, life" (this volume, 20).

Bear's chapter also gives us a clear picture of the logic of the norm at work and how its generative effects impact particular animals. As he notes in his discussion of EU bathing water regulations, "environmental management agencies are increasingly turning to techniques such as microbial source tracking (MST) to identify more accurately the sources—both spatial and species" of contamination. But the use of this quintessentially biopolitical technique takes place in a broader and much more complex context where "the disruptive—perhaps even transgressive—forces of water, wind and sun" (this volume, 93) make the evidentiary links between contamination and certain species often tenuous at best. Here, as always in the context of biopolitics, the relationship between legal institutions and norm is about managing risk in the form of the aleatory and the contingent, those unpredictabilities of events, bodies, and environments that the norm complicates by bringing deep, expert knowledge to bear upon them, posing new challenges, in turn, for legal institutions (Ewald 1990, 141–2). As Bear points out, these effects of the biopolitical coupling of law and norm are "uneven" in both space and time—even within the same species. "Whereas some (such as dogs) are represented as 'polluters' only during summer," he writes, "others (such as seagulls) might be increasingly discouraged year-round. Animals of the same species, meanwhile, can be treated very differently in close proximity to one another—for instance, where only one of two adjacent bays has been designated as bathing water" (this volume, 83).

Those dogs that are " 'polluters' only during summer" remind us—as does the whole of *Lively Legalities*—of something central to biopolitics, something already clear in the work of Michel Foucault, Jacques Derrida, Donna Haraway, and Niklas Luhmann, and amplified in Roberto Esposito's recent work on biopolitics as well: that the semantics of the "person" or the "subject" (who might, under an older juridico-political vocabulary, be the bearer of "rights") is inadequate to thinking this new biopolitical reality in which both human and nonhuman forms of life are enmeshed. Biopolitics operates, as Esposito puts it, not at the level of the "person," nor even at the level of the "body," but at the level of what he calls "flesh" (whether human or nonhuman), which is "the unitary weave of the difference between bodies," the "non-belonging, or rather the intra-belonging, that allows what is different to not hermetically seal itself up within itself, but rather, to remain in contact with its outside" (Esposito 2011, 121). From the vantage of the law and norm at work here, those dogs by the seaside discussed by Bear are not thinking and feeling individuals with wants, needs, and desires, nor are they bodies in what Deleuze would call the "molar" sense of the word; they are simply the bearers of certain microbes and parasites, possessing a status that changes from season to season precisely because of the operation of the norm and its expert knowledge practices that decompose and recompose what we used to call "the body" based on its "molecular" attributes, introducing a new kind of complexity into the regulatory equation.

In the end, all the chapters collected here are interested, either tacitly or explicitly, in the possibility of what has come to be called an "affirmative" rather than "thanatological" biopolitics of multispecies relations. In this light, the short-term, strategic advantages of what Janda and Lehun call "the projection of self upon the other" that we see at work in the arguments of animal rights thinkers such as Stephen Wise and Gary Francione are clear enough, and should not be discounted for the good they might do for some nonhuman creatures. But the asynchronicity between a new social reality that binds laws, life, and norms according to a new biopolitical logic and a juridico-political vocabulary inherited from an earlier historical moment poses a new kind of challenge: how "to redescribe things," as Andreas Philippopoulos-Mihalopoulos characterizes it, "in a way that neither absolves a body from the responsibility of situating itself, nor inebriates this body with the illusion of control of the assemblage" (this volume, 204). This new role of law must find its way in the recognition that no single agent—including a sovereign—can dictate the specific relations between life, law, and norms, nor can the "human," in the age of the Anthropocene and genetic engineering, be the fixed foot of the compass around which all such relations organize themselves. For this task, the vocabulary of "persons" and "rights," even though it forms the core of our inherited legal institutions, is far too blunt an instrument.

The same needs to be said, of course, for the ham-fisted distinction between "human" and "animal." And here, the ethnographic approach taken by many of the chapters in this volume will stand readers in good stead, by focusing our attention on how forms of life, and their articulation in relation to law and norm, are never generic, but are always highly overdetermined in any number of ways—a fact for which the category of "species," despite all its problems, is one (but only one) name. There's a world of difference between a tiger and a jellyfish, an orca and a herbivore, a python and parakeet—particularly in their life-world experience of captivity, wildness, property, domesticity, and so forth—but it is a not a difference that will be illuminated by the terms "person" or "animal." As Foucault himself recognized when he set out to deliver a year-long series of lectures on biopolitics, but instead ended up spending the year in a prolonged analysis of liberalism, we have to *first* ask after the specific forms and apparatuses (economic, scientific, legal, and legislative) in and through which "life" comes to be articulated as a social reality in the form of the "living" in all its empirical reality—its commodification, privatization, protection ("making live"), and so on—before we can ascertain what the "bio-" of "biopolitics" might mean (Foucault 2010). The issue, in other words, is not some transcendental, even theological principle called "life," but rather the "living" and the "lively."

References

Agamben, Giorgio. 1998. *Homo Sacer: Sovereign Power and Bare Life.* Translated by Daniel Heller-Roazen. Stanford: Stanford University Press.

Derrida, Jacques. 1990. "Force of Law: The 'Mystical Foundation of Authority.'" Translated by Mary Quaintance. *Cardozo Law Review* 11: 920–1046.

Esposito, Roberto. 2011. *Immunitas: The Protection and Negation of Life.* Translated by Zakiya Hanafi. London: Polity Press.

Ewald, Francois. 1990. "Norms, Discipline, and the Law." *Representations* 30 (Spring): 138–61.

Foucault, Michel. 1980. *History of Sexuality, Vol. 1: An Introduction.* Translated by Robert Hurley. New York: Vintage Books.

———. 2010. *The Birth of Biopolitics: Lectures at the Collège de France, 1978–1979.* Edited by Michel Senellart. Translated by Graham Burchell. London: Picador Books.

Luhmann, Niklas. 1995. *Social Systems.* Translated by John Bednarz, Jr. with Dirk Baecker. Stanford: Stanford University Press.

Rabinow, Paul and Nikolas Rose, eds. 2003. *The Essential Foucault.* New York: New Press.

Introduction

Lively Legalities

Irus Braverman

Thus far, scholars have relegated the legal investigation of nonhuman life, and of the animal question in particular, to the typically reformist discourse of animal rights. Within this discourse, legal rights are extended to certain nonhuman animals through the application of the same liberal framework that afforded human rights before it. *Animals, Biopolitics, Law: Lively Legalities* (in short: *Lively Legalities*) proposes a new subject of inquiry: lively legalities. The contributors—scholars from a variety of backgrounds and disciplines—try to envision what legal frameworks that move beyond the humanist perspective might look like. Indeed, this interdisciplinary collection orchestrates an attempt to acknowledge the myriad ways of living in the world, their inherent interconnections, and their manifestations in, and constitutions of, legal apparatuses.

Specifically, *Lively Legalities* asks what, in legal terms, it means to be human and nonhuman, what it means to govern and to be governed, and what are the ethical and political concerns that emerge from the project of governing human as well as more-than-human life. While the contributors take nonhuman animals as a departure point, they recognize that the questions articulated above also apply to non-animal life forms, aggregations of life, and ecological processes. Drawing on a vast array of expertise—from law, geography, and anthropology, through animal studies and posthumanism, to science and technology studies—the contributors consider the vast possibilities of lively legalities.

Questions and concepts

Lively Legalities focuses on three central questions. First, how can we move beyond the current humanist framework that treats animals as liberal

The green turtle (*Chelonia mydas*) has been listed as Endangered by the IUCN Red List since 2004. Photo by Brocken Inaglory, 2008. https://commons.wikimedia.org/wiki/File:Chelonia_mydas_is_going_for_the_air_edit.jpg.

subjects, and what might a posthumanist framework that does not attempt to make liberal subjects of nonhuman animals look like? Second, what important juridical insights do "animal questions," and nonhuman questions more broadly, offer at this time, controversially referred to as the Anthropocene? And, finally, how do animals (and lively nonhumans more generally) define our identity as humans, what does it mean to govern their lives and to "care better" for our interconnected communities, and how might these forms of pastoral power and biopower translate into law? The collection engages the following seven themes that we see as foundational for considering lively legalities: law and animality, legal materiality, the legal classification of the animal, property and ownership, the Anthropocene, and multispecies ethnographies/posthuman methodologies. I will address each theme in its turn.

Law and Animality. This volume takes as a starting point Cary Wolfe's argument in *Before the Law* that applying the human rights model to animals exposes a sad poverty of the imagination (2012, 14). We then take one step further to consider animal legalities, and the legalities of nonhuman life more generally, that move beyond the liberal traditions of human rights and welfare. Specifically, most of the contributors apply an ethnographic orientation to study the everyday properties of law in its dealing with animals in order to envision what thinking legally about animals might entail. This methodological disposition enables the various contributors to speak legally, rather than to speak about the law. The contributions illuminate various insights about law and the animal, ranging from law's attempts at classification and control; they also lend increased visibility to the distinctions between legal and extra-legal and between law and its states of exception.

Underlying the book collection is the argument that law is not simply a blank slate that reflects the changing relations between humanization and animalization. Instead, legal texts, cultures, and institutions tend toward and prescribe particular ideologies. In *Law and Nature* (2003), David Delaney asserts that formal law is "clearly on the side of those who position animals beyond the gap." He explains that "dominant, reductionist renderings of 'the animal' are internal to legal ideology and supported by legal forms" (220). Maneesha Deckha argues, similarly, that: "Law is an anthropocentric terrain. Not only is law the product of human actors, it entrenches the interests of humans over virtually all others and centers the reasonable human person as a main legal subject" (Deckha 2013, 1). In this sense, law's relationship to animality can teach us something important about law itself. The process of humanizing law and dehumanizing nature and animality demarcates the boundaries of law: law's sovereignty as dependent on its states of exception, what Jacques Derrida refers to as the beast and the sovereign (2009). The law–animal nexus also illuminates two important properties of law: that law is not fixed, and that it depends on the particular corporealities of its objects–subjects. Simultaneously, the law–animal nexus demonstrates that the life and death of an animal is not only biological or cultural but also legal.

Legal Materiality. Legal practitioners typically present law as abstract, immaterial, and universal. This has enabled them to perpetuate the mythology of equal representation, objectivity, and blind justice. Along these lines, many formal legal norms do not explicitly mention animals. When they are mentioned, animals tend to be either vilified or valorized. Christopher Bear's chapter shows, for example, how certain sanitary laws implicitly define animals as polluters and hence as a source of danger. *Lively Legalities* calls upon scholars to uncover the largely invisible roles that animals have been performing in legal norms and regulatory regimes. We aim to unveil the materiality of the law and demonstrate its powers as corporeal, emplaced, and localized. The process of detecting traces of materiality in law also enables the contributors of this volume to unravel those places that are not traditionally defined as law. Such is Elizabeth R. Johnson's realization that alongside its formal properties, law takes place in scientific discourses and encodings.

When as humans we try not to speak on behalf of animals and other nonhuman creatures, we must find a way to trace what it is that they are communicating. The act of tracing is therefore important for affording a fresh take on human–nonhuman interrelations. The term "traces" has come up in a variety of contexts in this collection: from law's tracing of bodies using their discharges in Bear's chapter, to tracing criminal activity through signs left in the scene, as explored by Adam Reed. Whereas such understandings of traces point to a continuum between human and nonhuman animals, they also reveal epistemological and ontological differences between forms of life. Andreas Philippopoulos-Mihalopoulos refers to the condition of the emergence of singularities as lively differences on a continuum as *rupture.* The idea of rupture is also manifest in Kathryn Gillespie's discussions of resistance and in Reed's epistemological distancing.

The Legal Classification of the Animal. Despite the rich literature on the question of the animal, the relationship between animals and law is still largely restricted to the domains of the natural sciences, embracing as truisms the scientific classification of animals into species and subspecies, their sorting into a Linnaean taxonomy, their categorization as domestic, captive, lab, or wild, and their relegation as such to particular geographical and emotional zones. With the exodus of animals from labs into the social realm, scholars are now challenged to envision a new "parliament of things" (Latour 1993) that reorders animals beyond their dualistic classification as subject/object and that allows them to assume a voice in a new social order (Braverman 2015b). To reflect this new vision of society that includes various forms of nonhuman life, a new way of thinking about law is required.

Through the years, myriad legal norms and institutions have attempted to order messy materialities through their classification. To classify the perceived messiness of nature, and of nonhuman animals within that, certain entities had to first be identified as such, named, and documented. *Lively Legalities* seeks to illuminate such classifications carried out through the law—effectively, law's "animal kingdoms"—and their claims for fixity and stability. The vast majority of what law defines as nonhuman animals (which is itself a contested category) has been classified into a restricted number of legal categories: wild, domestic, agricultural, pests, lab, and zoo animals (Braverman 2013). Each legal category is manifested by specific temporalities, materialities, and legal protections. Yet an animal's legal category is not always consistent, nor is it mutually exclusive. The physical mobility of animals is especially challenging to law's order: legal attempts to either freeze animals within their classificatory modalities or to reclassify them as part of a new order demonstrate the tense relations between the physical mobility of many animals and their legal immobility.

Another important aspect of ordering animals is that modern Western legal systems have, for the most part, adopted traditional scientific thinking and have typically created systems of governance that operate through species regimes. As I argue in my contribution to this volume, such species regimes enable both an abstraction—a grid over the Linnaean kingdoms (Foucault 1970)—and an embodiment—a personification of ecosystems, habitats, and populations. I offer that: "[s]ince humans understand themselves primarily as an exceptional species and therefore both relate to, and differentiate themselves from, other species—it is important to critically examine this lens and the work that it performs in the world" (this volume, 22). This critical examination analyzes how humans think of themselves as an exceptional species and, alternatively, how humans except themselves from ostensibly natural concepts like species altogether.

Alongside identifying modern Western law's tendency to classify nonhuman animals into categories and species, *Lively Legalities* also explores other forms of classification, including the foundational classificatory distinctions between human and nonhuman, between living and nonliving, and between plant and animal life. Additional forms of classification that emerge in the contributions are the renderings of animals as either captive (and domesticated) or wild (Chapters 6, 7, and 8) and the listing of species according to their level of endangerment (Chapter 1). Finally, the chapters also explore how the categories of legal and illegal (or non-legal) are projected onto animals, rendering them criminal, invasive, nuisance, pest, and so forth. Christopher Bear's chapter, for example, shows how water quality legislation impacts animals newly categorized as polluters, be they shoreline birds or domestic dogs (Chapter 4). These classifications are identified and problematized throughout this book as a response to the challenges posed by posthumanism at this particular moment in time.

Property and Ownership. Legal classifications are typically entangled with notions of property and ownership. In the United States, nonhuman animals are owned and thus "in principle no different from a parcel of land, a T-bone steak, a teddy bear, or a steel mill" (Delaney 2003, 220). Human animals, on the other hand, are assumed to have an inherent dignity that deems the property paradigm inapplicable, at least formally (Otomo and Mussawir 2012, 5). As a formal legal system, property establishes power not only over the owned object but also in relation to the nonowning legal subjects (ibid.). Traditional animal bodies are the apparent examples of such property regimes, but ownership and patenting are emerging as prevalent concepts also in the microbial world (Bear and Johnson, this volume).

Despite the traditional condemnation of animal ownership by many critical animal studies scholars, it should be noted that ownership is not always or necessarily antithetical to care and protection; indeed, being unowned can and has been at times a more precarious state of animal being—a *zoë*, if you will. In Chapter 8, Eben Kirskey explores similar assumptions about the private ownership of exotic pets in Florida. He toggles between the owners' attention to the lived experience of exotic birds, for example by taking care to not reproduce genetic defects, and the fact that this ownership over genetic material and the animal's body render the animal a commodity, as was evident at the snake convention he visited.

The Anthropocene. Lively Legalities proposes a sense of urgency in light of the life-changing conditions of the planet, adding to this a questioning of the existing legal and political structures and their current conceptualization, classification, and government of life. This era has recently been referred to, albeit controversially, as the Anthropocene (Braverman 2015a). At this time, questions regarding nonhuman life and law's ability to reflect on and respond to this life are becoming highly important.

The Anthropocene is a complex and paradoxical reference point: it embodies both humans' omnipresence and our responsibility. Exploring this paradox in the context of jellyfish, Elizabeth R. Johnson demonstrates how, despite the fact that the Anthropocene attributes to humans the ability to manipulate the environment on geological and climactic scales, jellyfish (and the various biotechnological developments in which they are bound up) exhort us to recognize our multifarious interrelation with and dependence on hosts of other organisms (Chapter 3). Similarly, Richard Janda and Richard Lehun explore the ways in which human laws, which deal with economic growth and consumption, have run unchecked to the extent that they conflict with nonhuman laws, a conflict marked by human impacts on global ecosystems. For Janda and Lehun, these effects of human law thus demand the recognition of the fragility of nonhuman law (Chapter 9).

Andreas Philippopoulos-Mihalopoulos' contribution, too, grapples with the paradox of human centrality implied by the concept of the

Anthropocene. He argues that although the global effects of humanity's actions do not denote centrality, it is our exceptional responsibility as humans to recognize our belonging to, and our dependence on, assemblages of others (Chapter 10). Many of the contributors query and flesh out this paradoxical quality of the Anthropocene, seeing it as a horrible opportunity to recognize and inhabit new lively legalities that enhance human life. Whatever we choose to name these times, legal responses to the particular challenges that they pose have until now been inadequate, or at least far from reflective. This collection underscores law's enhanced responsibility through an emphasis on relational and multispecies legalities. Specifically, we highlight throughout how law determines and is determined by the multispecies bodies who interact with it and with each other, creating networks and assemblages in which the human is decentered and implicated with others.

Biopolitical Regimes. Lively Legalities draws on Michel Foucault's work (1970; 1990; 2009) as well as on that of Roberto Esposito (2012), Cary Wolfe (2012), Donna Haraway (2008), Giorgio Agamben (1995; 2004), and Jacques Derrida (2008). These sources offer the context within which the present study of emerging legalities is both relevant and timely. A central theme that underlies this volume is biopolitics. As Cary Wolfe points out, to live under a regime of biopolitics is to live under a situation where we are all potentially animals before the law. In other words, animalization, as well as humanization, can be understood as a discursive, not just (or not at all) as a biological, technology. *Lively Legalities* similarly explores the biopolitical properties of governing nonhuman life, thereby exposing the political force of animalization. More specifically, we attend to the tensions between the individual, the species, and other forms of life. We perceive of the animal rights approach as one of myriad biopolitical approaches that, through furthering certain ideologies, create a hierarchy of value toward life. The contributors take varying stances toward these ideologies, providing a rich dialectic throughout the book.

Rather than presenting a unitary account of biopolitics, the contributors envisage multiple windows into biopolitics, identifying nuances and ruptures in this apparatus. For example, while my chapter identifies how the probability of survival or risk of extinction of a species are not black and white but rather gradations on a continuum, Johnson draws on Esposito's immunitary politics to identify how life and death are in themselves anthropocentric concepts that disregard other forms of life, including non-death. In Chapter 2, Jamie Lorimer's focus on probiotic biopolitics takes up Wolfe's (2012) call for an affirmative biopolitics and articulates a vision for ecosystem health through the introduction and protection of "keystone species," who perform specific ecological functions for the benefit of other species in their biomes (Chapter 2). Elan Abrell's focus on *zoë* and *bios* shows the movement into a kind of subjecthood for rescued exotic animals, even as they retain their property status. Finally, Abrell calls for a recognition of *animal sacer*, the ultimate state of exception for the animal, and discusses how animals can escape its confines (Chapter 7).

Multispecies Ethnographies, Posthuman Methodologies. It is hardly coincidental that many of the volume's contributors adopt a multispecies ethnography approach and endorse posthumanist methodologies. Utilizing cross-category analysis, we attempt to transcend the existing anthropocentric idioms to engender new lively legalities. Such multispecies ethnographies constitute a way of redefining the human along posthuman lines. We think of the posthuman predominantly as a methodology because of its diffused cross-disciplinarity (Wolfe 2012) and its futuristic temporality that considers a post-extinction human absence in order to introduce situated responsibilities in the present (Negarestani 2008). Reed's ethnography of the wildlife crime investigator in Scotland, Gillespie's documentation of bovine resistances in dairy farms, Kirksey's tracing of multispecies families of exotic pets in Florida, Lorimer's accounts of the Dutch rewilding project, Abrell's ethnography of the sanctuary, and my own ethnography of lists—share in common not only the desire to move away from a humanist account so as to take nonhuman life into consideration, but also the deployment of a grounded, local, relational, and situated methodology that considers the particularities of each instance as crucial for its conceptualization.

Indeed, *Lively Legalities* aims at bringing forth a multispecies legality observed from within an ethnography of posthuman transdisciplinarity and placed in the paradoxical era of the Anthropocene, with its reconceptualization of human responsibility. Ultimately, we aim for a novel and radical understanding of the connection between law and life. By acknowledging the myriad ways of being in the world, their inherent interconnections, and their manifestations in, and constitutions of, law, lively legalities extend the advocacy-oriented scholarship of animal rights to highlight how both animality and humanness are deeply embedded in the constitution of law and, reciprocally, how law is acutely relevant for constituting the animal. Indeed, while nonhuman life has rendered law's operations—in fact, its very existence as such—possible, law also constitutes animal life and renders it meaningful in a variety of ways.

A growing body of literature is currently emerging that addresses legalities from a nonhuman perspective. Yoriko Otomo's and Ed Mussawir's *Law and the Question of the Animal* (2012) brings together essays by legal scholars on law and animality, combining the theoretical and the practical to criticize the traditional animal rights and welfare approaches. Likewise, Ian Robertson's *Animals, Welfare and the Law: Critically Assessing the Role of Animals in Society* (2015) focuses on issues of human/nonhuman classification. Finally, Cary Wolfe's aforementioned *Before the Law* (2012) explores animal studies and animal rights through Foucauldian biopolitics as a way of thinking about the political and legal lives of human and nonhuman animals.

Drawing on such growing critical and theoretical interests, *Lively Legalities* presents a multidisciplinary engagement with the multiplicity of law and its biopolitical dimensions that moves beyond the premises of the rights or welfare traditions.

The book's structure

Lively Legalities opens with a foreword by Cary Wolfe and ends with an afterword by David Delaney. In between its pages are an introduction and ten substantive chapters.

In the book's foreword, " 'Life' and 'The Living,' Law and Norm," Cary Wolfe traces the relationship between the chapters in this volume. In particular, he shows the interconnections between law, norm, and biopolitics as those bear upon the regulation—the "letting die" and the "making live"—of nonhuman life at the dawn of the twenty-first century. Drawing on the work of Francois Ewald, Michel Foucault, Jacques Derrida, Roberto Esposito, and Niklas Luhmann, Wolfe foregrounds how the norm, in its operation in the form of expert knowledges produced under what Luhmann calls the "functional differentiation" of social systems that is characteristic of modernity, creates new kinds of complexity for legal institutions as biopolitics continues to pursue its fundamental logic of extending the reach of the political into heretofore ignored areas (i.e., "life" as the direct object of political power, regularization, optimization, and so on). According to Wolfe, *Lively Legalities* demonstrates how, under biopolitics, the control of life, the enhancement of life, the policing of life, the understanding of life, and the legal regulation of life assume a new order of complexity, one for which the indexing of law to sovereignty under earlier social and political logics is inadequate.

The book kicks off with an exploration of a prominent technology for the legal regulation of nonhuman life: the endangered species list. In this chapter, entitled "The Regulatory Life of Threatened Species Lists," I argue that threatened species lists are biopolitical technologies: they produce and reinforce underlying species ontologies by creating, calculating, and governing the boundaries between various nonhuman species. Such a differentiated treatment of the life and death of nonhuman species through their en-listing, down- and up-listing, multi-listing, and un-listing translate into the positive protection and active governance of such species. Listing threatened species thus becomes a way to affirm—and to justify—which lives are more and most important to save, thereby reifying the distinction between those who save (humans) and those who can only be saved (nonhumans).

Specifically, the last two decades have witnessed an explosion of national and global lists of threatened and endangered species. In 2010, at least 109 countries had produced a national list of threatened species and more than

25 listing systems of threatened species were used across North America alone. The IUCN Red List for Threatened Species is the first and most comprehensive attempt at the global listing of all threatened species and, increasingly, of all species. This chapter utilizes an empirical and ethnographic methodology to explore the nature of lists, and of the Red List in particular; it then proceeds to examine the biopolitical aspects of the Red List as well as its global, regulatory, scientific, and seductive powers.

In Chapter 2, "Probiotic Legalities: De-Domestication and Rewilding Before the Law," Jamie Lorimer offers a "third way" approach to the biopolitics of human–animal relations. He does so through examining the lively legalities of rewilding: a novel approach to nature conservation. Drawing on the work of Cary Wolfe, Lorimer argues that rewilding treads a path between the liberal approach to animal rights and the celebration of an undifferentiated "life" in forms of biocentric ethics. Focusing on the example of rewilding in the Netherlands, the chapter presents rewilding as a probiotic mode of biopolitics geared toward nurturing ecological processes while respecting valued forms of species difference. The chapter develops this analysis by reflecting on the tensions between rewilding and prevalent legalities for governing animal welfare, nature conservation, and biosecurity in Europe during the Anthropocene.

In Chapter 3, "Governing Jellyfish: Eco-Security and Planetary 'Life' in the Anthropocene," Elizabeth R. Johnson examines how jellyfish have been taken up as a "matter of concern" in contemporary scientific practices. Johnson shows that the entwining of humans and nonhumans in the era of climate change is not a smooth process, but involves what Rancière has referred to as a "repartitioning [of] the political from the non-political." Like the chapters before it, this chapter too draws on Foucault's writings, this time focusing on how jellyfish life is figured as an object of security. The chapter first describes how scientists, fisheries, and policy makers have struggled to make jellyfish and other forms of sea life objects of ecological securitization—part of a "bad" set of conditions and circulations—on a terrain that is more fluid than fixed. The chapter then proceeds to discuss how scientists and the pharmaceutical industry are sifting jellyfish and other Cnidaria into the category of social "good" through stem cell research. In conclusion, Johnson draws on the writing of Frederic Neyrat to consider how the science of jellyfish research might be directed differently: not toward a planetary extension of biological security, but toward inventing new forms of municipality that do justice to the munificence of life.

Continuing the examination of life's munificence and human categories of "good" and "bad" life, in Chapter 4, "Tracing Bacterial Legalities: The Fluid Ecologies of the European Union's Bathing Water Directive," Christopher Bear explores the implications of the European Union's (EU) 2006 Bathing Water Directive. This legislation, which is to be fully implemented by 2016, requires EU Member States to monitor bathing waters for levels of fecal bacteria, to communicate this information to the public, and to generate management strategies. While designed to benefit and protect human health, this law's implementation has important implications for animals, especially through their definition as "polluters." The chapter investigates how animals are made present in bathing waters, extending beyond bodily presence around beaches into becoming traces, as techniques are developed to monitor bacterial sources that involve animals topographically distant to the sea. Such new technological capacities reveal how animals' unruly lives can complicate the identification of their activities, surfacing issues of dispersal and fluidity. Bear's chapter also discusses how the relevant law both assumes and undermines other vital materialities such as wind, sun, and water. Although the Directive is open to engaging with actions by nonhuman actants, its associated management strategies tend to do so selectively. The chapter finally calls upon the emergent literature on lively legalities not to limit its attention to legislation that explicitly focuses on animals, but rather to explore the unintended and unexpected implications and manifestations of regulatory forms for other nonhumans.

Following up on the legal designation of certain animals and bacteria as polluters, Adam Reed's chapter, "Crow Kill," explores what happens when animals are defined as nuisance or pests from the standpoint of the animal welfare field investigator. Through a case study of crow killing in Scotland and the prosecution of a gamekeeper observed "inhumanely" dispatching wild birds caught in a legally registered cage trap on a shooting estate, the chapter examines the relationship between witnessing, detection, and reporting in wildlife crime. It explores the ways in which these responsibilities are distributed between a range of formal and informal legal actors, emphasizing the role of the animal welfare field investigator. Reed is especially concerned with the way that law's gaze plays out in this instance, from the original eye witnessing of the incident to the final criteria for legal judgment. Reed's chapter is also driven by a desire to explore the relationship between law in action and ethical feeling: it offers an ethnographic perspective on the lived experience of embodying an imagined space both inside and outside the law, and on the tension between, or conversion of, these states over time. "Crow Kill" is intended as one kind of anthropological contribution to the study of lively legalities, in this case figured as the capacity of legal complexes to both index and generate specific instances of human–animal relations.

Like most of the previous chapters, Kathryn Gillespie's "Nonhuman Animal Resistance and the Improprieties of Live Property" deploys an ethnographic methodology. Gillespie asks: if we take as a starting point that nonhuman species engage in resistant acts, what might be gained from taking this resistance seriously? Drawing on fieldwork in the dairy industry,

Chapter 6 argues that farmed animals resist from within their legal status as live property. Farmed animals are owned outright: they are the property of the humans who farm them. Gillespie argues that this status creates and maintains their exploitative conditions. In other words, that farmed animals are ownable in the first place is what enables their commodification and, specifically, the violent effects of commodifying their bodies for food. Cows raised for dairy, for instance, undergo invasive artificial insemination practices, their calves are separated immediately after birth, and they are subject to confinement, intensive milking, sale at auction, and eventual slaughter. But cows often resist their conditions of confinement and bodily appropriation. Gillespie argues that sustained attention to this resistance is an important way of resisting the anthropocentrism of law and that this can create new, multispecies legal regimes that respect the agency and alterity of nonhuman animals.

Next is Elan Abrell's Chapter 7, "Lively Sanctuaries: A Shabbat of *Animal Sacer.*" Drawing on two years of multispecies ethnography conducted at multiple animal sanctuaries in Texas, Hawaii, Florida, and New York, Abrell's chapter focuses on two prominent cases involving administrative efforts to relocate animals from private facilities to sanctuaries. The first case focuses on Tony the tiger, a 14-year-old Siberian–Bengal hybrid who has spent over a decade of his life living in a cage at the Tiger Truck Stop, next to US Interstate Highway 10. The second involves Lolita, an orca who has resided at the Miami Seaquarium for 44 years. The chapter examines how legal strategies function as techniques of pastoral power that enable animals to gain political lives, and thereby to move beyond the realm of *animal sacer*—the category occupied by animals-as-property discourses and the ultimate embodiment of the state of exception. Once in a sanctuary, these political lives develop further as human and nonhuman animals form multispecies assemblages that generate their own kinds of lively legalities.

In Chapter 8, "Multispecies Families, Capitalism, and the Law," Eben Kirksey draws on interviews with people who have formed multispecies families in Florida and other parts of the United States, finding a large network of humans who care for tropical birds, endangered frogs, venomous snakes, and lizards in their own homes. Kirksey argues that in Florida, exotic animals generally stand not *before the law,* as Cary Wolfe has it, but *beside the law,* in the moral milieu of the human home. Some animals, such as parrots, readily become members of human families, responding to our desires for touch and intimacy. When these social species are raised by humans from birth they often imprint on their primate caretakers—projecting their own species-specific norms of sociality and sexuality onto humans. Other kinds of critters, such as most snakes, fail to flourish in human households and will often try to resist captivity. Yet even those animals who are incorporated into the familial sphere and enfolded into relationships involving love and care are often abandoned amidst major life changes or sold on the open market as commodities. Flexible strategies for accumulating other species into human households, and then selling off valuable family members, has helped countless Floridians adapt to sweeping changes in political and economic landscapes. Kirskey argues that Florida stands out in the US legal landscape as a place where multispecies families that include diverse kinds of exotic animals proliferate within a *laissez-faire* economic environment.

The final two chapters, Chapters 9 and 10, provide a broad conceptual framework for the entire collection. In Chapter 9, "The Conflict of Human and Nonhuman Laws," Richard Janda and Richard Lehun start with the assumption that "we are in the Anthropocene." Humanity's collective impact, they argue, has become the dominant influence on the biosphere, leading to the destruction of the ecosystems upon which we depend. For the jurist, the Anthropocene involves a conflict of laws between those human laws governing our economic behavior and the nonhuman laws governing biogeophysical outcomes. This conflict produces an antinomical burden. Despite, and perhaps because of, their strong determinacy and persistence, human laws are no longer sustainable under the operation of nonhuman laws in the Anthropocene. Growing energy demands, met by increasing supply, have come to be in an antinomical relationship with the biosphere's regulatory response. By definition, this conflict of laws cannot be resolved; it can only be addressed though a reflexive reconfiguration of human norms. Nonhuman laws cannot be suspended, nor can we embrace multispecies legalities as a supervening source of legitimacy.

In the tenth and final chapter of the book, "Lively Agency: Law and Life in the Anthropocene," Andreas Philippopoulos-Mihalopoulos explores concepts of agency, law, and responsibility in the epoch of the Anthropocene. At the core of his exploration, Philippopoulos-Mihalopoulos offers the notion of *a life*, which he argues is not limited to animate beings but as a process of simultaneous connection and withdrawal that characterizes a body in relation to other bodies. The methodological tools for this exploration are Deleuze's concept of *a life*, Deleuze and Guattari's assemblage theory, postfeminist and new materialist thinking, and Spinozan ethics. The main question posed in this chapter is: How can lively agency be defined across human/nonhuman and animate/inanimate distinctions in a way that fleshes out a body's juridical responsibility? Philippopoulos-Mihalopoulos understands lively agency as an emergence that works across the animate-inanimate distinction. From this definition, a few questions emerge: Can there be an agency that is not legal? How does differentiation occur on the basis of flat ontology? And how should responsibility be defined in the Anthropocene? The chapter attempts to offer answers to the above questions on the basis of an ontological continuum of indistinguishability among bodies, which is paradoxically interposed with ruptures that bring in absolute difference as well as power inequalities.

Finally, in the book's afterword, "Lively Ever After: Beyond the Cult of Immateriality," David Delaney offers his reflections on the central legal themes addressed in the volume's chapters. Delaney describes what he calls the "cult of immateriality" that underpins dominant modern metaphysics and discusses ways in which law gives material effect to these ideological dispositions. He suggests that what is being called the Anthropocene is a condition that has been produced by and through distinctively modern, largely liberal, modes of legal thought and practice. Under these conditions, the world has become a "legal thing." Central to these dynamics are conventional conceptions of property, the associated constitution of (minded) subjects and objects, and the resultant structuring of power relations in accordance with the allocation of rights and non-rights. Delaney offers that to renounce the cult of immateriality and its foundational tenet that only humans (and gods) partake of the immaterial would facilitate the dissolution of the human/other-than-human dichotomy. It would also allow for the discernment of the materiality of law itself.

References

Agamben, Giorgio. 1995. *Homo Sacer: Sovereign Power and Bare Life.* Translated by Daniel Heller-Roazen. Stanford: Stanford University Press.

———. 2004. *The Open: Man and Animal.* Stanford: Stanford University Press.

Bennett, Jane. 2005. "The Agency of Assemblages and the North American Blackout." *Public Culture* 17 (3): 445–65.

Braverman, Irus. 2012. *Zooland: The Institution of Captivity.* Stanford: Stanford University Press.

———. 2013. "Animal Mobilegalities: The Regulation of Animal Movement in the American City." *Humanimalia* 5 (1): 104–35.

———. 2015a. *Wild Life: The Institution of Nature.* Stanford: Stanford University Press.

———. 2015b. "More-than-Human Legalities." In *The Handbook of Law and Society.* Edited by Austin Sarat and Patrcia Ewick, 307–21. West Sussex, UK: John Wiley & Sons.

Deckha, Maneesha. 2013. "Initiating a Non-Anthropocentric Jurisprudence: The Rule of Law and Animal Vulnerability under a Property Paradigm." *Alberta Law Review* 50 (4): 783–814.

Delaney, David. 2003. *Law and Nature.* Cambridge & NY: Cambridge University Press.

Derrida, Jacques. 2008. *The Animal That Therefore I Am.* New York: Fordham University Press.

———. 2009. *The Beast and the Sovereign, Vol. I.* Chicago: The University of Chicago Press.

Esposito, Roberto. 2012. *Terms of the Political: Community, Immunity, Biopolitics.* New York: Fordham University Press.

Foucault, Michel. 1970. *The Order of Things: An Archaeology of the Human Sciences.* New York: Pantheon Books.

———. 1990. *The History of Sexuality: An Introduction, Vol. I.* New York: Vintage.

———. 2009. *Security, Territory, Population: Lectures at the Collège de France, 1977–1978.* New York: Picador/Palgrave Macmillan.

Haraway, Donna. 2008. *When Species Meet.* Minneapolis: University of Minnesota Press.

Helmreich, Stefan. 2010. "How Like a Reef: Figuring Coral, 1839–2010." http://reefhelmreich.blogspot.co.uk/2010/11/stefan-helmreich.html.

Kirksey, Eben and Stefan Helmreich. 2010. "The Emergence of Multispecies Ethnography." *Cultural Anthropology* 24 (4): 545–76.

Latour, Bruno. 1993. *We Have Never Been Modern.* Translated by Catherine Porter. Cambridge: Harvard University Press.

Negarastani, Reza. 2008. *Cyclonopedia: Complicity with Anonymous Materials.* Melbourne: Repress.

Otomo, Yoriko and Edward Mussawir. 2012. *Law and the Question of the Animal.* London: Routledge.

Robertson, Ian. 2015. *Animals, Welfare and the Law: Critically Assessing the Role of Animals in Society.* London: Routledge.

Wolfe, Cary. 2012. *Before the Law: Humans and Animals in a Biopolitical Frame.* Chicago: University of Chicago Press.

Chapter 1

The Regulatory Life of Threatened Species Lists

Irus Braverman

> [A]nimals are divided into: (a) belonging to the Emperor, (b) embalmed, (c) tame, (d) suckling pigs, (e) sirens, (f) fabulous, (g) stray dogs, (h) included in the present classification, (i) frenzied, (j) innumerable, (k) drawn with a very fine camelhair brush, (1) et cetera, (m) having just broken the water pitcher, (n) that from a long way off look like flies.
>
> —Michel Foucault, *The Order of Things*, quoting from Borges' "a 'certain Chinese encyclopedia,'" p. xv

It is with the whimsy and wonder of the above quote that Foucault begins his great expedition into the order of things. "Out of the laughter that shattered," Foucault says, "all the familiar landmarks of my thought—our thought, the thought that bears the stamp of our age and our geography—breaking up all the ordered surfaces and all the planes with which we are accustomed to tame the wild profusion of existing things, and continuing long afterwards to disturb and threaten with collapse our age-old distinction between the Same and the Other" (1970, xv). It is not incidental, I shall argue here, that Foucault began his study of order with the project of classifying nonhuman animals in the form of a list. The divide between the "human" and the "animal" is foundational for identifying and distinguishing "us" from "them." As such, it provides the basis for the most fundamental classification of all—that between human and animal—and for the regulation of this classification through legal institutions that utilize listing technologies.

The age-old capacity of lists to make and resist order has become a topic of renewed attention as of late. A growing literature on lists describes their power to create and organize global connectivities (Staeheli 2012, 234), emphasizing their role in security regimes in particular (Amoore 2011; Leyshon and Thrift 1999). What has been overlooked in this wave of renewed

Black rhino (*Diceros bicornis*), 2008. The price of rhino horn on Korean markets increased by more than 400 percent within two years of their uplisting from CITES Appendix II to Appendix I, "which in turn coincided with a sharp increase in the poaching of black rhinos and in illegal trade in rhino horn" (Rivalan et al. 2007, 530). Photo courtesy of U.S. Fish and Wildlife Service.

attention, however, is the role of the list as a regulatory device for ordering human–nonhuman relations. This chapter will diverge from the anthropocentric focus of the existing literature on lists to explore the legal project of listing nonhuman species as "threatened" and "endangered." "All kinds of things become more interesting once we stop assuming that 'we' are the only place to begin and end our analysis," offer Hinchliffe and Bingham along these lines (2008, 1541). It is precisely toward such interesting valences around the seemingly dry and technical performance of the list that this chapter intends to direct attention. I will highlight the regulatory power of lists and their role in the grand project of ordering life: both human and nonhuman.

The last two decades have witnessed an explosion of national and global lists of threatened and endangered species (see, e.g., de Grammont and Cuarón 2006, 22). In 2010, at least 109 countries had produced a national red data book, national red list, or other national lists of threatened species (Miller 2013, 198) and more than 25 listing systems of threatened species were used across North America alone (2013, 192). The International Union for Conservation of Nature (IUCN) Red List for Threatened Species™ (hereafter, the Red List) is the "mother" of all threatened species lists, the first and most comprehensive attempt at the global listing of all threatened species. According to a prominent IUCN official, for the last five decades, the Red List has provided "a map of how to do conservation" (Lamoreux, interview).

Drawing on my previous work on the biopolitical dimensions of the Red List (2015a; 2015b), this chapter will explore the more and the less visible regulatory frameworks for listing threatened species through the Red List. Such explorations illuminate a number of common themes between human- and nonhuman-focused lists: visibility, translatability, comparability, inexhaustibility, simplicity, flexibility, credibility, objectivity, neutrality, technicality, and contagion. At the same time, these explorations also illuminate some of the differences between human and nonhuman lists: whereas various security lists (such as the secret drone "kill list," no-fly lists, and terrorist lists) identify humans who risk or threaten, threatened species lists typically identify nonhumans who are threatened.

The source of the differences between human- and nonhuman-focused lists is evident when examining them through a biopolitical lens: according to Foucault, only (certain) humans are privileged with political life. Animals and plants, along with all that is considered natural or wild, are relegated to the realm of biological life—namely, that which is killable. By contrast, this chapter applies the distinction between biological and political life also to the nonhuman context. Through their listing as threatened, certain species' lives are elevated to a political status, while the rest (initially, at least, the unlisted) remain biological, or mere, life (Braverman 2015c). In other words, whereas the rule for nonhumans is biological life and the threatened list is the exception, the situation is reversed in the case of humans, where the general rule is political life, and the list exceptionalizes and reduces such life to the biological realm.

Threatened species lists are thus both biopolitical and regulatory technologies: they (re)produce and reinforce underlying species ontologies by creating, calculating, and governing the boundary between the human and the nonhuman. Indeed, alongside their reinforcement of the biopolitical differentiation between various nonhuman species, threatened species lists also distinguish human from nonhuman species. Such a differentiated treatment of the life and death of nonhuman species through their en-listing, down- and up-listing, multi-listing, and de-listing translate into the positive protection and active governance of such species. Listing threatened species thus becomes a way to affirm—and to justify—which lives are more and most important to save, thereby reifying the distinction between those who save (humans) and those who can only be saved (nonhumans).

Despite their significant differences, the bulk of this chapter will examine several aspects of the nonhuman list that are highly applicable in the context of the human list, too. This exploration will utilize an empirical and ethnographic methodology to illuminate characteristics of the list that travel across the human-nonhuman divide but that may not be as obvious or visible when observed only in the human context. I will start by introducing the list in general, and the Red List in particular, and will then proceed to examine the biopolitical aspects of the Red List as well as its global, regulatory, scientific, and seductive powers.

The List

The word "list" originates from border, edge, boundary (from Old High German lîsta; OED 2013), but it also means lust and desire, or inclination. Dating back to Old English from before the twelfth century, *hlyst* also means "to listen" (OED 2013). "List-making is frequently seen as one of the fundamental activities of advanced human society," offer Bowker and Star (1994, 188), while Goody (1977) suggests that the first written records to exist were lists of kings and equipment. Belknap adds along these lines: "Lists have been used for varied purposes throughout history. Among other things, they serve to enumerate, account, remind, memorialize, order. Lists abound in various sizes, shapes, and functions" (2000, 40).

A grocery list, kill lists, sex offender lists, and lists of threatened species—all are consecutive configurations of discrete items linked by a common goal that assigns them meaning and functionality. Lists name, classify, document, and simplify; they aspire to comprehensiveness, comparability, consistency, and uniformity, and are structured to delineate boundaries, produce authority, and promote visibility. Making a list is a way of making something apparent (or heard, recall *hlyst*) that is not otherwise so. Related to and drawing upon these functions, certain lists also standardize and regulate. Whereas all lists rely on various forms of classification, effectively "sorting things out" (Bowker and Star 1999)—some also *prioritize*. With such lists, not only the listed items but also their particular order is significant. Threatened species lists are a good example of this dual function. Such lists also typically share the following characteristics: they are a *scientific* method for highlighting those *species* under higher *extinction risk* with the explicit or implicit goal of focusing attention on *conservation measures* designed to protect them (Possingham et al. 2002, 503; emphasis added).

The IUCN Red List of Threatened Species is by far the most influential and widely used method for evaluating global extinction risks. The IUCN has been producing red data books and red lists since 1963 (Lamoreux et al. 2003, 215). During the five decades of its use, the Red List of Threatened Species has evolved from a subjective expert-based system lacking standardized criteria to a uniform and global rule-based system (Miller 2013, 195; Mace et al. 2008). Despite (or as a result of) the insistence by many IUCN scientists on the Red List's non-prescriptive and apolitical character (Hoffmann, interview), it has had a profound influence on conservation laws and practices around the world (Possingham et al. 2002; Rodrigues et al. 2006). Specifically, the Red List has inspired the development of numerous national and regional red lists and has functioned as an important source for the Convention on International Trade in Endangered Species of Wild Fauna and Flora (CITES)—a powerful international convention on trade that determines whether and how commercial trade in certain species will be regulated. Why does the Red List have such enormous normative power, and how does it work in the world? To answer these questions, I will first explore the biopolitical properties of the Red List.

The Biopolitical List

Beyond their descriptive and declarative functions, threatened species lists normalize and regulate conservation and related actions; they also prescribe a series of material effects on specific animal bodies (Braverman 2015a). While recognizing these functions and their effects on the individual level, the power of threatened species lists emanates from their capacity to order life at the level of the biological *species*—what Foucault refers to as biopolitics (Foucault 1990). Thinking and governing through species regimes, and through compiling lists of threatened species in particular, enables both an abstraction—a grid over the Linnaean kingdoms (Foucault 1970)—and an embodiment: a personification of ecosystems, habitats, and populations. Since humans understand themselves primarily as an exceptional species and therefore both relate to, and differentiate themselves from, other species—it is important to critically examine the species lens and the work that it performs in the world.

For conservation scientists, the species is the foundational ontological unit through which life can be calculated and known (Braverman 2015c; Sandler 2012). Biermann and Mansfield reflect on the perspective of conservation experts that: "Managing individual nonhuman lives is meaningless in responding to the crisis of biodiversity loss; individual lives acquire meaning only when they advance the long-term well being of the broader population or are essential to sustaining key biological processes, especially evolution" (2014, 264). According to this way of thinking, the death of an individual gains meaning based on the level of endangerment of her or his species: once on the brink of extinction, the individual becomes larger than a singular life, and her or his death is therefore more than a singular death—it becomes the death of a life form, the death of nature (Braverman 2015c). Nonhuman life is measured numerically and valued according to its placement in the scheme of the threatened list.

At the same time, the deaths of so many other life forms who are not rare, charismatic, or visible enough to warrant the threatened designation fall outside the range of legal protections established by the list, or outside the list altogether. Such life forms are effectively "list-less": incalculable, unmemorable, and thus killable. Toward the end of this chapter, I argue that the conservation value of a species is defined through its inclusion and ranking in an ever-proliferating number of lists and that the regulatory power of such lists is constantly eroded as new lists take their place in defining what is even more threatened, endangered, or extinct.

While much recent biopolitical work emphasizes thanatopolitics or necropolitics, this chapter brings into focus an affirmative biopolitics (Rutherford and Rutherford 2013, 426), namely "the ways in which biopolitics can be more about life than death, about inclusion rather than exclusion" (429). What happens to those listless lives that fall outside the realm of the threatened list does not configure into this account, which focuses instead on the viability of the listed. But such a focus on the affirmative does not entail a disavowal of death. Quite the contrary, "to *make live* does not mean to avoid death altogether but to manage death at the level of the population. In a biopolitical regime, death is transformed into a rate of mortality, which is open to intervention and management. This transformation erases the fact that not all life is equally promoted" (Biermann and Mansfield 2014, 259). I will discuss such erasures later, in the context of the scientific powers of the list.

The Global List

In its aspiration for a totalizing regime, the Red List illuminates the utility of the list form for furthering global classification schemes. "The IUCN Red List assesses the status of species at a global level because this is the scale at which extinction occurs," explain Mace and other prominent architects of the Red List (Mace et al. 2008, 1437). Lists are not only a way of channeling communication flows; they also "do the global" in their work as boundary objects that operate across time and space in an attempt at universal standardization.

The Red List "does the global" in a number of ways. First, it produces simple and visible links between otherwise loosely connected species, geographies, temporalities, and risks. "A global list deals with the global by adding, combining, and possibly ordering items—without the obligation to create a totalizing signifier of the global" (Staeheli 2012, 234). The use of species as the foundational unit of threatened lists—effectively rendering them the "currency of conservation" (Lamoreux, interview)—is not only ideological, as emphasized earlier, but also pragmatic. Species are the most common, visible, and easily measured unit for assessing the state of biodiversity. The Red List's visibility is an important factor in its global efficiency. Indeed, threatened species are "among the most visible and easily understood symbols of the rising tide of extinctions," making them an "emotive and politically powerful measurement of biodiversity loss" (Miller 2013, 192; see also Wilcove 2010).

In addition to utilizing species units, the Red List's visibility is enhanced through the list's color-coded visualization of danger (the *red* list) and its clear topology of endangerment, as well as through its adoption of "catastrophe-governance" that focuses on raising alarm by identifying and quantifying threats and extinction (Aradau and van Munster 2011, 85–106). John Lamoreux of the National Fish and Wildlife Foundation is a member of the IUCN and actively engaged in the red list assessments. He argues that "birders are famous for making lists: *you have to be able to see what you saw.* There's almost a listing mentality" (interview). Beyond these apparent functions, Lamoreux points out that the Red List is also important as a "rallying cry." "As an organization, you know what you stand for if you make a list of what's important," he tells me. The Red List, and threatened lists more generally, are thus a technology for the identification, differentiation, and visualization of certain forms of life with the goal of mobilizing universal support and political and legal action that aim to prevent (certain) nonhuman extinctions.

To serve as an effective technology for mobilization, the Red List must be easily translatable into various contexts—a "pan-linguistic device" (Staeheli 2012, 240). Red List Unit Programme Officer Rebecca Miller focuses on the broad functionality of lists as she writes: "The principle aim of a threatened species assessment is to estimate a species' risk of extinction in a comparable, repeatable, transparent, and objective manner" (Miller 2013, 191). The list's power as a global technology also derives from its plasticity (Belknap 2000, 35) and homogeneity, which promote equality and comparability among species. The Red List is "applied to grasshoppers as well as blue whales," John Lamoreux tells me accordingly. "There's something about the applicability across all groups that's just truly amazing," he adds.

By 2013, the IUCN Species Survival Commission network—the central scientific body of the IUCN that is comprised of thousands of scientists and experts from around the world—evaluated the global threat status of 71,576 species of animals, plants, and fungi (IUCN 2013c). The aim: to assess and appropriately categorize every living species on earth (ibid.).

This global scope of the Red List demonstrates how lists "promise order as well as open-endedness, exhaustiveness as well as infinite addition" (de Goede and Sullivan forthcoming, 3). The generic list's "logic of infinite addition" (Staeheli 2012, 234) is an important element of the threatened species list as well and is exemplified to the extreme in the Red List context. Mike Hoffmann of IUCN's Species Survival Commission clarifies that the Red List is not just about registering *threatened* species, but about registering *all* species. "You can't talk about the status of biodiversity globally unless you've assessed everything," he tells me in an interview. A 2014 *Science* article by Stuart Pimm and others illuminates the massive scale of this project. According to these authors, while an estimated 1.9 million animal species have been described and documented, between 2 and 11 million animal species are still unknown. Some further argue that uncertainties in insect and fungi numbers make stating a plausible range for the number of unknown species impossible (Pimm et al. 2014, 987).

The Regulatory List

The Red List is especially powerful for its simplicity and comprehensiveness: "you want a category system that at the end of the day is relatively simple to implement," Hoffmann explains in our interview. The simplicity factor is intimately related to the aforementioned heightened comparability that the Red List affords. Generally, the assumption is that the simpler the categories and criteria, the more they can be applied across the board to regulate the various taxa on the list. Indeed, the criteria and categories "are designed to apply whether you are a mammal or a bird or a fungus or a plant or whatever you are" (Hoffmann, interview). For example, Criterion D requires a threshold of fewer than 50 mature individuals (IUCN 2001)—a number that applies to all taxa, from fungi to whales. Thus a "one size fits all" approach can be quite problematic. The IUCN cautions, for example, that: "The choice of scale at which range is estimated may thus, itself, influence the outcome of Red List assessments and could be a source of inconsistency and bias. It is impossible to provide any strict but general rules for mapping taxa or habitats; the most appropriate scale will depend on the taxon in question, and the origin and comprehensiveness of the distribution data" (IUCN 2001).

Nonetheless, the central idea of the Red List "was to come up with one system that is applicable across all taxa, and you can therefore make *comparisons* across your different taxonomic groups" (Hoffmann, interview).

In addition to its role in constructing a governable platform of comparability between different taxa, the Red List also provides comparability within particular taxa over time. It makes possible grand calculations such as this one: "On average, 52 species of mammals, birds, and amphibians move one category closer to extinction each year"; or this: "the deterioration for amphibians was equivalent to 662 amphibian species each moving one Red List category closer to extinction over the assessment period, the deteriorations for birds and mammals equate to 223 and 156 species, respectively, deteriorating at least one category" (Hoffmann et al. 2010, 1507; see, e.g., Figures 1.1 and 1.2). The capacity of the Red List to facilitate comparisons across previously disconnected units and fields corresponds with what has been described elsewhere as "a new mode of hyperconnectivity," whereby "[e]very item can now be combined with every other item" (Staeheli 2012, 240). The basic order of the list thus generates "a virtual space for recombinations, inventions, and narratives" (ibid.).

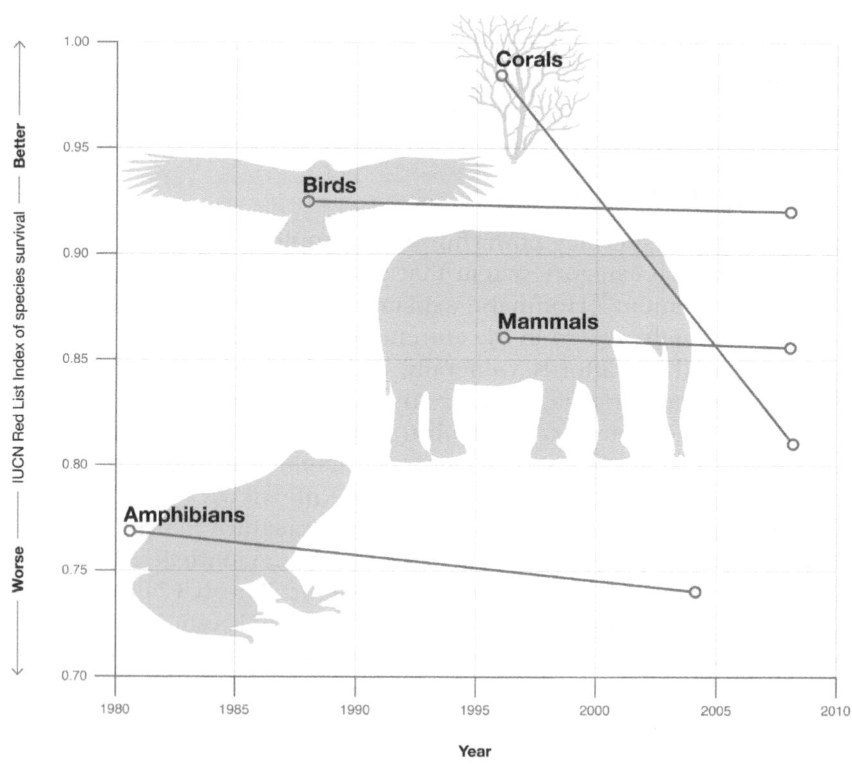

Figure 1.1 From the IUCN website: "The Red List Index for reef-forming corals, birds, mammals, and amphibians. Coral species are moving toward increased extinction risk most rapidly, while amphibians are, on average, the most threatened group." http://www.iucnredlist.org/about/summary-statistics. Used with permission.

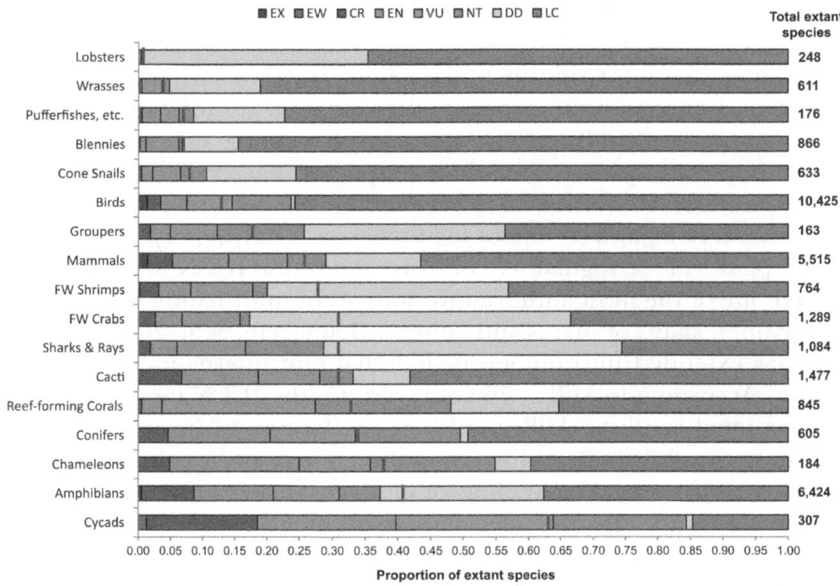

Figure 1.2 From the IUCN website: "The proportion of extant (i.e., excluding Extinct) species in *The IUCN Red List of Threatened Species. Version 2015.2* assessed in each category for the more comprehensively assessed groups. Taxa are ordered [to] show the best estimate for proportion of extant species considered threatened (CR, EN, or VU). . . . The numbers above each bar represent the total number of extant species assessed for each group. **CR** - Critically Endangered, **EN** - Endangered, **VU** - Vulnerable, **NT** - Near Threatened, **DD** - Data Deficient, **LC** - Least Concern." http://www.iucnredlist.org/about/summary-statistics. Used with permission.

The Red List's regulatory powers lie also in its touted objectivity, transparency, and repeatability (namely, that if another expert were to conduct the assessment he or she would reach the same listing status; Brooks, interview). Nonetheless, it is not free from biases. According to Hoffmann, the biggest source of bias is when scientists want to list "their" species as threatened, "because they're worried that if it's not, they're not going to get money." The reverse also happens, with researchers who prefer that their species be listed as Least Concern "so that they can collect their species, put it in a specimen jar, and do research on it." "Our job," Hoffmann tells me, "is to be the neutral, objective, adjudicators of that process." IUCN's Standards and Petitions Subcommittee is the particular adjudicator in cases of disagreement over a Red List designation. According to Hoffmann, they are "the experts in the criteria, and what they say . . . would essentially be considered gospel" (interview).

This brings me to consider the Red List's authority. Barney Long of the World Wildlife Fund and the IUCN tells me that "when you say this species is red listed by the IUCN as Critically Endangered, everyone automatically agrees and accepts that. There's no conversation, because the experts have agreed that it is Critically Endangered" (interview). These lists are so important, Long continues, because they are a means for conservationists to communicate with the public, and serve as a source of advice for policy makers on how to protect and manage species. The credibility of the list, it is inferred, creates a front behind which disparate conservation groups can unite, serving as a source of legitimacy, as a rallying cry, and also as a shared platform for regulatory controls. Today, the IUCN Red List is considered one of the most authoritative sources of information on the global conservation status of plants and animals (Lamoreux et al. 2003). Its influence has extended into numerous national and international regulatory systems. According to Miller, 76 countries use the IUCN methodology for their national red lists (Miller 2013, 197). Because of its effectiveness in governing the global efforts for saving threatened species, the Red List has emerged as the central technology of modern conservation.

Then there are also the adverse and unintended effects of particular listings, which point to the unpredictability of governing across global and temporal scales. Brian Horne of the Wildlife Conservation Society tells me in an interview that collectors often "want the rare, and the unusual and different." Hence, when turtle breeders learned that a certain turtle species was soon to be listed under CITES' Appendix I, their prices for that animal increased dramatically: "[t]he turtle went from being a hundred dollar turtle to [costing] one thousand dollars" (see, e.g., Figure on page 2, this volume). Another result is that once a species is downlisted (i.e., it is classified as less threatened), "you become a victim of your own success . . . because suddenly there's less funding sources available," which in turn translates into less protection (Bennett, interview). A final example of unintended consequences is that the price of black rhino horn on Korean markets increased by more than 400 percent within two years of their uplisting from CITES Appendix II to Appendix I, "which in turn coincided with a sharp increase in the poaching of black rhinos and in illegal trade in rhino horn" (Rivalan et al. 2007, 530; see, e.g., Figure on page 18, this volume). The listing process produced by officials in one corner of the world has thus translated into the life or death of the relevant nonhuman animals in other corners of the world.

The Scientific List

In addition to the simplicity, comparability, and translatability of threatened species lists, their global power, mobility, and ubiquity derive from their configuration as scientific, technical, and quantitative, and therefore as neutral and apolitical. According to the Guidelines for Appropriate Uses of IUCN Red List Data: "The IUCN Red List is developed through contributions from a network of thousands of scientific experts around the world. . . . It uses a scientific process based upon objective criteria. Assessments are impartial, independent, and not politically driven. . . . The IUCN Red List is therefore a synthesis of the best available species knowledge from the top experts" (IUCN 2011). The insistence on the part of conservationists that the Red List is never political but only scientific exposes the underlying ideal "that science describes nature (and nature alone) and that politics is about social power (and social power alone)" (Bowker and Star 1999, 46). The list's visibility, accessibility, and transparency simultaneously serve to conceal its underlying political features and value-based judgments.

In 1994, the IUCN revised its expert-based risk-ranking system into a data-driven quantitative system and finalized these categories and criteria in 2001 (IUCN 2014; Mace et al. 2008). To provide a global index of biodiversity and to identify those species most in need of conservation attention, IUCN scientists have stressed that "the classification system must be objective and transparent. It also needs to be applicable to a variety of species and habitats; standardized to yield consistent results independent of the assessor or the species being assessed; accessible to allow a variety of species experts to use it; scientifically defensible; and reasonably rigorous (i.e. it should be hard to classify species inappropriately)" (Mace et al. 2008, 1427). Another scientist writes that the current Red List is designed to provide "a standardized, consistent, and transparent method for assessing extinction risk, thereby increasing the objectivity and scientific credibility of the assessments" (Miller 2013, 195). Yet some scientists reject the Red List's claim of scientific objectivity. James Watson is president-elect of the Society of Conservation Biology and head of the Climate Change Project at the World Conservation Society. He says about the rigid criteria of the Red List, and of threatened lists more generally, that "[a]t the end of the day, all listings are arbitrary: they're not driven by the laws of physics, they're actually created . . . by humans trying their best to develop the most appropriate categories according to the best available knowledge" (interview).

Currently, the Red List classifies taxa into nine categories: Extinct (EX), Extinct in the Wild (EW), Critically Endangered (CE), Endangered (EN), Vulnerable (VU), Near Threatened (NT), Least Concern (LC), Data Deficient (DD), and Not Evaluated (NE) (IUCN 2014). The evaluation system consists of one set of criteria that are applicable to all threatened species (namely, species included in the categories of Critically Endangered, Endangered, and Vulnerable) and that measure the symptoms of endangerment (but not the causes). Five criteria, listed A through E, are used to categorize taxa within these threatened categories. The criteria are: A) a reduction in population size; B) a small, reduced, fragmented, or fluctuating geographic range; C) a decline in size of an already small population; D) a very small or restricted population; and E) a quantitative analysis indicating the probability of extinction. To be listed as Critically Endangered, for example, a species must decline by 90 percent or more, cover less than 100km^2, or contain fewer than 50 mature individuals (IUCN 2014). A species need only satisfy one criterion to be listed. Although the other categories are included in the list's database, species classified within them are not assessed in the same manner as those within the threatened categories.

Each of the categories contains a list of species, which can be traced in the Red List's online database, with one exception: the category of Not Evaluated (NE) contains no data. Mike Hoffmann explains: "NE just indicates that no attempt to evaluate the status of the taxon has been made. In reality, any species not on the Red List (i.e., more than 90 percent of species) is NE" (e-mail communication). A related concept is the "undescribed species." The IUCN Guidelines state that "The listing of undescribed species on the IUCN Red List is discouraged, but in exceptional circumstances these may be included" (2014, 5). Hoffmann explains: "Nearly all undescribed species are implicitly not evaluated, with a few rare exceptions when conditions outlined in the guidelines are met and an attempt has been made to evaluate the undescribed species against the categories and criteria." Generally, the further away from extinction the species is ranked, the less visible it is from the list's perspective—and the more "list-less" it becomes.

The Red List example demonstrates the close, if not inseparable, relationship between lists and databases—indeed, how the list may become a database (de Goede and Sullivan forthcoming, 6). The Red List is one such hybrid database-list; it operates by translating analogous flows in risk levels and flexible forms of life into fixed digital categories. Easily distinguishable from one another, these categories serve as the basis for myriad regulatory actions. In this sense, the Red List is a technique of government: a sophisticated system that rests both on the binary of inclusion (of all known species) and exclusion (of the unknown) as well as on a differentiation among a set of distinct categories, determined through algorithmic calculations of probability.

While the Red List's categories and criteria are "one size fits all," species are, by their very nature, diverse. To be listed, this diversity must be identified and measured. IUCN trainers guide assessors on how to interpret the categories and criteria across taxa so that they meet the thresholds. Hoffmann tells me about the assessors that, "[t]hey might be field biologists, taxonomists, academics, government personnel, park managers, or any one of a number of people." The process of figuring out whether a species meets the risk thresholds is complicated and not always clear-cut. Often, the final status depends on the tendencies of the particular assessors. According to Hoffmann, the central challenge facing the Red List's administration is that of assessors being either too evidentiary or too precautionary: "You either want perfect data, and therefore you are less likely to list something as threatened, so everything's going to go into Data Deficient—or you're very precautionary, you think everything's at risk, and so you throw it into a threatened category. Ideally, you want somewhere in the middle of those two things" (interview). Since scientists tend to be very evidentiary, Hoffmann continues, they often experience difficulty when working with the Red List, which is built "to give fuzzy numbers" (interview).

"Not all threatened species are created equally," Hoffmann further explains in a statement that points to the actual impact of a Red List designation, what legal scholars often call "law in action," in contrast to the "law [here, the list] on the books." Lamoreux explains, for example, that "even if you list a whole lot of dragonflies on the Red List, they're not going to suddenly get as much attention as a panda." He clarifies, accordingly, that "they're not all equal in the eyes of conservation funding or conservation action" (interview). Hoffmann is first to admit that "we have lots of biases," explaining that the system is "still very much biased towards vertebrates" and that "plants, fungi, and invertebrates are underrepresented" (interview). Watson notes, similarly, that of 1,600 species on the Australian threatened list, only 35 percent receive government funding for conservation. "The things which get money are birds and mammals, and the things which don't get money are butterflies and plants," he tells me in an interview.

Even the listing of a species as threatened, then, does not promise this species equal protection in relation to other listed species. Myriad criteria, as well as other more or less formal lists, determine which species are politically and legally defined as more or less worth saving. "We've got a long way to go," Hoffmann says about the current state of the Red List. Conservation biologist Arne Mooers adds that "the conservation biology community [itself] mistakenly considers probabilities of extinction as representing worth" (interview). For this reason, certain conservation biologists have been advocating for alternative or additional lists that would openly justify the de facto priorities adopted by countries, organizations, and institutions, which, they argue, would make these priorities more scientific and transparent (Possingham et al. 2002).

Alongside its reliance on fixed standards, the Red List also enables flexibility. Specifically, the number of species listed in each category changes every time it is updated—on the books, every five years. This is a result of various factors, including species being assessed for the first time, species being reassessed and moved into a different category of threat, and taxonomic revisions. The IUCN distinguishes genuine from non-genuine reasons (in other words, "real" from "technical" changes in threat levels that result from error, taxonomic revisions, or changes in threshold definitions) for revising a listing (IUCN 2013). The ever-changing nature of the list makes it even more potent, as no protection, or un-protection, is never fixed or settled. Thus, scientists are engaged in an ever-listing process.

This depiction of the Red List resonates with the characterization of lists in general as inherently ambivalent in that "criteria for selection are not fixed at the outset, but evolve during the list's use" (Staeheli 2012, 237). Indeed, neither the manifold modifications in species' status nor the more radical changes in the list's criteria and its modes of calculation detract from the power of the Red List. Rather than a weakness, moreover, the Red List's shifting foundations in fact enhance its credibility. Such changes also cannot be detected through a simple reading of the list. As Staeheli argues, "[r]eading a list does not reveal these myriads of small changes, struggles, and ambivalences . . . the list looks perfect in itself, a homogenized and objectivized collection of cleanly separated items, in a space out of time" (ibid.). The decisions made in the course of the Red List's construction are therefore "forever lost to the historical record. . . . In fact, their history is considered by most to be boring, trivial, and unworthy of investigation" (Bowker and Star 1999, 17).

The Seductive List

I have already explored the Red list's biopolitical, global, regulatory, and scientific properties. Lastly, I would like to explore the Red List's contagious, or seductive, qualities. It has already been acknowledged that lists produce an urge for more lists, highlighting "the contagious nature of list-making" (Staeheli 2012, 243), apparently classified by the Diagnostic and Statistical Manual of Mental Disorders (DSM) as "glazomania" (Cagen 2007). The obsession with lists is nowhere more apparent than in the conservation context, where threatened lists and other priority lists for conservation proliferate by the day, alongside narratives on skyrocketing rates of extinction. Long explains that in addition to the Red List for species, the IUCN is currently developing priority lists for ecosystems and protected areas, resulting in three separate conservation lists within the IUCN alone.

Of the various threatened species lists, some "are designed purely to evaluate risk of extinction, whereas others focus on ranking species to receive priority conservation attention" (Miller 2013, 194). Accordingly, certain countries produce at minimum two separate lists. This, in order "to prevent blurring the line between extinction risk assessment, which is a scientific endeavor, and conservation priority setting, which is very much a value-based judgment" (103). Such a dual existence of scientific and political lists both constructs and reinforces the ostensibly apolitical nature of the scientific list, which is then juxtaposed with the social nature of the political list. Another challenge that arises in this context is intra-list incompatibility. Although the majority of conservation lists are generically referred to as threatened or endangered species lists, the determination of what classifies a species as endangered or threatened can differ greatly from list to list. These differences have engendered quite a bit of confusion, not only on the part of conservationists but also on the part of policy makers and the public.

If the Red List focuses on identifying all threatened species from an ever-growing list of known species, other lists supplement this by identifying alternative targets for maintaining biodiversity. In this way, despite the terminological challenges, "lists intersect, feed on each other, become consolidated, disseminated, stretched and translated" (de Goede and Sullivan forthcoming, 11–12). For example, the Alliance for Zero Extinction (AZE) aims to identify all sites around the globe that serve as the single remaining location for a species that is listed as Endangered or Critically Endangered under the IUCN Red List (AZE 2013). Of 20,934 such species, the AZE mapped 920 species in 588 sites, implying that these are the world's *most* threatened species (ibid.). Mike Hoffmann explains that, "These are the places where, if you don't do something here, now, for this species, you're going to lose a species" (interview).

Despite their common origin in, and their immense drawing on, the Red List, the various conservation lists differ in their perspective on what is most important about life and thus on what is most worth saving—whether rarity in numbers, unique territorial configurations, or evolutionary (phylogenetic) variation. Rather than a bifurcated understanding of life versus death, then, conservation lists parse the life of species into complex orderings according to their extinction risks, effectively establishing a gradation of animal bodies according to the perceived worthiness of their lives. Even among those species who are deemed threatened, categories and criteria thus prioritize the ones who are perceived to be *the most threatened of all*: those whose lives are even more, and finally most, worth saving (Braverman 2015a; 2015b; 2015c).

Alongside the staggering proliferation of lists, a critique of existing listing processes as the exclusive metrics of conservation is currently emerging among scientists. In the words of James Watson of the World Conservation Society: "The conservation field is dominated by ecologists who really like to make lists." But "conservation is also not just about *listing* something," he continues, "it is about *doing* something." "This is not a failure of the list itself, it's the failure of the conservation community to develop other metrics beyond the list" (Watson, interview). Joseph et al. (2009, 328) argue along these lines that the existing listing approach in conservation typically "ignore[s] two crucial factors: the cost of management and the likelihood that the management will succeed" (see also Bottrill et al. 2011; Possingham et al. 2002; Walsh et al. 2012). Such critiques merely hint at the vast possibilities for problematizing, challenging, and "torquing" (Bowker and Star 1999, 27; 190) threatened species lists in ways that resist their authority and their seemingly automatic application. "The trick is to question every apparently natural easiness in the world around us and look for the work involved in making it easy," suggest Bowker and Star (1999, 39).

Conclusion

Foucault contends that, "Order is at one and the same time, that which is given in things as their inner law, the hidden network that determines the way they confront one another, and also that which has no existence except in the grid created by a glance, an examination, a language; and it is only in the blank spaces of this grid that order manifests itself in depth as though already there, waiting in silence for the moment of its expression" (1970, xx). Listing a threatened species provides such a grid over the animal and plant kingdoms, giving particular forms of life a name, a number, a map, a database, and a threat rank—all establishing their "inner law" and uniqueness, and thereby elevating them from the listless abstraction of other, unknown, forms of life. The threatened species list is thus a biopolitical technology par excellence.

As part of the threatened species list's prominent biopolitical features, this chapter has illuminated the global, regulatory, scientific, and seductive dimensions of this list. Although my list of the list's dimensions is not exhaustive by any means, it nonetheless provides a sense of why the Red List and other threatened species lists carry such immense regulatory force in global conservation narratives. Conservationists typically believe that life—embodied in species units—must be assessed, calculated, and ranked if it is to be protected and saved. And while conservation is about saving life, it is also about sorting out and regulating which life should be privileged in this endeavor. The life that is worth conserving obtains meaning through both an infinite calculus and a proliferating number of lists.

Interviews

Bennett, Elizabeth. Vice President for Species Conservation, Wildlife Conservation Society. On-site, New York City, NY, December 20, 2013.

Brooks, Tom. Head, Science and Knowledge Unit, IUCN. Skype, January 25, 2014.

Hoffmann, Michael. Senior Scientific Officer. Species Survival Commission, IUCN. Skype, January 9, 2014; e-mail communication, June 26, 2015.

Horne, Brian. Turtle Conservation Coordinator, Wildlife Conservation Society. Skype, January 9, 2014.

Lamoreux, John. Biodiversity Analyst, National Fish and Wildlife Foundation. Telephone, January 7, 2014.

Long, Barney. Director, Species Protection and Asian Species Conservation, World Wildlife Fund. Skype, January 9, 2014.

Mooers, Arne. Professor of Conservation Biology, Simon Fraser University. Skype, January 6, 2014.

Watson, James. President-elect, Society of Conservation Biology; Head, Climate Change Program, the Wildlife Conservation Society (WCS). Skype, January 27, 2014.

References

Amoore, Louise. 2011. "Data Derivatives: On the Emergence of a Security Risk Calculus of Our Times." *Theory, Culture and Society* 28 (6): 24–43.

Aradau, Claudia and Rens van Munster. 2011. *The Politics of Catastrophe: Genealogies of the Unknown.* London: Routledge.

AZE. 2013. *Alliance for Zero Extinction.* http://www.zeroextinction.org/.

Belknap, Robert. 2000. "The Literary List: A Survey of Its Uses and Deployments." *Literary Imagination* 2 (1): 35–54.

Biermann, Christine and Becky Mansfield. 2014. "Biodiversity, Purity, and Death: Conservation Biology as Biopolitics." *Environment and Planning D: Society and Space* 32: 257–73.

Bottrill, Madeleine, Jessica Walsh, James Watson, Liana Joseph et al. 2011. "Does Recovery Planning Improve the Status of Threatened Species?" *Biological Conservation* 144 (5): 1595–601.

Bowker, Geoffrey and Susan Leigh Star. 1994. "Knowledge And Infrastructure in International Information Management." In *Information Acumen: The Understanding and Use of Knowledge in Modern Business.* Edited by Lisa Bud-Frierman, 187–213. London: Routledge.

———. 1999. *Sorting Things Out: Classification and Its Consequences.* Cambridge, MA: MIT Press.

Braverman, Irus. 2015a. "En-Listing Life: Red is the Color of Threatened Species Lists." In *Critical Animal Geographies.* Edited by Rosemarie Collard and Kathryn Gillespie, 184–202. London: Routledge/Earthscan.

———. 2015b. "Is the Puerto Rican Parrot Worth Saving? The Biopolitics of Endangerment and Grievability." In *Economies of Death.* Edited by Kathryn Gillespie and Patricia Lopez, 73–94. London: Routledge/Earthscan.

———. 2015c. *Wild Life: The Institution of Nature.* Stanford: Stanford University Press.

Cagen, Sasha. 2007. *To-Do List: From Buying Milk to Finding a Soul Mate, What Our Lists Reveal About Us.* New York: Fireside.

Foucault, Michel. 1970. *The Order of Things: An Archeology of the Human Sciences.* New York: Vintage Books.

———. 1990. *The History of Sexuality: An Introduction, Volume 1.* New York: Vintage Books.

de Goede, Marieke and Gavin Sullivan. forthcoming. The Politics of Security Lists. *Environment and Planning D: Society and Space*: 1–22.

Goody, Jack. 1977. "What's in a List." In *The Domestication of the Savage Mind,* 52–111. Cambridge: Cambridge University Press.

de Grammont, Paloma and Alfredo Cuarón. 2006. "An Evaluation of Threatened Species Categorization Systems Used on the American Continent." *Conservation Biology* 20 (1): 14–27.

Hinchliffe, Steve and Nick Bingham. 2008. "Securing Life: The Emerging Practices Of Biosecurity." *Environment and Planning A* 40 (7): 1534–51.

Hoffmann, Michael, Craig Hilton-Taylor, Ariadne Angulo, Monika Böhm et al. 2010. "The Impact of Conservation on the Status of the World's Vertebrates." *Science* 330 (6010): 1503–9.

IUCN, 2001. *IUCN Red List Categories and Criteria, Version 3.1.* Gland, Switzerland and Cambridge, United Kingdom: IUCN Species Survival Commission, IUCN.

———. 2011. *Guidelines for Appropriate Uses of IUCN Red List Data.* http://www.iucnredlist.org/documents/RL_Guidelines_Data_Use.pdf.

———. 2013. *IUCN Red List Summary Statistics.* http://www.iucnredlist.org/about/summary-statistics.

———. 2014. *Guidelines for Using the IUCN Red List Categories and Criteria, Version 11.* http://jr.iucnredlist.org/documents/RedListGuidelines.pdf.

Joseph, Liana, Richard Maloney and Hugh Possingham. 2009. "Optimal Allocation of Resources among Threatened Species: a Project Prioritization Protocol." *Conservation Biology* 23 (2): 328–38.

Lamoreux, John, H. Resit Akçakaya, Leon Bennun, Nigel Collar et al. 2003. "Value of the IUCN Red List." *Trends in Ecology and Evolution* 18 (5): 214–5.

Leyshon, Andrew, and Nigel Thrift. 1999. "'Lists Come Alive': Electronic Systems of Knowledge and the Rise of Credit Scoring in Retail Banking." *Economy and Society* 28 (3): 434–66.

Mace, Georgina, Nigel Collar, Kevin Gaston, Craig Hilton-Taylor et al. 2008. "Quantification of Extinction Risk: IUCN's System for Classifying Threatened Species." *Conservation Biology* 22 (6): 1424–42.

Miller, Rebecca. 2013. "Threatened Species: Classification Systems and Their Applications." In *Encyclopedia of Biodiversity* 2nd edition. Volume 7. Edited by Simon Levin, 191–221. Waltham, MA: Academic Press.

OED Online. 2013. Oxford: Oxford University Press.

Pimm, Stuart, Clinton Jenkins, Robin Abell, Thomas Brooks et al. 2014. "The Biodiversity of Species and Their Rates of Extinction, Distribution, and Protection." *Science* 344 (6187): 987–98.

Possingham, Hugh, Sandy Andelman, Mark Burgman, Rodrigo Medellín et al. 2002. "Limits to the Use of Threatened Species Lists." *Trends in Ecology and Evolution* 17 (11): 503–7.

Rivalan, Phillipe, Virginie Delmas, Elena Angulo, Leigh Bull et al. 2007. "Can Bans Stimulate Wildlife Trade?" *Nature* 447 (31): 529–30.

Rodrigues, Ana, John Pilgrim, John Lamoreux, Michael Hoffmann et al. 2006. "The Value of the IUCN Red List for Conservation." *Trends in Ecology and Evolution* 21 (2): 71–6.

Rutherford, Stephanie and Paul Rutherford. 2013. "Geography and Biopolitics." *Geography Compass* 7 (6): 423–34.

Sandler, Ronald. 2012. *The Ethics of Species: An Introduction.* Cambridge: Cambridge University Press.

Staeheli, Urs. 2012. "Listing the Global: Dis/Connectivity Beyond Representation?" *Distinktion: Scandinavian Journal of Social Theory* 13 (3): 233–46.

Walsh, Jessica, James Watson, Madeleine Bottrill, Liana Joseph and Hugh Possingham. 2012. "Trends and Biases in the Listing and Recovery Planning for Threatened Species: An Australian Case Study." *Oryx* 47 (1): 134–43.

Wilcove, David. 2010. "Endangered Species Management: The US Experience." In *Conservation Biology For All.* Edited by Navjot Sodhi and Paul Ehrlich, 220–35. Oxford: Oxford University Press.

Chapter 2

Probiotic Legalities: De-Domestication and Rewilding Before the Law

Jamie Lorimer

> What is needed here then . . . is a third way, one that can think life and norm together, without falling back on either the lexicon of "the person" or, at the other extreme, the radically dedifferentiating discourse of "life" which is unworkable both philosophically and pragmatically.
>
> —Cary Wolfe, *Before the Law*, p. 58

Introduction

In his 2012 book *Before the Law: Humans and Other Animals in a Biopolitical Frame*, Cary Wolfe appeals for a new philosophical foundation for animal studies and explores ethical and political strategies for critical legal intervention. He starts by identifying the twin deficiencies of the existing approaches. The first is with the model that extends liberal forms of rights to animals by virtue of their similarity to human norms such that (some) animals become honorary persons. The second deficiency he identifies is with the hyperbolic celebration of an undifferentiated "life" that he finds in the Deleuzian biophilosophy of Esposito and its popular incarnations in forms of biocentric ethics.

Wolfe suggests that both approaches neglect the material specificities of humans and nonhumans, most significantly their variegated abilities to "respond" in socio-ecological encounters and the politico-ethical responsibilities this demands. He welcomes the generative and affirmative take on biopolitics offered by Esposito, which helps address the dystopic thanatopolitics he finds in Agamben. But he argues that Esposito offers unworkable criteria for a pragmatic biopolitics for living (and eating and dying) well with animals. This is because Esposito's position requires an impossible (even anti-humanist and certainly apolitical) suspension of the human

Large grazers at the OVP. Photo made by GerardM. Licensed under Public Domain via Wikimedia Commons, https://commons.wikimedia.org/wiki/File:GroteGrazers.JPG.

immunitary impulse to protect the self. Such a suspension, he argues, offers us no grounds to differentiate between Ebola and elephants, for example, and neglects the unequal political ecologies that configure who gets infected or trampled.

Instead, Wolfe argues that "the performative structure and logic of immunity indemnification is precisely the condition of possibility for any possible affirmation, thus opening the community to its others" (2012, 103). From here he draws on Derrida to suggest that:

> hospitality, *to be* hospitality, to be real, must be something "determinate" and "conditioned"; my laws will not protect you if they aren't. But this act of selection and discrimination, in its contingency and finitude, is precisely what opens it to the other and to the future. This is why discrimination, selection, self-reference, and exclusion cannot be avoided (ibid.).

Wolfe's book is as much a critical and cautionary account of current biopolitical thought as it is a manifesto for how to think nonhuman animals (and humans) in other ways. It also lays the foundations for further posthumanist praxis in search of a middle ground between nonhuman ontologies of immanence and animal personhood.

In this chapter, I develop Wolfe's analysis by exploring a possible legal manifestation of Wolfe's "third way," affirmative biopolitics. The central aim of the chapter is to outline "probiotic legalities" for human–nonhuman relations. My concept of the probiotic extends Heather Paxson's (2008) notion of the "post-Pasteurian," which she identifies in recent microbiological enthusiasms for raw milk cheese. Paxson explains that "post-Pasteurians work hard to distinguish between 'good' and 'bad' microorganisms and to harness the former as allies in vanquishing the latter. Post-Pasterianism takes after Pasteurianism in taking hygiene seriously. It differs in being more discriminating" (2014, 118). A probiotic legality describes comparable thinking in the macrobiome, identifying biopolitical technologies for securing and managing the circulation of life through the selective cultivation and suppression of desired systemic properties. It involves an ecologized politics, recognizing the entangled agencies of species within wider vital processes—for example by mobilizing "keystone species" to deliver ecosystem services. Probiotic approaches can be counterpoised to the antibiotic tendencies that characterize modern legalities that tend toward purification, simplification, stability, linearity, and control (Latour 1988; Gandy 2004).

I outline the concept of probiotic legalities in the context of nature conservation, focusing on an example of ongoing efforts to "de-domesticate" large herbivores and "rewild" a novel ecology in the Netherlands. Claiming, civilizing, commodifying, and saving the wild have long been legal concerns

(Whatmore 2002; Delaney 2003); and the wild—understood here as the inherent tendencies of life to differentiate or become otherwise—has frequently been the subject of acts of violence in the name of these concerns. In enacting lively legalities, life often becomes a resource, a risk, or, in certain (largely, though not exclusively, human) cases, the property of an individual person. The probiotic legality outlined below circumvents this legal trinity of resource/risk/personhood. To explain how it does so, I map the fraught intersections between rewilding and prevalent legalities for managing nonhuman life in Europe. I focus specifically on tensions with existing legalities for securing species' populations (biodiversity), for ensuring the sanctity of human bodies, property, and agricultural systems (biosecurity), and for protecting nonhuman personhood (animal welfare).

Rewilding

Rewilding has emerged in the last 30 years as a new approach to nature conservation. This is a variegated and contested movement (Jørgensen 2015), whose advocates nonetheless share an aim to shift the focus in conservation from exposing and managing extinctions toward the (re)introduction of absent species and functions (Lorimer et al 2015). Such proactive interventions aim to restore or even enhance degraded and inhabited ecologies. Rewilding shifts the historical references that inform conservation to prehistorical (rather than premodern) benchmarks, arguing that such systems provide more functional, abundant, and resilient ecologies to guide future conservation in the Anthropocene (Donlan et al. 2006; Marris 2011; Monbiot 2013).

A growing awareness of the "trophic cascades" (Estes et al. 2011) caused by the absence (either local or global) of certain "keystone species" has granted certain animals significant agency in the practice of rewilding. These animals are valued primarily for their functional roles within wider ecologies: as predators, grazers, decomposers, et cetera. In North America, the focus has largely been on predators (Foreman 2004), and the actual and potential roles these play in controlling the grazing habits and the size and structure of populations of species lower down the trophic pyramid. Wolves are the prominent example of keystone species. Their reintroduction to Yellowstone had desired landscape-scale vegetation impacts due, in part, to their predation of abundant elk but also to "the ecology of fear" their presence has created and the impacts of this on herbivore grazing dynamics (Ripple and Beschta 2004).

In Europe, the focus has been more on reintroducing large herbivores like "primitive" breeds of cattle and horses, along with deer, bison, beaver and boar. These animals figure as "ecological engineers," whose unfettered, "naturalistic" grazing and browsing has the potential to recreate the dynamic, diverse, and resilient forest–pasture landscapes understood to predominate in pre-agricultural Holocene Europe (Vera 2000). A suite of such animals have been introduced into a range of nature reserves and are being promoted for the management of the growing areas of forest and agricultural land currently being abandoned in central and eastern Europe (Navarro and Pereira 2012). Efforts are currently underway to "back-breed" the aurochs (the extinct animal from which domestic cattle are descended) to create a more authentic bovine grazer (Goderie et al. 2013).

The Oostvaardersplassen

The Oostvaardersplassen (OVP) is the central example of the European model of rewilding by naturalistic grazing. This 5,600-hectare nature reserve is located on a polder just outside Amsterdam in the Netherlands. A polder describes land reclaimed from the sea. This site was drained in the 1950s and forms part of the largest artificial island in the world, and was largely given over to housing, agriculture, and industry. The area that now constitutes the reserve was earmarked for an oil refinery, but for a range of economic and hydraulic reasons, it was colonized by migratory geese and soon became recognized as a haven for wetland birds. The area was designated as a nature reserve in 1986.

The OVP is strongly associated with Frans Vera—a paleoecologist, conservationist and former employee of Staatsbosbeheer, the statutory agency charged with managing the reserve. From his observations of the ecological dynamics associated with geese grazing at OVP, Vera developed a radical hypothesis about the paleoecology of Europe and a controversial proposal for its future conservation (Vera 2000). He challenged prevalent accounts of the Holocene paleoecology of Europe, which identify the closed canopy, high forest as the climax ecological state for temperate ecosystems and argue that low intensity agriculture opened up the forest to create the conditions that support valued biodiversity. In contrast, Vera argued that the landscape would have been kept open by large herbivores, whose grazing would have generated a "cyclical turnover" of vegetation creating a "shifting mosaic" of forest-pasture landscapes (Vera 2000). For Vera, valued wildlife survived in spite of premodern agriculture and thus conservation policy should focus less on supporting farming and more on creating space for naturalistic grazing.

The OVP has become the experimental site to test this hypothesis and to demonstrate conservation by naturalistic grazing (Vera 2009). In the 1980s, herds of hardy, but nonetheless formerly domesticated, cattle and horses were purchased and released into the reserve, along with herds of deer. Initially, they were left to fend for themselves—living, breeding and dying in what was promoted as a "Serengeti behind the dykes" (Van den Belt 2004, 311). The hope was that these animals would "de-domesticate" themselves, discovering new behaviors and creating novel ecologies akin to their prehistorical antecedents. By grazing, dying, and decomposing they would begin to address the trophic simplification associated with modern agriculture.

The OVP experiment has generated a series of ecological surprises—including the arrival of the Netherlands' first vulture and sea eagles (the latter now nesting below sea level). The recorded ecological dynamics at the site have yet to offer definitive evidence in support of Vera's hypothesis, which is widely contested by other scientists (Svenning 2002). Nonetheless, the OVP has become a popular ecotourism destination, catalysed in part by the production of a big budget wildlife documentary film in 2013.[1] The film both inspired and legitimized a wider movement seeking to replicate the naturalistic grazing pioneered at the OVP across other sites in Europe.[2]

The 30 years since the emergence of the project has seen many political controversies and involved extensive public and private dispute, some litigation, and a fair amount of new legislation. These controversies are analytically and politically generative and help shed light on the legalities of governing "the return of the wild." Through these disputes, and through their legal manifestations in particular, advocates of rewilding have come to better understand, refine, and justify their activities. I have explored these controversies elsewhere, mapping their fraught intersections with four prevalent modes of "bovine biopolitics," namely: agriculture, welfare, biosecurity, and conservation (Lorimer and Driessen 2013). I further develop this analysis in this chapter, specifying the lively legalities of rewilding by focusing on the *legal* practices involved in reconciling tensions at the interface of rewilding with animal welfare, nature conservation, and biosecurity. Each of these biopolitical frameworks has well-established and hard fought legalities that the OVP rewilders have come up against in their efforts to promote their experiment.

Rewilding and Welfare

The most well-known dispute about rewilding at the OVP relates to questions of animal welfare. The OVP is a bounded reserve; the introduced animals cannot leave. This is fertile land, and so the populations of herbivores grew fast. The OVP currently accommodates about 3,500 red deer, 1,100 horses and 350 cattle. Although wolves have started to return to Germany and have been spotted in the Netherlands, in the OVP there are no predators that would trouble the cows and horses. By the late 1990s, the OVP animals were beginning to die of starvation due to the harsh winters. The site is overlooked by a commuter rail line and has roads on raised dykes on several of its borders. It is very visible to the general public. Because of its high visibility, the welfare of the starving animals soon became a source of concern for animal welfare advocates.

The opposition to the OVP herbivore management policy was led by the Dutch Society for the Protection of Animals (*De Dierenbescherming*) that argued that these animals are still domestic and should therefore be subject to forms of care we extend to such animals. The 1976 European Convention for the Protection of Animals Kept for Farming Purposes (Council of Europe 1976) specifies animal welfare standards that require animals to be kept free from hunger, thirst, discomfort, pain, injury, and disease. Invoking this Convention, the welfarists argued that the cattle and horses should be given supplementary food in the winter, offered shelter from the extreme winter weather, and provided with veterinary care.

The rewilders contested this argument. Drawing comparisons with free-ranging populations of herbivores in places like the Serengeti, they argued that supplementary feeding would unnaturally extend the lives of animals within the herd, create conflict, and encourage breeding, thus interfering with the aggregate social dynamics that have developed amongst the cattle and horses. They suggested that death by starvation is a normal part of wild life for large herbivores—downplaying the significance of predation. Finally, they proposed that such deaths are not painful but form part of an important social process through which reproduction in a herd is controlled.

The case was brought to court in 2007. Legal representatives for the welfarists offered a multifaceted case, challenging the classification of the cattle and horses (but not deer) as wild and seeking to reposition them as either captive, game, or laboratory animals (Rechtbank's-Gravenhage 2006). The legal argument came to focus on questions of property, ownership, and responsibility. In Dutch law, humans are responsible for the welfare of what they call "kept" animals (Rechtbank's-Gravenhage 2006). The legal term "kept" is also a territorial, ethological, and ultimately phenomenological classification that codifies appropriate relationships. Lawyers for Staatsbosbeheer successfully argued that these animals were no longer kept, as they were not "held" by their clients (the term "held" implies a relationship of physical control). The cattle and horses at OVP are not tagged (and thus individuated) and have not been handled for more than 20 years. Occasionally injured or especially troublesome animals have been shot but there is no infrastructure or experience at the reserve for catching or tranquilizing animals. Because they could literally no longer "hold onto" their animals, the judge found that Staatsbosbeheer had no legal obligation to comply with agricultural animal welfare legislation.

Once livestock, these were now wild (or at least feral) animals. Property rights had been formally relinquished, the animals de-commodified and responsibility derogated. This is a rare (perhaps even unique) event in the history of human–cattle and human–horse legalities. Cattle and horses have been abandoned or deliberately introduced to support colonial settlement or future expeditions (Ritvo 1987). To the best of my knowledge, they have never been given up willingly in a court of law. Outside the courtroom, this result quickly turned into a public relations disaster. Emaciated charismatic animals starving to death behind high fences in the suburbs are not easily tolerated—however wild they may be. The government had to find a compromise: it assembled an international commission of scientists and ethicists to arrive at an acceptable solution. The International Commission for the Management of the Oostvaardersplassen (ICMO) has so far produced two reports—ICMO (2006) and ICMO2 (2010)—the most recent of which outlined the current policy, providing a curious hybrid of existing legislation and practice. The report attributed the problem of overpopulation to the absence of predators and a reserve warden was ordered to proactively cull those cattle and horses adjudged to be unable to survive the winter. Between 30 and 60 percent of the population has been killed in this way every year. This predator model of animal management was to be performed with the "eye of the wolf." However, the ethology of free-ranging cattle and horses in the presence of wolves has not been well studied; the two species have not co-existed in such conditions in Europe for at least 250 years. To judge cattle welfare, the OVP authorities refined their own experience of watching herbivores through an engagement with the embodied expertise, behavioral criteria, and associated legislation developed to assess dairy and beef cattle. Recognized systems exist for scoring the condition of domestic cattle (Grandin 2010), though as these often require proximity, touch, and individual familiarity with cattle bodies they were not altogether operational at the OVP.

In "becoming-wolf" and deciding how to kill cows, the authorities thus turned to the practice, technologies, and regulations that codify humane forms of hunting. Cows and horses were shot with a silenced, high-calibre rifle from the cab of the ranger's truck, ideally when they became separated from the herd (as is common when they become unwell). The small size of the reserve makes it unsuitable for the reintroduction of wolves. Additionally, current European legislation prohibits the introduction of predator and prey into a fenced enclosure the size of OVP, as wolves may use fences to catch herbivores (Sandom et al. 2012). Such legislation would also likely rule out the de-domestication (or retraining) of dogs as wolf surrogates to create the ecology of fear so valued at Yellowstone (see above). This option has not been considered, not least because hunting with dogs is illegal in many parts of Europe. No one seems sure what should be done if a wolf found its way to the OVP independently, which is looking increasingly possible as the wolf makes its return to Western Europe (Seddon et al. 2014). Although the cattle and horses have become partially subject to the forms of care and control associated with both agricultural and game animals, they maintain their feral/wild status. It would be illegal for members of the public to either feed or hunt these animals—unlike, for example, cattle on proximal farmland or the deer in the neighbouring Veluwe forest.

The heat of political controversy forced a blending and morphing of practices, criteria, and legislation. Drawing together norms associated with the farm and the hunting reserve has enabled the emergence of a novel mode of biopolitics. For advocates, this embodies many of the philosophical and ethical principles advocated by Wolfe in his quest for a "third way" introduced above. A group of ethicists and applied philosophers who have been advising the Dutch government have argued that the eye of the wolf, population management model respects the welfare of individual animals, but understands them as parts of both wider social groups and a dynamic, more functional ecology (Klaver et al. 2002; Korthals et al. 2002; ICMO2 2010). This model thus expands on the atomized figure of animal personhood at the center of proposals for feeding and veterinary care that were made by some opponents of the OVP experiment. At the same time it also mitigates the aggregate level of suffering associated with high levels of geriatric animal life (and death) associated with a resource rich ecology lacking its apex predators.

The eye of the wolf model offers a lively legality that conceives wildness on a continuum, rather than as an impossible pure ideal (Keulartz 2009). It also shows wildness as a multiple, related to the specific ethological and ecological properties of specific nonhuman constituents—in this case, cattle and horses. It seeks to replace relations of domination with those of trust, trust that animals (and their ecologies) will flourish with a relinquishing of human control (Klaver et al. 2002). The status quo at the OVP is still far from ideal as a result of the limited size of the reserve. Along these lines, Kymlicka and Donaldson (2014) point to the animals' lack of an "exit option" as a major impediment to their flourishing and thus as the exemplary possibilities of the OVP experiment.

Rewilding and Biodiversity Conservation

In addition to these debates about animal welfare, political and legal tensions also emerged at the intersections between the process-oriented understanding of ecology that is at the heart of the OVP rewilding experiment and the powerful legislative framework that enacts biodiversity conservation around species composition. This legislation is embodied in the European Species and Habitats Directives, a pan-European legislation that designates a network of protected areas, commonly referred to as Natura 2000. This legislation expresses the equilibrium, "compositionist" model of nature (Callicott et al. 1999), which is at the heart of European conservation (Lorimer 2015) and values landscapes associated with premodern agricultural pasts, rather than the prehistorical benchmarks at the heart of rewilding.

Natura 2000 identifies a list of rare and threatened species and habitats whose populations and acreages are to be secured. Statutory conservation bodies—like Staatsbosbeheer—are legally required to monitor and manage designated areas so that the target indicators of valued natures are maintained in "favourable condition." In practice, this means counting and caring for *species*. Birds are the flagship denizens of the species-focused legal landscape. They are the best-known and most watched of all European taxa and their conservation is the best resourced (Lorimer 2006).

By contrast, rewilders at OVP (and elsewhere) are generally less interested in species as such (i.e., discrete units); they are more concerned with their ecological roles as the instigators of particular, valued functions: grazing, predation, decomposition, et cetera. They argue that conservation delivered by keystone species generates more "self-willed," adaptive, and resilient ecologies better equipped for accelerated climate change. They also argue that naturalistic grazing can be significantly cheaper than subsidizing forms of low-intensity agriculture—a practice that currently constitutes a significant part of the EU Common Agricultural Policy (Merckx and Pereira 2015). Rewilders accept that species provide intuitive, accessible, and charismatic means for monitoring ecological dynamics and promoting causes, but argue that they figure secondary to ecological change. Local extinction matters less than systemic dysfunction. Here form is secondary to process.

In 1989, the OVP was designated as a Special Protection Area for birdlife. Technically, this placed an obligation on the site managers to count the populations of rare birds and manage in their specific interests. In 1996, local birdwatchers, unconnected to and often antipathetic toward the management of the OVP, began to notice significant declines in the populations of spoonbills on the reserve. Spoonbills are a priority species under the Birds Directive; their population in the OVP crashed from 300 to zero. Attention was raised through the media and accusations were made that the decline was due to the lack of responsible predator management (Bosman 1996). The build-up of dead animal bodies on the reserve was believed to be encouraging the growth in the population of foxes that would eat the eggs and young of ground nesting birds—like spoonbills. Local bird enthusiasts noted that Staatsbosbeheer were not monitoring their bird populations and were not explicitly managing in their interests. They argued that they were not complying with their legal obligations. In the ultimate transgression of orthodox European biodiversity conservation, they enquiries revealed that Staatsbosbeheer did not even have an action plan: there were no quantified management targets to which they could be held accountable.

With this disclosure and in the face of pressure from the influential bird lobby, Staatsbosbeheer was forced to act. This time, the case never came before the courts. Instead, the international commission charged with resolving the animal welfare controversy was also asked to look into the conservation situation. Their report largely agrees with Staatsbosbeheer's conservationist critics, demanding that more be done to comply with Natura 2000. Calls were made for an improved "statement of management objectives" and a "system of environmental monitoring," including "analysis and modeling to identify current processes, predict future trends and to set thresholds to acceptable change" (ICMO 2006, 13). The senior scientist in charge of the reserve was charged with drafting a management plan to try and bring the OVP into line with prevalent practice.

The resulting document (Staatsbosbeheer 2011) makes for an awkward reading, offering a masterpiece of bureaucratic and ecological linguistics to shuttle between legal commitments to species and the rewilding commitment to processes. The management plan emphasizes both stability and change and seeks to articulate the complicated pragmatics of monitoring an uncertain, nonlinear system. The broad challenge this document faces is to justify the type of open-ended forms of science and management that have come to characterize rewilding in terms that can detect and anticipate trends that might undermine its future functioning, assessed over a variety of different geographies and temporalities. For example, desired population totals for protected species, like the spoonbill, are specified within ranges to allow for temporal and spatial variations.

The OVP conservation controversy subsided when it was discovered that the spoonbills had moved out from the reserve and returned in future years. Nonetheless, the dispute forced rewilders to refine, specify, and better secure their policy. These negotiations also shed important light on the mode of biopolitics that rewilding has sought to enact. This dispute illustrates how Dutch rewilding orients and specifies a commitment to the flourishing of nonhuman difference in relation to entrenched political commitments to species and habitats. In so doing, it avoids the extreme forms of biocentrism of which Wolfe is critical, by attending to the ecological (and less successfully, the political) specificities necessary to secure particular valued functions and relations. This is a relational or ecologized biopolitics committed to the conservation of "keystone" forms of life.

The centrality of species to environmentalism and animal studies is somewhat overlooked in Wolfe's account. The biopolitical implications of a species ontology are not central to his analysis, although they have been discussed elsewhere (Braverman 2015; Biermann and Mansfield 2014). Species offer a further dimension to Wolfe's (perhaps somewhat simplistic) binary that I outlined in my opening quotation. Species do not fit Wolfe's two categories of life as animal person or as dedifferentiated flux. Instead, species figure as populations—here incarnated as both sentient life forms and ecological agents. In mobilizing species, the rewilders at the OVP seek to modify an ascendant preoccupation in conservation with the diversity and quantity of system forms to create space for systemic properties—like resilience, abundance, and connectivity. This involves acknowledging the cultural, ethical, and ecological significance of the species and habitat forms through which such properties are delivered. There is a novel and still nascent conservation biopolitics emerging at the OVP, which is premised on letting an ecology flourish, even if this means letting some forms of species' life die.

Rewilding and Biosecurity

Death is more central to the third and final set of tensions in this story, which relates to the biosecurity implications of rewilding. There are two important and connected dimensions to consider here. The first relates to the risks posed to human life and property by the bodily presence of predators (wolves), large and sometimes aggressive herbivores (cattle, bison, horses), and organisms capable of significant landscape modification (like beaver and boar). The second biosecurity concern relates to the potential of these animals (and their carcasses) to act as reservoirs, hosts and vectors for zoonotic and other animal diseases with the potential to jeopardize human life, or more commonly the hygiene and security of agricultural systems.

The first set of biosecurity concerns figures most prominently with the reintroduction of predators, like the wolf, and largely account for the species' near eradication in Europe and North America. Anxieties about wolf predation continue to trouble efforts to reintroduce and conserve the species in North America and Europe (Nilsen et al. 2007; Buller 2008). Although the actual risks are often overplayed, animals like wolves provide the most visceral illustration of the human immunitary impulse to protect bodies, kin, and property. The return of predators exemplifies some of deficiencies that Wolfe identifies with forms of biocentric ethics, which fail to offer grounds for securing the human and thus extending hospitality to nonhuman others.

But this immunity impulse is not unwavering. The return of the wolf illustrates how this animal's status has changed dramatically over the last 100 years (Emel 1998). There are ongoing efforts to develop modes of co-existence or even conviviality with wolves that begin to acknowledge their claims to space and resources—though not to human flesh. For example, schemes exist to compensate pastoralists affected by wolf predation, and to train dogs to guard flocks and tourists in European alpine regions (Haraway 2008, 40). Additionally, there has been substantial investment in wider education, marketing, and development programs. These seek to enhance the wolf's economic potential for (often marginal) affected populations and to flag their wider cultural significance to nonlocal populations. In biopolitical terms, we might understand the re-evaluation of the wolf as a recognition of the pathogenic (or auto-immune) risks of the anthropocentric and antibiotic immunity impulse of modern thought, which seeks the eradication of risky nonhuman difference. Tolerating or even valuing wolves offers glimpses of a probiotic model of immunity (or community, to use Esposito's terms; 2011) that takes the specificities of wolves seriously to both harness their ecological, economic, and cultural virtues and to respect their own rights to a full life.

Concerns with being eaten are less prominent with naturalistic grazing and have not featured in debates over the management of the OVP. The herbivores are constrained within the reserve and tend to avoid people. Instead, tensions relate more to the second set of biosecurity regulations governing the risks that the large herbivores might pose as disease carriers, as a result of their differential immunity in comparison to more domesticated neighbouring kin. Although the animals themselves are relatively immobile, they are frequently exposed to human and other animal disease vectors that link the reserve to other populations: birds, tourists, water and wind connect the site to its wider environment.

In the wake of a series of animal health crisis (e.g. foot and mouth disease, BSE, and bovine TB), European biosecurity legislation stipulates a series of regulations that challenge the type of naturalistic grazing enacted at the OVP. For example, all cattle in the European Union must be individuated by attaching two distinctive, numbered yellow ear tags. Each animal must be checked regularly for disease and have a "passport" that remains with it throughout its life in order to track animal movement and disease spread. Agricultural animals are frequently vaccinated against disease and may receive antibiotics. Regulations also prohibit leaving cattle and horse carcasses to decay in the field and stipulate that bodies should be disposed of through sanitary mechanisms. Finally, regulations over the control of invasive, noxious, or pest species may also impel rewilders to eradicate various self-willed arrivals (e.g., ragwort or even wild boar).

Many of these regulations contravene the desired mode of rewilding at the OVP. For example, tagging, monitoring, and inoculating cattle are expensive practices that require cattle that are amenable to human contact. For cattle to be tagged they would need to be "held" and thus habituated to people in ways that would undermine their ethological and ecological integrity (and the arguments that allow alternative forms of welfare outlined above). Second, rewilders argue that dead animal bodies are an important functional input to their desired ecology. Carrion and decomposition support diverse microbial, invertebrate, avian, and mammalian ecologies rarely found in the European countryside. For example, the OVP's resident sea eagle population is dependent on the presence of bountiful carrion.

Finally, rewilders promote the OVP as a hub in a wider ecological network (Baerselman and Vera 1995). They map the site as connected to a national and then pan-European network of reserves and corridors. This requires the OVP to be permeable, relinquishing departees and remaining hospitable to new arrivals. Such nonhuman mobilities are relatively unproblematic in the case of large birds. They are more challenging with wild boar, which are endemic in the Netherlands, have remarkable abilities to circumvent human barriers, and can carry disease.

To enable the OVP experiment to proceed, the rewilders have had to secure a series of "exemptions" from European biosecurity legislation. These are provisions that can be granted nationally to cover a specific territory or time period. They are understood as temporary, but in practice may persist indefinitely to help handle hybrid and liminal circumstances like the OVP and other sites of animal captivity (Braverman 2012). Perhaps the most notable exemption granted to the OVP excludes the cattle and horses from ear tags, passports, and individualized monitoring. The OVP cattle and horses are among an extremely small number of animals in Europe to be granted this (suspended) legal status. On the one hand, this measure can be understood as an easing of the immunitary logics and divided geographies that currently characterize European biosecurity legislation (Hinchliffe et al. 2012; Hinchliffe and Ward 2014)—creating spaces and relations for living with bovine and equine microbiologies without rigid hygienic precautions. However, this is a fragile compromise; it is hard to see the OVP herds and other wildlife being exempted from culling if there were an outbreak of a disease that threatened human and/or agricultural security.

There has been less flexibility to date in relation to the regulations for the removal and disposal of the animal carcasses. Where it is possible, the Staatsbosbeheer have been obliged to remove the bodies of the cattle and horses that die on the reserve—either as a result of natural causes or from the predator simulation model. As they remain unequivocally "wild" animals in the eyes of Dutch law, dead deer can be left to rot (Figure 2.1). This is also the case for animals that die in the more swampy parts of the reserve. Recently, the Dutch Food and Consumer Product Safety Authority have issued a positive recommendation for a trial that involves leaving a number of horse/cattle carcasses *in situ*. The Minister of Economic Affairs, Agriculture and Innovation will make a decision on this in the near future and there is some optimism at the reserve about a future return of further processes of death and decay.

Biopolitical exceptions are a hot topic in social theory and feature prominently in Wolfe's *Before the Law*. It is interesting to consider the status of the "states of exception" operational at OVP in the context these recent writings—not least, because some animal advocates in the Netherlands have drawn explicit comparison between the reserve and a concentration camp (Keulartz 2009). As with others arguing in this vein, they suggest that the suspension of biosecurity and animal welfare laws for these captive animals involves the relegation of individual cattle and horses to the status of a forms of "bare life," stripped of political status and made to suffer as biological resources. But for wilding advocates these exemptions permit the emergence of a novel form of bios—or valued life—pegged less to the

Figure 2.1 A dead deer shot in the Oostvaardersplassen because it was too weak to survive. The deer are decapitated to prevent trophy hunters entering the nature reserve. "OP dood hert" 2 by GerardM. Licensed under Public Domain via Wikimedia Commons, https://commons.wikimedia.org/wiki/File:OP_dood_hert_2.jpg#/media/File:OP_dood_hert_2.jpg.

sanctity of the human-like individual and more to the flourishing of a multispecies ecology. It is precisely the legal state of exception from the strictures of existing welfare, conservation and biosecurity legislation that enables a politics for this bios to emerge. Here, the exception offers a temporary and legal political tool for experimentation, in contrast to the illegal (for Agamben) states of exception associated with recent and historic forms of human captivity and violence.

A Probiotic Legality?

This chapter has sought to position and differentiate rewilding in relation to some of the most prevalent modes of biopolitics that govern animal life in Western Europe. In so doing, it has suggested that the lively legalities of this form of rewilding might offer a "third way" biopolitics akin to that which Cary Wolfe appeals for in *Before the Law*. The chapter has developed the conceptual engagement with questions of immunity that characterizes Wolfe's work to offer a largely positive reading of the potential of rewilding.

In conclusion, I would like to specify how this might be understood as a probiotic alternative.

Probiotic biopolitics can be counterpoised to the anthropocentric and antibiotic logics that characterize most modern approaches to managing life, including those that grant legal status to a subset of anthropomorphic entities. Probiotic biopolitics can also be differentiated from the inoperable hyperbolic enthusiasms for the singular dedifferentiated life that Wolfe finds in the work of Esposito. Although rewilding is more aligned with the immanent and posthumanist ontology at the heart of Esposito's work, probiotic approaches recognize the political and ethical significance of the human, the power relations that bisect this category, and the importance of other forms of life.

More specifically—and in contrast to popular uses of the term in the marketing of dietary supplements—the probiotic refers to ecologized forms of biopolitics, which seek to manage a dynamic system. Here the political target is not exclusively the security of persons, or even of populations of species, but the functioning and flourishing of an ecology. This is a juggling act, involving a pluralist awareness of the ontological politics that underpins nature conservation (Lorimer 2015). In the case of the OVP, the welfare of individual cattle and horses must be considered alongside their relationships to the herd they comprise, the organisms that are affected by their grazing, defecating and dying, and thus the wider ecological assemblage in which they have been deployed as keystone ecological engineers. The animals' suffering and deaths matter, but these are evaluated in the context of more abstract functional concerns for resilience, adaptation, and connectivity, for example. As it stands, the OVP secures the welfare of human populations, herds of cattle and a lively, flourishing and unique ecology. It is premised on an immunity impulse that is becoming hospitable to various others: a probiotic model of immunity as multispecies community that recognizes the specific and differentiated agencies of nonhumans and takes seriously the risks and responsibilities these pose.

The legalities surrounding the governance of OVP offer one tentative, incomplete but nonetheless generative answer to the problem of wildness. But as I have argued elsewhere (Lorimer and Driessen 2013), the OVP is not a posthumanist or political utopia, nor is it a universal and final juridical solution to this problem, because it is always already traced with the automaticity and mechanicity of a reaction. It is a "line," to use Derrida's formulation, that is always already "multiple" and nonlinear, always folded and in motion, always under erasure. We must choose, and by definition we cannot choose everyone and everything at once. But this is precisely what ensures that, in the future, we will have been wrong. Our "determinate" legal acts now will have been shown to be too determinate, revealed to have left someone or something out (2012). Instead, it is useful to conceive of the lively legalities that govern the OVP as an open-ended legal experiment that is exposed to ecological surprises, political events, and the generative controversies to which these can give rise. The OVP can offer valuable insights for law and conservation in the Anthropocene, when the end of nature and the politicization of natural science undermine any hard wiring of environmental governance to universal and immutable natural laws.

Notes

1 This film was called *De Nieuwe Wildernis* (The New Wilderness).
2 See www.rewildingeurope.com.

References

Adams, William. 1997. "Rationalization and Conservation: Ecology and the Management of Nature in the United Kingdom." *Transactions of the Institute of British Geographers* 22 (3): 277–91.

Baerselman, Frank and Frans Vera. 1995. *Nature Development: An Exploratory Study for the Construction of Ecological Networks.* The Hague: Ministry of Agriculture, Nature Management and Fisheries.

Biermann, Christine and Becky Mansfield. 2014. "Biodiversity, Purity, and Death: Conservation Biology as Biopolitics." *Environment and Planning D: Society and Space* 32 (2): 257–73.

Bosman, Andrea. 1996. "Is het Goed dat de Lepelaar uit de Oostvaardersplassen is Verdwenen of Juist Niet?" *Trouw.* 4 June. www.trouw.nl.

Braverman, Irus. 2012. *Zooland: The Institution of Captivity.* Stanford: Stanford University Press.

———. 2015. *Wild Life: The Institution of Nature.* Stanford: Stanford University Press.

Buller, Henry. 2008. "Safe from the Wolf: Biosecurity, Biodiversity, and Competing Philosophies of Nature." *Environment and Planning A* 40 (7): 1583–97.

Callicott, John Baird, Larry Crowder and Karen Mumford. 1999. "Current Normative Concepts in Conservation." *Conservation Biology* 13 (1): 22–35.

Council of Europe. 1976. *European Convention for the Protection of Animals Kept for Farming Purposes.* http://conventions.coe.int.

Delaney, David. 2003. *Law and Nature.* Cambridge: Cambridge University Press.

Donlan, Josh, Joel Berger, Carl Bock, Jane Bock et al. 2006. "Pleistocene Rewilding: An Optimistic Agenda for Twenty-First Century Conservation." *American Naturalist* 168 (5): 660–81.

Emel, Jody. 1998. "Are You Man Enough, Big and Bad Enough? Wolf Eradication in the US." In *Animal Geographies: Place, Politics and Identity in the Nature-Culture Borderlands.* Edited by Jody Emel and Jennifer Wolch, 91–117. London: Verso.

Esposito, Roberto. 2011. *Immunitas: The Protection and Negation of Life.* Malden MA: Polity Press.

Estes, James, John Terborgh, Justin Brashares, Mary Power et al. 2011. "Trophic Downgrading of Planet Earth." *Science* 333 (6040): 301–6.

Foreman, David. 2004. *Rewilding North America: A Vision for Conservation in the 21st Century.* Washington DC: Island Press.

Gandy, Matthew. 2004. "Rethinking Urban Metabolism: Water, Space and the Modern City." *City* 8 (3): 363–79.

Goderie, Ronald, Woulter Helmer, Henri Kerkdijk-Otten and Stefan Widstrand. 2013. *The Aurochs: Born to be Wild.* Zutphen, The Netherlands: Roodbont.

Grandin, Temple, ed. 2010. *Improving Animal Welfare: A Practical Approach.* Wallingford, UK: CABI Publishing.

Haraway, Donna. 2008. *When Species Meet.* Minneapolis: University of Minnesota Press.

Hinchliffe, Steve, John Allen, Stephanie Lavau, Nick Bingham et al. 2012. "Biosecurity and the Topologies of Infected Life: From Borderlines to Borderlands." *Transactions of the Institute of British Geographers* 38 (4): 531–43.

Hinchliffe, Steve, and Kim J. Ward. 2014. "Geographies of Folded Life: How Immunity Reframes Biosecurity." *Geoforum* 53 (May): 136–44.

Hodder, Kathy, John Bullock, Paul Buckland and Keith Kirby. 2005. "Large Herbivores in the Wildwood and Modern Naturalistic Grazing Systems." *English Nature Research Reports.* Peterborough: English Nature.

ICMO. 2006. *Reconciling Nature and Human Interests: Advice of the International Committee on the Management of Large Herbivores in the Oostvaardersplassen.* The Hague: Wageningen.

ICMO2. 2010. "Natural Processes, Animal Welfare, Moral Aspects and Management of the Oostvaardersplassen." *Report of the Second International Commission on Management of the Oostvaardersplassen.* The Hague: Wageningen.

Jørgensen, Dolly. 2015. "Rethinking Rewilding." *Geoforum* (online). http://dx.doi.org/10.1016/j.geoforum.2014.11.016.

Keulartz, Josef. 2009. "Boundary Work in Ecological Restoration." *Environmental Philosophy* 6 (1): 35–55.

Klaver, Irene, Josef Keulartz, Henk Van Den Belt and Bart Gremmen. 2002. "Born to Be Wild: A Pluralistic Ethics Concerning Introduced Large Herbivores in the Netherlands." *Environmental Ethics* 24 (1): 3–21.

Korthals, Michel, Josef Keulartz, Henk Van Den Belt, Irene Klaver et al. 2002. "Battles of Nature: The Ethical Side of Grazing with Large Herbivores." *Vakblad Natuurbeheer* 41 (May): 43–5.

Kymlicka, Will and Sue Donaldson. 2014. "Animals and the Frontiers of Citizenship." *Oxford Journal of Legal Studies* 34 (2): 201–19.

Latour, Bruno. 1988. *The Pasteurization of France.* Cambridge, MA: Harvard University Press.

Lorimer, Jamie. 2006. "What About the Nematodes? Taxonomic Partialities in the Scope of UK Biodiversity Conservation." *Social and Cultural Geography* 7 (4): 539–58.

———. 2014. "Wild Experiments at the Oostvaardersplassen: Rethinking Environmentalism in the Anthropocene." *Transactions of the Institute of British Geographers* 39 (2): 169–81.

———. 2015. *Wildlife in the Anthropocene: Conservation after Nature.* Minneapolis: University of Minnesota Press.

Lorimer, Jamie and Clemens Driessen. 2013. "Bovine Biopolitics and the Promise of Monsters in the Rewilding of Heck Cattle." *Geoforum* 48 (8): 249–59.

Lorimer, Jamie, Chris Sandom, Paul Jepson, Chris Doughty et al. 2015. "Rewilding: Science, Practice, and Politics." *Annual Review of Environment and Resources* 40 (1): 150902153650003. DOI:10.1146/annurev-environ-102014-021406.

Marris, Emma. 2011. *Rambunctious Garden: Saving Nature in a Post-Wild World.* New York: Bloomsbury USA.

Merckx, Thomas, and Henrique Pereira. 2015. "Reshaping Agri-Environmental Subsidies: From Marginal Farming to Large-Scale Rewilding." *Basic and Applied Ecology* 16 (2): 95–103.

Monbiot, George. 2013. *Feral: Searching for Enchantment on the Frontiers of Rewilding.* London: Penguin Books Limited.

Navarro, Laetitia and Henrique Pereira. 2012. "Rewilding Abandoned Landscapes in Europe." *Ecosystems* 15 (6): 900–12.

Nilsen, Erlend, EJ Milner-Gulland, Lee Schofield, Atle Mysterud et al. 2007. "Wolf Reintroduction to Scotland: Public Attitudes and Consequences for Red Deer Management." *Proceedings of the Royal Society B: Biological Sciences* 274 (1612): 995–1003.

Paxson, Heather. 2008. "Post-Pasteurian Cultures: The Microbiopolitics of Raw-Milk Cheese in the United States." *Cultural Anthropology* 23 (1): 15–47.

———. 2014. "Microbiopolitics." In *The Multispecies Salon.* Edited by Eben Kirksey, 115–21. Durham: Duke University Press.

Rechtbank's-Gravenhage. 2006. "Uitspraak in Kort Geding Over de Noodzaak tot Bijvoeren van Grote Grazers (o.a. Edelherten) in de Oostvaardersplassen in Het Licht van Wettelijke Zorgplichten." LJN: AV4486, KG 06/171. 13 March.

Ripple, William and Robert Beschta. 2004. "Wolves and the Ecology of Fear: Can Predation Risk Structure Ecosystems?" *BioScience* 54 (8): 755–66.

Ritvo, Harriet. 1987. *The Animal Estate: The English and Other Creatures in the Victorian Age.* Cambridge MA: Harvard University Press.

Sandom Chris, Joseph Bull, Susan Canney and David Macdonald. 2012. "Exploring the Value of Wolves (*Canis lupus*) in Landscape-Scale Fenced Reserves for Ecological Restoration in the Scottish Highlands." In *Fencing for Conservation.* Edited by Michael Somers and Mathew Hayward, 245–76. New York: Springer.

Seddon, Philip, Christine Griffiths, Pritpal Soorae and Doug Armstrong. 2014. "Reversing Defaunation: Restoring Species in a Changing World." *Science* 345 (6195): 406–12.

Staatsbosbeheer. 2011. *Managementplan Oostvaardersplassengebied 2011–2015.* Driebergen, the Netherlands: Staatsbosbeheer.

Svenning, Jens-Christian. 2002. "A Review of Natural Vegetation Openness in North-Western Europe." *Biological Conservation* 104 (2): 133–48.

Van Den Belt, Henk. 2004. "Networking Nature, or Serengeti Behind the Dikes." *History and Technology* 20 (3): 311–33.

Vera, Frans. 2000. *Grazing Ecology and Forest History.* Wallingford, UK: CABI.

———. 2009. "Large-Scale Nature Development—the Oostvaardersplassen." *British Wildlife* 20 (5): 28–36.

Whatmore, Sarah. 2002. *Hybrid Geographies: Natures, Cultures, Spaces.* London: Sage.

Wolfe, Cary. 2012. *Before the Law: Humans and Other Animals in a Biopolitical Frame.* Chicago: University of Chicago Press.

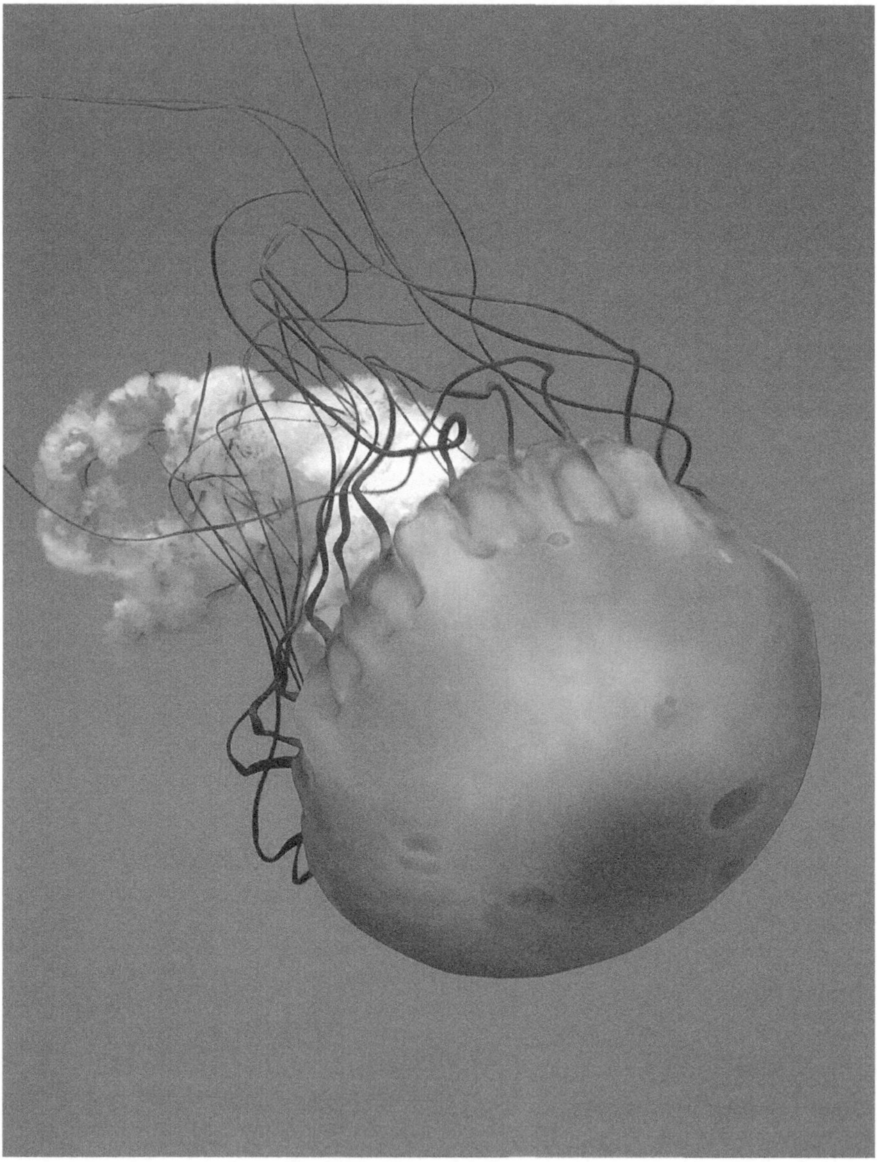

Chapter 3

Governing Jellyfish: Eco-Security and Planetary "Life" in the Anthropocene

Elizabeth R. Johnson

> "Why do you like jellyfish so much?" I asked.
>
> "I don't know. I guess I think they're cute," she said. "But one thing did occur to me when I was really focused on them. What we see before us is just one tiny part of the world. We get into the habit of thinking, this is the world, but that's not true at all. The real world is in a much darker and deeper place than this, and most of it is occupied by jellyfish and things . . . Two thirds of the earth's surface is ocean, and all we can see of it with the naked eye is the surface: the skin. We hardly know anything about what's beneath the skin."
>
> —Haruki Murakami, *The Wind-Up Bird Chronicle*, p. 225

> We see the emergence of a completely different problem that is no longer that of fixing and demarcating the territory, but of allowing circulations to take place, of controlling them, sifting the good and the bad, ensuring that things are always in movement, constantly moving around, continually going from one point to another, but in such a way that the inherent dangers of this circulation are canceled out.
>
> —Michel Foucault, *Security, Territory, Population*, p. 65

Jellyfish fill Toru Okada with dread. Having once encountered a swarm—or "smack"—of jellyfish on an ocean swim, a trip to the aquarium leaves the protagonist of Haruki Murakami's *Wind-Up Bird Chronicle* slumped on a bench, battling a rising panic. His wife-to-be is astonished. "I can see it in your eyes," she says. "They've gone out of focus. It's incredible—just from looking at jellyfish" (1999, 225). Her experience—captured in the epigraph above—is just as incredible. Through her eyes, jellyfish bring into

---

Pacific sea nettle (*Chrysaora fuscescens*) at the National Aquarium in Baltimore, Maryland. Photo by Elizabeth R. Johnson, December 2014.

relief the other-worldly character of the world that we inhabit. Much more than "cute," jellyfish give form to what is "beneath the skin" of the earth.

Enabled by advances in jellyfish husbandry, exhibits like the one described in Murakami's novel have proliferated over the past two decades. Aquarium-goers around the world now similarly experience the profound weirdness of jellyfish bodies. Eva Hayward (2012) has explored how looking at the alien-like bodies of jellyfish might open up new ways of relating to other organisms, creating the potential to alter our sense of what does—and what might—come to matter. These are organisms, she writes, that are encountered "viscerally rather than intellectually, sensuously rather than conceptually" (184). We cannot touch them without inviting distress, but through looking at a distance we nevertheless might, as Karen Barad writes, become more intimate with the infinite alterity that "lives in, around, and through us, by waking us up to the inhuman that therefore we are" (Barad 2012, 217–8).

Similarly, Stacy Alaimo has drawn on Jacques Rancière to speculate on how scientific representations of jellyfish may ignite a "redistribution of the sensible." Such redistribution, for Rancière, would ostensibly transform our aesthetic, ethical, and political commitments. For Alaimo, jellyfish pulse beyond the "visible, the sayable, the thinkable [to] disrupt and confuse categories with their . . . mode of being" (151). Alaimo borrows from Cary Wolfe to figure jellyfish as creatures "before the law" (Wolfe 2012). Their uncanny shapes and being-ness elude signification, making them difficult to frame by juridical–legal structures. Unlike charismatic organisms—polar bears or sea turtles—that are easily enrolled in regimes of species protection or an extended conception of rights, the seemingly fluid continuity between jellyfish and the marine substrate that gives them life makes them difficult to individualize and practically impossible to judge. They do not conform to accepted frameworks of animal ethics. Do they suffer? Do they respond? The way their bodies process information—through a neural network rather than a centralized nervous system—make it difficult to know. Often, even their animality is called into question. Alaimo speculates that the challenge presented by jellyfish bodies may heighten our consideration of networks of entanglement and elicit "posthuman modes of environmentalist concern" (Alaimo 2013, 140).

As Toru Okada's wife notes, this is incredible: "just [by] looking at jellyfish" we may alter our sense of what matters, shifting ethical frameworks and giving new shape to environmental politics. Gazing upon their bodies might offer a sense of the "liveliness" that Andreas Phillippopoulous-Mihalopoulos references in this volume, a liveliness that recasts our sense of responsibility in the world. But our lives with jellyfish go well beyond the spectacle of the aquarium. Scientists have made their proteins and peptides circulate outside their bodies, into those of mice, pigs, and other organisms to make perceptible genetic differences by encoding them with jellyfish fluorescence.

Jellyfish stem cells are similarly studied and extracted, woven into cosmetic treatments to reduce the signs of aging. Meanwhile, multiple species of jellyfish seem to be reproducing in the wild at alarming rates: swimmers like the fictional Okada and fishing boats encounter smacks with ever-greater frequency. Jellyfish, therefore, seem to have come into focus as part of our social and material existence as never before.[1]

Examining scientific practice and language rather than aesthetics, I find that jellyfish and their study are not eroding "humanist claims to sovereign knowledges" (Alaimo 2013, 155) but are instead becoming part an ongoing respatialization of those claims. In what follows, I show how the science of jellyfish research has become part of changing spatial practices of biological governance, consistent with the nomination of "the Anthropocene" as our current era. While a universalized human problematically stands at the center of this proposed geologic stratum, the era's nomination also references our deep entanglement with other organisms, organisms who respond—positively and negatively—to our manipulations of the earth. Jellyfish are emblematic of this shift in planetary awareness. Scientists tie the growth of their populations to anthropogenic climate change and ecological degradation; their uptake in the cosmetic and biopharmaceutical industries integrates their liveliness to our own even more tightly. As a result, these organisms are paradoxically figured both as the uncontrollable agents of a coming apocalypse and as a vehicle of biopharmaceutical innovation that will enable humans to attain immortality. The science of jellyfish therefore crystalizes what philosopher Frederic Neyrat considers one of most pressing paradoxes of the Anthropocene: that we are increasingly driven to recognize our own mortality and finitude—as individuals and as a species—but continue to organize our social lives (at least in the West) as if we are immortal (Neyrat and Johnson 2014). This tendency and its corresponding focus on a particular understanding of human survival has prompted an expanded discourse and practice of securitization into new spaces and into the bodies of nonhuman organisms.

A return to Foucault's lectures published in *Security, Territory, Population* (2009) provides a useful touchstone for considering this respatialization of security. There, Foucault described how the object of power shifted in the nineteenth and twentieth centuries. "Fixing and demarcating the territory" gave way to controlling the circulation of things, "sifting the good and the bad," to ensure the enhancement of human populations (2009, 65). The literature on biopolitics has primarily paid attention to how this transition has played out on and over human bodies. The rise of biopower meant that attending to "limits and frontiers, or fixing locations" was no longer the predominant expression of power. Human health, behavior, everyday routines and social relationships also became the objects of governance. This is a story that is rehearsed with some frequency. However, Foucault also made plain that the rise of biopower entailed more than a management of human bodies. It also required close attention to the management of lively things, their circulation, and their interconnections across space (Foucault 2009; Crampton and Elden 2007). In his lectures, Foucault referred to this as the management of a milieu: the rise of biopolitics also involved "making possible, guaranteeing, and ensuring circulations: the circulation of people, merchandise, and air, etcetera" (Foucault 2009, 29). This required attention to the details of natural processes, particularly those related to agricultural production. While Foucault's milieu was largely limited to those things easily recognized as objects of human consumption, others since have detailed the centrality of nonhuman bodies—predominantly livestock, viruses, and captive animals—and their circulations within a biopolitical frame (Shukin 2009; Braun 2007; Hinchliffe et al. 2012; Wolfe 2012; Braverman 2012). This literature makes clear that contemporary biopolitics demands the knowledge and management of a socio-biological system that is more-than-human. In the process, organisms once considered distant and alien are studied, mapped, and enrolled as objects of ecological threat and ecological security.

Through examining how jellyfish are taken up in the aquarium and in scientific practice, I shed light on the changing relationship between securing life and the space of juridical territory. I show how the entwining of human and nonhuman concerns in this era of climate change and ecological degradation is not a smooth process, but involves what Rancière has referred to as a "repartitioning [of] the political from the non-political" (Rancière 2011, 4). In the first part, I show how jellyfish are being figured as agents of ecological devastation alongside the human behaviors that facilitate them. I further explore the legal and practical limitations of securing life in a more-than-human space—the three-dimensional space of the living sea, which both extends and exceeds the boundaries of territorial jurisdiction and the law. I describe how scientists, fisheries, and policy makers have struggled to make jellyfish and other forms of sea life objects of ecological securitization—one part of a "bad" set of conditions and circulations—on a terrain that is more "fluid" than "fixed." In part two, I take up how scientists and the pharmaceutical industry are sifting jellyfish and other Cnidaria in the category of social "good" through stem cell research. In the conclusion I draw on the writing of Frederic Neyrat to consider how the science of jellyfish research might be directed differently—not toward a planetary extension of biological security, but to "invent a new form of municipality that does justice to the munificence of forms of life" (Neyrat 2010, 37).

Beyond the Aesthetics: Jellyfish "Behaving Badly"

Having read Alaimo and Hayward's accounts of jellyfish encounters, I had anticipated a visceral, transformative experience when in the winter of 2014 I toured the jellyfish exhibit of the National Aquarium in Baltimore. To be sure, each of the many jellyfish housing units, also called kreisels, glowed with ethereal beauty of several species (see, e.g., Figure 3.1 below). Some floated orange against a turquoise background. Others were lit with blue florescent light. Each provoked distinct sensations. But alongside these otherworldly denizens of our world, I also found a narrative I was not expecting: one of danger and ecological insecurity.

Figure 3.1 Moon jellyfish, *Aurelia Aurita*, float at the National Aquarium in Baltimore, Maryland. Photo by Elizabeth R. Johnson, December 2014.

The title of the aquarium exhibit offered the first clue: "Jellies Invasion: Oceans Out of Balance." As it suggests, scientists and the media have enrolled jellyfish as bioindicators of ailing oceans. In her recent book *Stung!* (2013), for example, marine biologist Lisa-Ann Gershwin describes jellyfish as exploiters of already fragile ecologies. She argues that the more frequent blooms witnessed in recent years indicate that overfishing and pollution are having catastrophic effects on populations of larger marine species. While organisms considered valuable to human life—and general biodiversity—suffer in low-oxygen, high-acidity environments and warming temperatures, jellyfish thrive. Their gelatinous bodies store oxygen and, unlike those made of muscle and fat, they seem unaffected by the accumulation of radiation or other toxins (Gershwin 2013). Fewer organisms "higher" on the food chain mean that plankton, copepods and other small marine organisms—jellyfish food—have grown in abundance. Since the 1990s, for example, moon jellyfish populations have thrived in the Gulf of Mexico's so-called "dead zone," an area often animated by organism too small or strange to be considered human food. These creatures seem to take advantage of conditions that denigrate other forms of life.

More than a symptom, jellyfish are also a threat. In the text surrounding the aquarium's kreisels, visitors not only read of stinging tentacles, but also of "voracious appetites," "formidable" predatory capacities, tendencies of prolific reproduction, and an ability to "gobble up" all of the sea's plankton. As an article in the *Smithsonian Magazine* reported in 2010, "all around the world, jellyfish are behaving badly" (Tucker 2010, n.p.). Framed as the perpetrators of ecological insecurity, jellyfish appear as demons of the sea. Indeed, the growing frequency of blooms does seem to impinge on anthropocentric values in several ways. In the short term, jellyfish threaten the world's fisheries. When they bloom, jellyfish consume enormous amounts of prey in a relatively short period. They are themselves, however, consumed only by an ever-smaller number of threatened predators like leatherback sea turtles, leading scientists to refer to them as "trophic dead ends" (Gershwin 2013). According to Gershwin, jellyfish threaten already fragile tuna populations and could "starve the whales to extinction" (Gershwin 2013, 134). And they not only threaten ecologies, but also put built infrastructures at risk. Going back decades, one can read about smacks infiltrating the intake systems of nuclear power and desalination plants around the globe, causing power outages and millions of dollars in damage (Tucker 2010, n.p.; Vanzi 1999). Fishing boats are also compromised, as "jellyfish masses" can break nets and jam engines "beyond repair" (National Science Foundation 2008, n.p.).

But jellyfish themselves are only part of this story. Curators of the "Jellies Invasion" exhibit also highlighted how human behavior was responsible for blooms, ultimately "tipping the balance of the earth's aquatic ecosystems." Each bit of information about the dangers jellyfish pose to fisheries and marine biodiversity was paired with a list of "what *you* can do" to limit their continued expansion. Promoted practices included cleaning boat bottoms, limiting fish consumption, supporting "green" legislation, and reducing the use of household fertilizers. According to one journalist, "there's a queasy sense among scientists that jellyfish just might be avengers from the deep, repaying all the insults we've heaped on the world's oceans" (Tucker 2010, n.p.). These connections suggest that "we"—or, at least the excrement of twenty-first century civilization—are becoming jellyfish.

We might be tempted to read these stories of jellyfish–human connectivity optimistically. The exhibition's attention to links between human behavior and marine ecologies suggests a growing awareness of the tight meshwork of human and nonhuman life. Indeed, inquiry into jellyfish ecologies seems to confirm what so many cultural theorists have been arguing all along: that nonhuman life is not "outside" of social life, but intimately woven within it (Latour 1993; Haraway 2007; Barad 2012). Accordingly, we might be hopeful that such exhibits may spark a reformed sense of responsibility. But rather than prompting the kind of dis-orientation experienced by Alaimo and Hayward, the National Aquarium exhibit illuminates an ongoing re-ordering of space that follows well-traveled contours. Alongside the spectacle of jellyfish bodies, the stories told of these organisms and their connection to social life are made part of a security apparatus that increasingly enrolls biological sciences and marine ecologies in new ways. In the section that follows, I show how jellyfish are made to appear at once as the effects of human action and, at the same time, a lively object—alien in its destructive capacity—that needs to be studied so that it might be cast out of a "polite," more-than-human, society.

Eco-security: Governing Sea Space, Sea Life

Ensuring the circulation of grain and other material resources that sustain human life has always entailed the management of nonhuman organisms, including their elimination from socio-ecological systems. Consider, for example, how invasive species like Kudzu or even simply "weeds," have long been cast as enemies of a "civilized" society, defined in decidedly anthropocentric terms (Comaroff and Comaroff 2001; Neely 2010). Today, who and what matter in these efforts has expanded precipitously, engendering growing apparatuses of ecological security that are planetary in scope. As Stephen Hinchliffe and his co-authors have noted, these techniques of ecological control involve making "more life through continuously expanding circulations, and . . . intensifying entanglements" (2012, 13). Nonhuman organisms enter and exit regimes of management anew, some as threats, others as "good" ecological citizens that perform "services" we deem conducive to lived environments (Robertson 2011). If, as Rancière writes, "politics is a way of repartitioning the political from the non-political," jellyfish—and their ocean milieu—are currently part of an associated respatialization as territorial logics of governance are extended to the seas and to the complicated entanglements of ecological relations therein (Rancière 2011, 4).

The ocean and its (inedible) inhabitants have long been thought to exist "outside" of socio-political life, as an alien space. In Carl Schmitt's *Nomos of the Earth*, the seas were a nonplace, devoid of significant matter and distinct from the orderable space of the land. He famously noted, accordingly, "on the waves, there is nothing but waves" (Schmitt 2003 [1950], 42–3). As Philip Steinberg's work has shown, however, the seas have historically been brought in and out of regime of spatial ordering, in and out of the territorial rubrics of containment associated with sovereign power and the juridical–legal infrastructure of nation-states (2009). From the early seventeenth century on, the majority of nations treated the seas and their resources under the doctrine of *mare liberum*, or "freedom of the seas" (Grotis 1916 [1609]). This doctrine was meant to ostensibly guarantee access to the world's oceans, afford unobstructed navigation for all, and declare the ocean's resources a global common. A growing need for international cooperation after World War II prompted the United Nations to draw the seas into a more structured framework by creating the Geneva Conventions on the Law of the Seas in 1958. The Convention continued to ensure "innocent passage" and freedom of navigation for all states, while also determining criminal and civil jurisdiction and defining piracy on the high seas. A more detailed update followed three decades later, on the heels of a changing relationship to ocean resources—particularly advances in deep-sea oil drilling, waste dumping, and the collapse of various fisheries—and became effective in 1994.[2]

The 1958 and 1994 Conventions attempt to render the seas manageable by fixing them as an extension of territorial space. This is reflected no better than in the name given to the 12 nautical miles that extend beyond the shoreline: the "territorial sea." Sovereign economic rights are also granted within "exclusive economic zones" that extend another 200 miles beyond the shore. These zones gives states sovereign control over the natural resources beneath the seabed as well as living resources that move about within the ocean's fluid substrate. States are thereby given authority to allocate fishing licenses, determine limits and quotas, and ensure "conservation and promoting of optimum utilization of [highly migratory] species throughout the region, both within and beyond the [Zone]" (United Nations 1994, Part V, Article 64).[3] The seas outside the exclusive economic zones ostensibly remained under the doctrine of *mare liberum*, free and "open to all states" (UN 1994, Part VII, Article 87). The resources within the high seas—referred to as "The Area"—are therefore not governed by sovereign states (UN 1994, Part XI, Article 136). Instead, activities that take place in "The Area" are, according to the Convention, to "be carried out for the benefit of mankind as a whole, irrespective of the geographical location of States, whether coastal or land-locked" (UN 1994, Part XI, Article 140).

The Convention is designed to ensure that the movement of humans in and across the world's waters produces "good" circulations. But the sea is not a locale to be administered through the organization of social and spatial processes. Rather, it is fluid matter constituted, as Steinberg notes, "through its very geophysical mobility" (2013, 165). The fluid movement of that matter—like jellyfish themselves—is difficult to comprehend or articulate within the language of governance that we have developed on firmer land. Despite these difficulties, concerns over ecological health drive attempts to manage the seas' geophysical mobility and the circulation of its contents. The twelfth part of the 1994 Convention, for example, meant to ensure the "Protection and Preservation of the Marine Environment," prohibits the release of known toxic substances and other forms of pollution. It also attempts to delimit the circulations of unknown or potential harms. In the words of the Convention:

> States shall take all measures necessary to prevent, reduce and control pollution of the marine environment resulting from the use of technologies under their jurisdiction or control, or the intentional or accidental introduction of species, alien or new, to a particular part of the marine environment, which may cause significant and harmful changes thereto (Part XII, Article 196).

Jellyfish and their ecologies have been made visible in part by placing them within the extended territorial logic of securitization that is similarly reflected in UN doctrine. In one of Gershwin's most striking passages, for example, she compares the spread of *Mnemioposis*—a species of comb jellyfish that prompted the collapse of several commercial fisheries and the endangerment of fish life in the Caspian Sea—with that of the Third Reich. As she writes, *Mnemioposis's* movement from the Caspian to the Mediterranean "reads like diary notes of Hitler's army: try the northern route, stopped dead by the winter cold—try the southern route, success—push further—keep going, almost there—reach the target, spread out—conquer. . . . *Mnemiopsis* has spread through the seas of the Mediterranean Basin like cancer—in all directions . . . aggressively . . . lethally" (Gershwin 2013, 62; ellipses in the original).

Gershwin's rather extreme demonization of *Mnemioposis* figures these organisms as an enemy to be fought, as if on a battlefield terrain similar to that encountered on land. In her work, this anthropomorphism operates metaphorically. But scientists and local governments in South Korea have taken up the call to do battle with jellyfish in practice, attempting to regulate their circulation according to the same logic of territorial securitization. To fight this "enemy," they have developed and deployed the "Jellyfish

Elimination Robotic Swarm," or JEROS, a group of jellyfish-killing robots that can shred up to 900 kilograms of jellyfish per hour (Robinson 2013; Love 2014). The creation of JEROS and Gershwin's language express what Hinchliffe et al. refer to as the "will to closure" through which undesirable elements can be charted on a map-able terrain, cut off in order to render complex ecologies safe—for humans (2012, 2). But neither jellyfish nor the fluid substrate in which they live conform to such a terrain. Neither their movements nor their life cycles operate according to predictable rhythms. Rather, blooms emerge in relation to environmental conditions that are—often from season to season—in flux.

The Science of Securing an Emergent Threat

Like the viral pathogens that Hinchliffe et al. analyze, marine ecologies circulate as part of a "radically uncertain" future (2012, 536). The three-dimensional and deeply interconnected network of emergent properties in the sea makes sifting the "good" from the "bad" an uneasy task. Consider, for example, how harmful algae blooms serve as emergent and supposedly deadly feature of ocean ecosystems that are beyond our control (Schrader 2010). In light of this radical uncertainty in the seas, Steinberg suggests that attempts to order the oceans require a fuller appreciation of it "as a uniquely fluid and dynamic space" as well as "an epistemology that views the ocean as continually being reconstituted by a variety of elements: the non-human and the human, the biological and the geophysical, the historic and the contemporary" (2013, 157). Beyond patrolling bays with jellyfish-shredding robots and the scripting of formal legal doctrine, an epistemology of and for the ocean and its elements is currently developing within laboratories and scientific practice, changing the spatial dynamics of security practices by operating them on and through knowledge of nonhuman life cycles.

While the aquarium insists on making recommendations about "what *you* can do" to delimit the spread of these "invaders," scientists and policy makers are exploring ways to take jellyfish out of circulation not by changing human behavior, but by intervening in jellyfish lifecycles. Scientists have observed that both jellyfish and hydra pass from a larval stage into a colonial polyp stage, in which they live as sea anemones do, affixed to a substrate. Here, the organisms reproduce through asexual cloning. Given the "right" conditions, that is where they would remain, continuing asexual reproduction indefinitely, making these colonies functionally immortal. But changes in the amount of iodine in the water, the number of hours of daylight, water temperature, or food availability prompt them to undergo metamorphosis en masse, creating the blooms that "threaten" ocean ecologies. But while the media seems already to have accepted that jellyfish behavior has taken a turn for the antisocial, precisely what prompts blooms, how they connect to anthropogenic change, and even whether they are on the increase, are all unclear. The recent attention to jellyfish as a threat, however, has already ensured an increased investment in research on their lifecycles in order to remedy the unpredictability of blooms.

Several recent studies have worked to identify the proteins that catalyze metamorphosis in some particularly prolific species. For example, scientists at Okinawa Institute of Technology have used that data to artificially induce metamorphosis in moon jellyfish (*Aurelia aurita*) populations (Fuchs et al. 2014). A primary investigator in the project has suggested that inducing metamorphosis in winter would spark a massive die off and eliminate blooms the following year (*The Life Cycle of a Jellyfish, and a Way to Control It* 2014). Given these findings, scientists have speculated on the ability to control moon jellyfish populations in a mid-sized bay. Such research is on the frontlines of eliminating "bad" circulations of the sea, not through a "will to closure" but by a manipulation of environmental and biological conditions.

What is described above is one of many ways in which practices and logics of securitization are extended to a planetary scale. The language of a speculated jellyfish apocalypse and its attendant practices acknowledge these seemingly otherworldly organisms as an integral and agential (if not mindful) part of the unfolding of the ecologically precarious present. But while jellyfish act according their own, often-indecipherable movements, humans have also drawn them into regulative regimes reshaped around them. The fluid space of ocean ecologies, including the life cycles of jellyfish, now requires close surveillance of its emergent properties. And, when necessary, these and other organisms necessitate the punitive management of their reproductive practices. The science of jellyfish ecologies has therefore engaged in taking the regulatory sphere "out of place," whereby political action takes shape across new landscapes and logics of control (Rancière 2011, 4).

But jellyfish circulate in social life in other ways, beyond the prohibition of their reproduction and movement. Humans also seek to harness their reproductive capacities as a means toward biotechnological innovation, expanding how and where they circulate and intensifying our socio-biological entanglements with them. Here, jellyfish and their kin are not derided, but lauded. Their "generative" capacities offer the hope that we might short circuit ecological insecurity by learning to live as they do.

Securing Human Life: Living as Jellyfish, Forever

The earliest Cnidaria, in both polyp and medusa forms, emerged during the latter stages of the Pre-Cambrian period, approximately 565 million years ago. Though there are no evidentiary links between modern species and the earliest of these gelatinous forbearers, fossils of mid-Cambrian jellyfish show the same level of complexity as those extant today (Cartwright et al. 2007). In the context of current ecological change and the larger geologic record, it would seem then that these organisms possess an ability to persist while others suffer and die—a trait that humans seem ever more eager to adopt. Accordingly, efforts to secure and enhance human life also intersect with jellyfish outside of the seas, as investment in the science of jellyfish life cycles suggests that humans might like to become jellyfish by harnessing the regenerative capacities of their stem cells.

Human stem cells are pluripotent in development—embryonic stem cells differentiate to produce the different elements of the body. Adult stem cells are more limited; they are multipotent at best. Hematopoietic stem cells, for example, produce our different blood cells. The stem cells of several nonhuman animals possess more flexible capacities for regeneration. Zebra fish, flies, and mice, for example, can all regenerate portions of injured tissues through a processes of cell de-differentiation and re-differentiation, when specific cells reproduce as stem cells to create a new line. Cnidarians are one of the few known (at least at the moment) phyla that can undergo transdifferentiation, whereby any cell type can reproduce as another. Tentacle cells can produce mouth cells, mouth cells can generate oral arm cells. Some Cnidarian species undergo processes of transdifferentiation in whole or in part at different stages of their life cycle (Rinkevich 2009). The species *Turriptosis dohrnii*—a type of hydra—has received considerable press over the past two years for its so-called immortality (Rich 2012). Under the right conditions, *Turriptosis* can change the direction of its development, morphing from their "adult" form back into the "juvenile" polyp form. Other species of Cnidaria undergo similar processes. *Stephanoscyphus plaulophors* will transdifferentiate from ephyra to the larval stage and then develop into polyps; the polyps of *Cassiopea andromeda* produce buds that behave exactly like sexually produced larvae (Frank et al. 2009).

For obvious reasons, Cnidarians have become important to stem cell research. In fact, hydroids were subjects of the study that led to the first description of stem cells in 1883 by August Weismann (Frank et al. 2009). Today, they have gained currency in stem cell research again primarily because they enable scientists to study totipotent stem cell development *in vivo*, i.e., as they undergo mitosis in the organisms itself. This sheds important light on how cells regenerate and differentiate in "real life." Stem cell therapies that might harness the capacities of Cnidarians for regeneration offer hope for healing damaged organs, muscles, and other tissues as well as aid in the process of developing synthetic tissues *in vitro*.

Cnidarian cells are also unique in that they do not undergo the processes of aging that "plague" humans: they lack the elements of a cell that limit how many times it can reproduce. This too has sparked the imagination of scientists, in particular pharmaceutical biologists and chemists looking to repair damaged tissue, put an end to processes of aging, or "solve death."[4] This knowledge has already stepped out of the experimental laboratory into the commercial sphere, as several cosmetic companies now advertise skin creams that will transfer the hydra's "immortal" properties into human skin. A recently patented "Anti-wrinkle hexapeptide" called JUVELEVEN™, for example, draws on the "renewal and longevity" of the "remarkable" hydra in order "to repair and delete DNA damage that occurs along the years; rejuvenating and regenerating skin cells" (JUVELEVEN Anti-Wrinkle Hexapeptide 2014). The study of Cnidarian stem cells has therefore also managed to regenerate the ancient dream of a fountain of youth. But rather than a mysterious geographical location, that dream is now embodied in these invertebrate sea creatures (Rosenthal 2008, n.p.). Here, the practice of securing life—the assurance that our bodies will be bound to the earth indefinitely—is taking shape through a distributed network of laboratories attempting to suture together human and nonhuman bodies.

Regardless of the viability of these dreams, the science that strives to make humans live like jellyfish is part of a shift in how the elements of life are governed. The identification of peptides and proteins like JUVELEVEN opens up avenues for the privatization and patenting of life's processes. As Sheila Jasanoff (2012) has described, molecular life—the tissues, cells, and other elements of human and nonhuman organisms—now circulate according to international legal frameworks that adjudicate the authority to own the processes of life's (re)generation. As Jasanoff writes, these processes preform an ontological surgery on life itself. National patent laws attribute ownership to life that has been extracted from organisms and reproduced in laboratories. United States' case law—for example *Diamond v. Chakrabarty* and *Moore v. The Regents of the University of California*—has ensured that ownership over biological materials could be attributed to the scientists who make meaning of and circulate them as part of an international network of knowledge production (Jasanoff 2012). This process reconfigures how "life" operates as an object of management. For example, while Cnidarian stem cells are often studied *in vivo*, cell materials like the JUVELEVEN hexapeptide now circulate outside their bodies, having been endowed with patents and, accordingly, assigned capitalist value. By attempting to enfold human and animal life at the molecular level, we have reconfigured biomaterials as objects of legal concerns, regulating them as a form of what Kaushik Sundar Rajan refers to as "biocapital" (Rajan 2012; Goldstein and Johnson 2015).

The Politics of Jellyfish Science: Beyond the Sensible

While "just looking at jellyfish" produces a sense of awareness, even wonderment at "what's beneath the skin of the earth," scientific practices are currently in the process of ensuring the earth's more inscrutable elements are drawn into governmental frameworks. Following how jellyfish circulate amid those practices reveals some of the messy respatializations that are taking shape in the shadow of climate change and in the context of the Anthropocene.

The two pathways through which jellyfish life has entered into social practices of governance and knowledge production that I have described here are paradoxical. On the one hand, jellyfish bodies and behaviors are studied in order to control and limit their populations. Wild, in the three-dimensional space of the sea, jellyfish circulate and reproduce "badly." Accordingly, they are made an object to be reined in. On the other hand, scientists are attempting to harness jellyfish capacities for life in order to ensure the continuation of our own life as humans. In laboratories and commodities, extracted elements of jellyfish biology circulate as part of "good" projects in innovation. Here, the "inherent dangers of" jellyfish circulation are canceled out (Foucault 2009, 65). Neyrat's (2014) paradox of the Anthropocene is brought to life in these two registers of becoming jellyfish. Their ecologies teach us that our life conditions are on the cusp of getting increasingly unfortunate; they force us to question the still-persistent hierarchy that places humans at the apex of life; they goad us to the realization that we are more fragile, more vulnerable, more reliant on dynamic and varied forms of life than many other organisms on earth. Yet, at the same time, the science of jellyfish life cycles and stem cells gives us license to deny all of that: to deny the multiform conditions that forge our life and the very necessity of our mortality. This tendency is not limited to the practices of jellyfish science; it is the tendency upon which technological fixes of geo-engineering and biotechnology—now multibillion dollar industries in the United States and Europe—are selected as a legitimate path toward determining our collective global future.

Neyrat's paradox is based on a split image of human life. On one hand, we envision ourselves as connected, part of a circulation of life and resources. On the other, we appear as bearers of a life that capable of becoming "indestructible" (Rosenthal, quoted in Short 2012). Through these contradictory practices, we find evident a belief that creating the conditions for immortal life inside the human body will remedy illnesses located elsewhere—in complex and often imperceptible ecologies. In an extension of the apparatuses of population control and public health that Foucault described, we now participate in a politics of planetary, eco-securitization that extends from the land into the seas and into the life cycles of organisms, changing shape accordingly. This is an environmental politics *for* life that legitimates not only the exclusion and "letting die" of others, but also the genocide of humans and the wholesale extinction of ecological systems. It is a kind of politics that, as Neyrat describes, is based on the conditions of "survival." As he writes: "The prefix 'sur'—in both the French 'sur-vie' and in the English 'survival'—involves the idea of after and beyond" (Neyrat and Johnson 2014, n.p.). This means that humanity can believe in her survival—the perpetuation of living over and beyond the earthly limits of life—while she simultaneously destroys the planet. That is, she can believe that "her life is out of reach, definitively unscathed" by the earth and its entanglements (ibid.). Life can accordingly be secured "out there" through the management of other life and "in here" through the prolonging of our own biological life. In both cases, it is our connection to the earth and its other inhabitants that is, once again, denied. Confronting this political and ecological condition and deciding on a different future—and a different politics—will require a rethinking of these terms, a decoupling of a politics *for* life from a politics of survival.

If Alaimo and Hayward have shown how looking at jellyfish might open up to another way of considering our connection to nonhuman organisms, following the practices of jellyfish science might offer us another way of considering life altogether. Thinking with a-typical forms of nonhuman life—life as something other than a linear progression into death—might be necessary if we are to redraw the boundaries of our collective imaginary. If we are to organize new forms of "municipality" that do justice "to the *munificence* of forms of life," we might begin here, by reconfiguring the parameters of life and death itself (Neyrat 2010, 37). The scientific studies of life cycles and pathways to death in marine invertebrate may help us to do just that. They challenge the human-centered relationship between life and death as juxtaposed and fixed on linear developmental trajectories. By enlivening the study of invertebrate life cycles in new ways, we may find resources that encourage us to view death not as the end of life—and therefore something to be militated against—but as internal and integral to all life. In so doing, we might begin to better engage with the earth's multi-faceted forms of life not as objects to be managed, but as co-habitants with whom we make and to whom we do justice.

Acknowledgments

This chapter owes much to the detailed editorial eyes of Irus Braverman and Caitlin McIntyre as well as wonderfully generous comments from Jamie Lorimer and the others in this collection. Many of the ideas here emerged in the course of conversations with Astrid Schrader and through our collaboration on the Unsettling Life/Death project.

Notes

1 Scientists classify jellyfish among over 10,000 sessile and motile organisms within the phylum Cnidaria. The term "jellyfish" is often used colloquially to refer to all medusoid Cnidaria. Scyphozoa, or "true jellyfish" are the most recognizable of these, but the phylum also includes Hydrazoa and Cubazoa.

2 The Convention entered into force after its ratification by sixty nation-states.

3 Given that lively ocean resources are not so easily affixed within zones, enacting this authority is difficult and often contingent on multi-scalar agreements between different economic sectors (see, e.g., St. Martin 2005; Baird and Quastel 2011).
4 This has been the highly publicized new endeavor of Google, which is now investing in bio-pharmaceutical research to racially extend the human lifespan (McCracken 2013).

References

Alaimo, Stacy. 2013. "Jellyfish Science, Jellyfish Aesthetics: Posthuman Reconfigurations of the Sensible." In *Thinking with Water*. Edited by Cecilia Chen, Janine MacLeod, and Astrida Neimanis, 139–64. Montréal: McGill University Press.

Baird, Ian and Noah Quastel. 2011. "Dolphin-Safe Tuna from California to Thailand: Localisms in Environmental Certification of Global Commodity Networks." *Annals of the Association of American Geographers* 101 (2): 337–55.

Barad, Karen. 2012. "On Touching—The Inhuman That I Therefore Am." *Differences* 23 (3): 206–33.

Braun, Bruce. 2007. "Biopolitics and the Molecularization of Life." *Cultural Geographies* 14 (1): 6–28.

Braverman, Irus. 2012. *Zooland: The Institution of Captivity*. Stanford: Stanford University Press.

Cartwright, Paulyn, Susan Halgedahl, Jonathan Hendricks, Richard Jarrard et al. 2007. "Exceptionally Preserved Jellyfishes from the Middle Cambrian." *PLoS ONE* 2 (10): e1121.

Comaroff, Jean and John Comaroff. 2001. "Naturing the Nation: Aliens, Apocalypse and the Postcolonial State." *Journal of Southern African Studies* 27 (3): 627–51.

Crampton, Jeremy and Stuart Elden. 2007. "Space Knowledge and Power: Foucault and Geography." In *Space, Knowledge, Power*. Edited by Jeremy Crampton and Stuart Elden, 1–16. London: Ashgate.

Foucault, Michel. 2009. *Security, Territory, Population*. New York: Palgrave MacMillan.

Frank, Uri, Gunther Plickert and Werner Müller. 2009. "Cnidarian Interstitial Cells: The Dawn of Stem Cell Research." In *Stem Cells in Marine Organisms*. Edited by Baruch Rinkevich and Valeria Matranga, 33–60. London: Springer Science & Business Media.

Fuchs, Björn, Wei Wang, Simon Graspeuntner, Yizhu Li, Santiago Insua, et al. 2014. "Regulation of Polyp-to-Jellyfish Transition in Aurelia Aurita." *Current Biology* 24 (3): 263–73.

Gershwin, Lisa. 2013. *Stung!: On Jellyfish Blooms and the Future of the Ocean*. Chicago: University of Chicago Press.

Goldstein, Jesse and Elizabeth Johnson. 2015. "Biomimicry: New Natures, New Enclosures." *Theory, Culture, Society* 32 (1): 61–81.

Grotis, Hugo. 1916 [1609]. *The Freedom of the Seas*. New York: Oxford University Press.

Haraway, Donna. 2007. *When Species Meet*. Minneapolis: University Of Minnesota Press.

Hayward, Eva. 2012. "Sensational Jellyfish: Aquarium Affects and the Matter of Immersion." *Differences* 23 (3): 161–96.

Hinchliffe, Stephen, John Allen, Stephanie Lavau, Nick Bingham et al. 2012. "Biosecurity and the Topologies of Infected Life: From Borderlines to Borderlands." *Transactions of the Institute of British Geographers* 38 (4): 531–43.

Jasanoff, Sheila. 2012. "Taking Life: Private Rights in Public Nature." In *Lively Capital*. Edited by Kaushik Sunder Rajan. Durham: Duke University Press.

JUVELEVEN™ Anti-Wrinkle Hexapeptide. 2014. *Erase10*. Retrieved from https://erase10.com/juveleven-anti-wrinkle/.

Latour, Bruno. 1993. *We Have Never Been Modern*. Cambridge: Harvard University Press.

"The Life Cycle of a Jellyfish, and a Way to Control It." 2014. *Phys.Org News*. http://phys.org/news/2014–01-life-jellyfish.html.

Love, Dylan. 2014. "These Jellyfish-Killing Robots Could Save the Fishing Industry Billions Per Year." *Business Insider*. http://www.businessinsider.com/jellyfish-killing-robot-2014–6#ixzz3QzEYDGVd.

McCracken, Harry. 2013. "Google vs. Death." *Time Magazine*, September 11.

Murakami, Haruki. 1999. *The Wind-Up Bird Chronicle*. New York: Vintage.

National Science Foundation. 2008. "Jellyfish Gone Wild: Environmental Change and Jellyfish Swarms. A Multi-Media Report by the NSF." http://www.nsf.gov/news/special_reports/jellyfish/textonly/index.jsp.

Neely, Abigail. 2010. "'Blame it on the Weeds': Politics, Poverty, and Ecology in the New South Africa." *Journal of Southern African Studies* 36 (4): 869–87.

Neyrat, Frederic. 2010. "The Birth of Immunopolitics." *Parrhesia* 10: 31–8.

Neyrat, Frederic and Elizabeth Johnson. 2014. "The Political Unconscious of the Anthropocene: A Conversation with Frederic Neyrat by Elizabeth Johnson." *Environment and Planning D: Society and Space (Online)*. http://societyandspace.com/2014/03/20/frederic-neyrat-the-political-unconscious-of-the-anthropocene-interview-by-elizabeth-r-johnson/.

Rajan, Kaushik. 2012. *Lively Capital: Biotechnologies, Ethics, and Governance in Global Markets*. Durham: Duke University Press.

Rancière, Jacques. 2011. "The Thinking of Dissensus: Politics and Aesthetics." In *Reading Rancière*. Edited by Paul Bowman and Richard Stamp, 1–17. London: Continuum Press.

Rich, Nathanial. 2012. "Can a Jellyfish Unlock the Secrets of Immortality." *New York Times*, 28 November.

Rinkevich, Baruch and Valaria Matranga. 2009. *Stem Cells in Marine Organisms*. London: Springer Science & Business Media.

Robertson, Morgan. 2011. "Measurement and Alienation: Bringing Ecosystems to Market." *Transactions of the Institute of British Geographers* 37 (3): 386–401.

Robinson, Wills. 2013. "The Jellyfish Mincer: Terrifying Robot which Can Devour 900kg of Fish an Hour Could Help Save Millions of Dollars a Year." *Daily Mail*, October 3. http://www.dailymail.co.uk/sciencetech/article-2442737/Jellyfish-killer-Robot-destroy-900kg-fish-hour-save-industry-millions.html#ixzz3QzGD6dKZ.

Rosenthal, Nadia. 2008. "Stem Cells and the End of Aging, a Lecture at the Howard Hughes Medical Institute." February 9, 2008. https://www.youtube.com/watch?v=KcjXBO90b9k.

Schmitt, Carl. 2003 [1950]. *Nomos of the Earth*. New York: Telos Press.

Schrader, Astrid. 2010. "The Time of Slime." *Environmental Philosophy* 9 (1): 71–93.

Short, Michael. 2012. "Go Forth and Multiply—and Regenerate." *The Sydney Morning Herald,* October 1. http://www.smh.com.au/federal-politics/go-forth-and-multiply—and-regenerate-20120930-26tmq.html.

Shukin, Nicole. 2009. *Animal Capital.* Minneapolis: University of Minnesota Press.

St. Martin, Kevin. 2005. "Disrupting Enclosure in New England Fisheries." *Capitalism, Nature, Socialism* 16 (1): 63–80.

Steinberg, Philip. 2009. "Sovereignty, Territory, and the Mapping of Mobility: A View from the Outside." *Annals of the Association of American Geographers* 99 (3): 467–95.

———. 2013. "Of Other Seas: Metaphors and Materialities in Maritime Regions." *Atlantic Studies* 10 (2): 156–69.

Tucker, Abigail. 2010. "Jellyfish: The Next King of the Sea: As the World's Oceans Are Degraded, Will They Be Dominated by Jellyfish?" *Smithsonian Magazine.* August 2010: http://www.smithsonianmag.com/40th-anniversary/jellyfish-the-next-king-of-the-sea-679915/?all.

United Nations. 1994. "Convention on the Law of the Sea." http://www.un.org/Depts/los/convention_agreements/texts/unclos/unclos_e.pdf.

Vanzi, Sol Jose. 1999. "Giant Pangasinan Jellyfish Caused Luzon blackout." *Philippine Headline News Online.* December 12. http://www.newsflash.org/1999/12/ht/ht000992.htm.

Veron, Jen. 2008. "Mass Extinctions and Ocean Acidification: Biological Constraints on Geological Dilemmas." *Coral Reefs* 27 (3): 459–72.

Wolfe, Cary. 2012. *Before the Law: Humans and Other Animals in a Biopolitical Frame.* Chicago: University of Chicago Press.

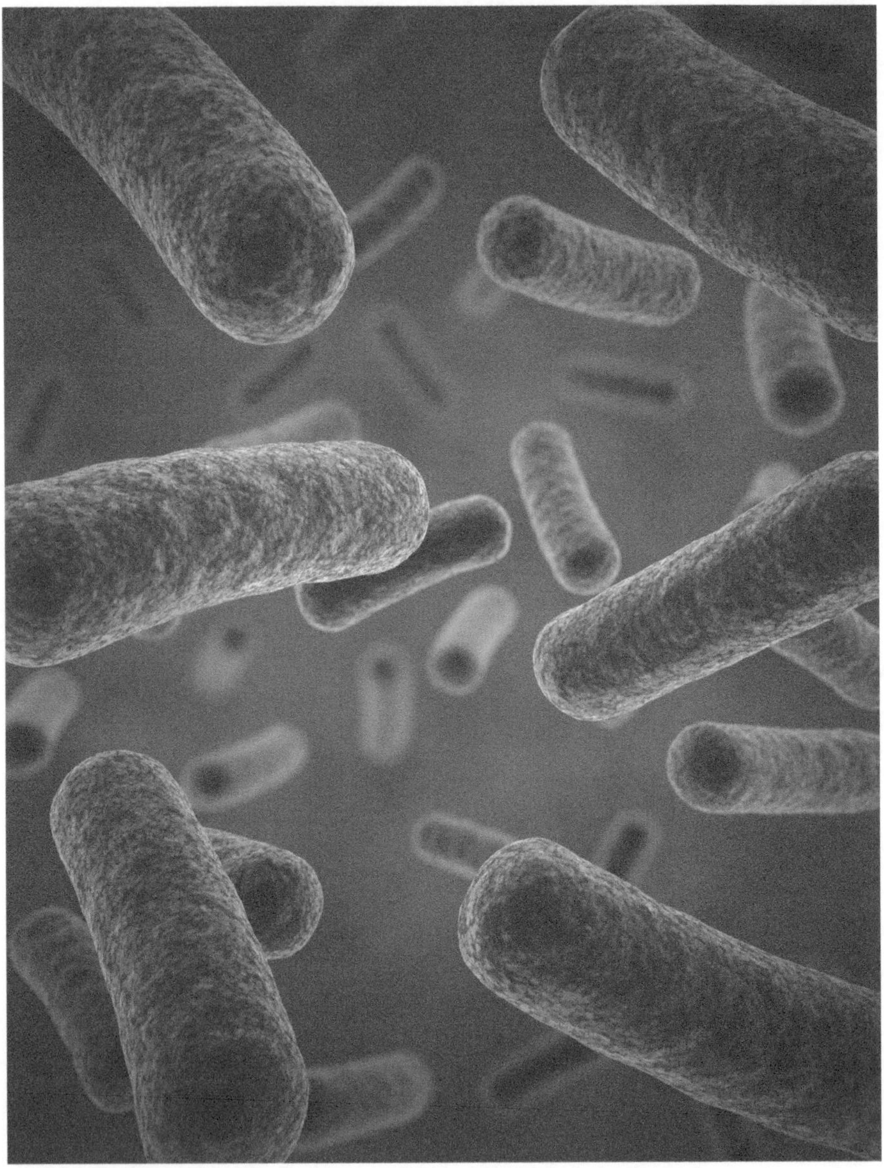

Chapter 4

Tracing Bacterial Legalities

The Fluid Ecologies of the European Union's Bathing Water Directive

Christopher Bear

Introduction

In 2006, the European Union introduced a revised Bathing Water Directive[1] (2006/7/EC). Aiming to "preserve, protect and improve the quality of the environment and to protect human health" (Chapter 1, Article 1.2), the Directive will be implemented fully by the start of 2016. Replacing the 1976 Bathing Water Directive [76/160/EEC]), the new Directive requires European Union Member States to monitor their bathing waters for the presence and concentration of faecal bacteria, and to produce "profiles" of each designated site to inform potential bathers and future management strategies. The revisions have been celebrated by many environmentalists and bathing groups for setting considerably tougher standards than the previous version, with the intention of producing safer water for humans to swim in, and for standardizing the communication of water quality assessments to members of the public. At the same time, the revisions have been contested by local politicians, who were concerned about the economic impacts of failing to meet the new requirements (e.g., Pilmoor 2013), and by specialist recreational groups (e.g., Surfers Against Sewage 2014) that felt that the legislation did not go far enough. Although the Directive's focus is on the control of faecal bacteria, its implications for nonhuman life have rarely been at the center of public debate.

In exploring the Directive's implementation, my chapter responds to David Delaney's concerns over how "entities . . . are made meaningful in distinctively legal ways and practically situated with respect to distinctively legal manifestations of relations of power" (2015, 98). The first focus of the chapter, therefore, is on how the Directive co-produces new representations of nonhuman animal life around legally designated bathing waters.

Escherichia coli. Credit: spawns, Thinkstock.

Although the Directive itself makes no mention of animals, authorities responsible for its implementation have increasingly framed them as "polluters" in their search for ways to reduce levels of water-borne faecal bacteria. This distinction between "animals" and "bacteria" is somewhat arbitrary, given that all animal bodies are composed of bacteria (Margulis and Sagan 1986). Nonetheless, for the purposes of this chapter, I maintain the distinction, exploring particularly the framing of animals as producers, carriers and distributors of bacteria.

However, the making-meaningful of animals extends beyond representation and does not lie solely in the hands of humans. Second, therefore, the chapter responds to Irus Braverman's (2015, 308) invitation to make visible "the largely invisible roles that animals have long performed in regulatory frameworks." In this particular instance, animals are far from visible in the regulatory framework, leaving considerable scope for managers and policy makers to decide whether and how to include them. When they are made visible in the implementation, it is rarely through a need to offer them protection—the legislation's focus is on the protection of humans—but more often through a desire to control them. In this way, the chapter is about the becoming-law of animals: how the Directive makes animals visible, legible, and governable. Doing so involves not only animals and associated bacteria in and around the designated bathing water sites themselves, but also those that are topographically distant.

Third, the chapter explores the application of new technologies and approaches in making distant animal bodies and their "incriminating" traces visible. For instance, farm slurry or bird excrement from urban centers have often been categorized rather vaguely as "diffuse source pollution" (e.g., SEPA 2014). In implementing the Directive, environmental management agencies are increasingly turning to techniques such as microbial source tracking (MST) to identify more accurately the sources—both spatial and species—of faeces. Such approaches attempt to render the unruly lives of animals manageable and carry an air of objectivity and certainty. However, additional actants and forces, such as water and sun, complicate such certainty, affecting the life, death, dispersal, and impact of bacteria.

The underlying theme of movement highlights the flow of law itself—the becoming-animal of law, in other words—as the Directive extends beyond the designated bathing water sites, following the flow of bacteria-infused animals and that of bacteria that emanate from them. Law here is not "a thing," but "a dynamic, shifting, often contradictory, multi-point process" (Delaney 2015, 97). Acknowledging the vital materialities of "bathing waters" thus complicates the notion and stability of water quality and highlights the potential of advocating a "less fixedly human and more risky approach to boundaries, to political actors and to political outcomes" (Buller 2014, 314). This chapter's analysis shows along these lines that while the Directive is "pointillist" (Doel 1999) in tone—namely, it focuses on bounded spaces and measurements taken at fixed spatial and temporal points—such pointillist undertones are destabilized by the vital materialities and deterritorializing movements of animals, bacteria, and water. Although the revised Directive is open to engaging with such "liveliness," management strategies and policies tend to do so very selectively, showing their willingness to control, or even eradicate, certain animals in an effort to improve the quality (as enacted through approved scientific measurement techniques) of waters, but tending to ignore other forces, such as the sun and wind. This results in "politics of blame" around water quality, which sit uneasily between "a strategic understatement of material agency" and an acknowledgment of "the distributive quality of agency" (Bennett 2005, 464). Although issues of blame and responsibility are not expressed explicitly in the Directive, they nonetheless emerge implicitly through law in action, which forms the chapter's focus.

Drawing on a review of documentary sources on the Directive's implementation in the United Kingdom, I provide an overview of the legislation, examining the specific form of water quality it enacts. Subsequently, I examine how the legislative revisions have affected the treatment of animals in and around designated bathing waters, before extending the chapter's focus on animals to those that are topographically distant and made visible through the detection of their bacterial traces. Finally, I expand the chapter's analysis of "lively legalities" to nonhumans other than animals and bacteria, exploring how the movement of water, along with the influence of sun and weather, disrupts the assessment of its quality.

Enacting Water Quality

The Bathing Water Directive is one of a number of reference points for bathing water quality in Europe—other formalized enactments include the "Blue Flags," which have appeared on beaches across Europe since 1987 (and globally since 2001), and the annual *Good Beach Guide* (Marine Conservation Society 2014). These overlapping formalizations enact bathing water quality in multiple ways. There is also a temporal dimension to bathing water quality's multiple enactments, as the formalizations draw on embodied knowledge (such as surfers' bodily responses to the presence of faecal bacteria, subsequently communicated through campaigns) and on changing scientific understandings. This section provides a brief overview of the revised legislation, highlighting the emergent concept of water quality.

The original Bathing Water Directive was introduced in 1976 in response to concerns over "severe water pollution problems" around Europe (Benson and Jordan 2014, 48). This earlier legislation monitored ten parameters: total coliforms, faecal coliforms, salmonella, enteroviruses, pH, color, mineral oils, surface active substances [detergents], phenols, and transparency. Mandatory standards were established for each parameter, alongside more stringent "guideline" values (which Member States should "endeavour . . . to observe" [Council Directive 76/160/EEC], but which were not mandatory). In practice, some of these parameters were more significant than others. As the UK's Department for the Environment, Food and Rural Affairs (DEFRA 2008) notes: "[c]ases of non-compliance with the physico-chemical parameters are extremely rare so compliance in the United Kingdom each year is normally determined by the extent of pollution by total and faecal coliform bacteria." The focus, in other words, has tended to be on the presence of faeces, rather than on any other form of pollution. Figure 4.1 shows the changing levels of compliance with the Directive across the European Union since 1990, with the percentage of coastal waters meeting the mandatory standards rising from around 80 percent in 1990 to almost 97 percent by 2013 (European Environment Agency 2014a, 13).

Viewed through illustrations such as Figure 4.1, the original Directive could be celebrated as a considerable success (e.g., DEFRA 2008). Alongside

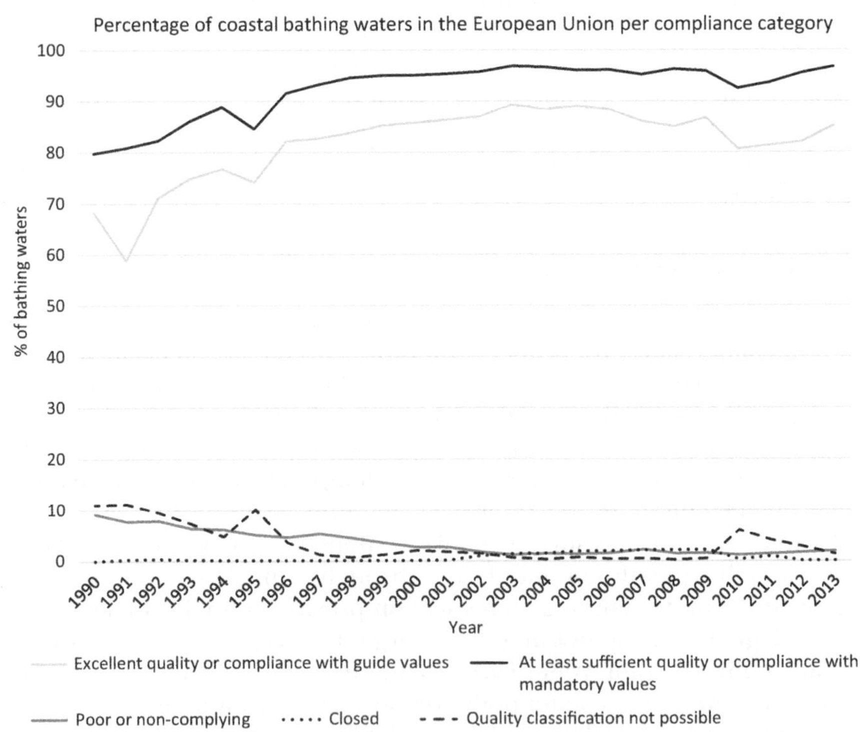

Figure 4.1 Percentage of coastal bathing waters in the European Union per compliance category. Redrawn using data courtesy of European Environment Agency, 2014b. Used with permission.

other legislation, such as the Urban Waste Water Treatment Directive (91/271/EEC), the Bathing Water Directive has directly led to changing approaches to the management of sewage, and of agricultural runoff in particular (Jones 2008). These changes have been celebrated widely, especially by authorities wanting to promote the quality of their beaches to potential tourists. Simultaneously, the original Bathing Water Directive was subjected to criticism, especially from campaign groups such as Surfers Against Sewage, which argued that they continued to be affected (and, indeed, infected) by contaminated waters (Surfers Against Sewage 2014). By the mid-1990s, broader concerns were raised that, in spite of growing compliance, there had "been less additional improvement of coastal bathing water quality" as time had progressed, and that the original Directive no longer reflected current scientific understanding or technical and management capabilities (Commission of the European Communities 2000, 16). Although Figure 4.1 is suggestive of a scientifically measurable quality, visceral demonstrations of bodily impacts highlighted shortcomings. Through the 1990s, scientific arguments were used increasingly to argue that the standards were somewhat arbitrary and were not suitably focused on their goal of protecting human health (Commission of the European Communities 2000, 16). Within the original Directive, therefore, the quality of water was a far from stable concept.

The revision of the Directive was prompted by four concerns in particular: that certain parameters had become either outdated or irrelevant; that monitoring of waters was being carried out purely to check compliance, rather than to develop understanding; that methods of analysis had not been standardized, leading to results that were not comparable; and that "[m]icrobiological analysis requires considerable time which means that, in case the water sample is confirmed to be non-compliant, any (re)action to address that non-compliance will be too late and people might have been exposed to pollution" (Commission of the European Communities 2000, 16). These concerns formed the focus of the revision process.

A revised Bathing Water Directive came into force in 2006. According to the European Environment Agency (2014a, 7), the new Directive "simplifies management and surveillance methods" by requiring the monitoring of only two types of bacteria, intestinal enterococci and *Escherichia coli*, thereby replacing the previous spectrum of ten parameters (United Kingdom Parliament 2008, 4). Alongside this simplified monitoring, the revisions replaced the former mandatory and guideline standards with a four-stage classification system: poor, sufficient, good, and excellent. Starting in 2016, any bathing waters classified as "poor" "must display a sign advising against bathing during the bathing season . . . giving a reason based on water quality" (DEFRA 2010, 7). These new classifications relate to the Directive's emphasis on the importance of communicating the data to the general public in a clear way so as to inform their decisions about whether or not to bathe. Management authorities must, therefore, produce "profiles" for each designated Bathing Water, that will:

(a) contain a description of the physical, geographical and hydrological characteristics of –

    I. the bathing water;
    II. any other surface water in the catchment area of the bathing water where the surface water could be a source of pollution for the bathing water;

(b) identify and assess the causes of pollution that might affect bathing water quality and pose a risk to bathers' health;
(c) assess the potential for cyanobacterial proliferation;
(d) assess the potential for the proliferation of macro-algae or phytoplankton;
(e) if assessment under point (b) shows that there is a risk of short-term pollution, supply the following information:

    – the anticipated nature, frequency and duration of short-term pollution;
    – details of any remaining causes of pollution, including management measures taken and the time schedule for their elimination;
    – management measures taken during short-term pollution and the identity and contact details of bodies responsible for taking such a decision;

(f) identify the location of the monitoring point (DEFRA 2010, 11).

The profiles will be established on the basis of data collected over four consecutive years: "to assess a quality of bathing water for 2013, for instance, data from 2010 to 2013 are used" (European Environment Agency 2014a, 9). The profiles must be based on a minimum of one sample per month during the bathing season (Annex IV, 1), with additional samples to be taken during any short-term pollution events (Environment Agency n.d., 2). In addition to these longer-term profiles, the relevant authority should also alert potential bathers to any short-term pollution risks, with advice "made available . . . in an easily accessible place in the near vicinity of each bathing water" (Article 12).

Beyond simplifying the communication of information about water quality, the revised Directive also introduces more stringent standards: whereas 97.6 percent of bathing waters met the mandatory standards in 2010, if the same samples were subjected to the standards set by the revised Directive, only 88 percent of those waters would meet the new "sufficient" classification (DEFRA 2012). According to DEFRA (2010, 7), this new sufficient classification is approximately twice as stringent as the former mandatory pass, whereas the new "excellent" classification is approximately twice as stringent as the former "guideline" standard. The new Directive is aimed at creating direct comparability across Europe through dictating the methods of data collection and analysis.

Two central points emerge from this section. First, that water quality is enacted in multiple ways, whether through bodily encounters, or dialogue and contestation between scientific knowledge, political and legal discourse. Second, and related to this, is that the mandatory assessment of quality has changed over time. Discussion of these regulatory shifts is often centered on a trajectory toward greater stringency (e.g. Kinver 2013; Natural Resources Wales 2014). By contrast, in the next two sections I show that this is not a simple linear path; rather, it has highly variable impacts on who (or what) is to be blamed for the changing quality of bath water.

Siting Water Quality

The legislation designates specific sites as bathing waters; it applies, in other words, not simply to all coastal waters, nor to where people swim occasionally, but to an ever-changing and contested list of legally designated sites. Specifically, Article 1.3 defines the scope of the Directive as applying to "any element of surface water where the competent authority expects a large number of people to bathe and has not imposed a permanent bathing prohibition, or issued permanent advice against bathing." In this section, I focus on how the revision of the Directive has affected, if indirectly, the treatment of animals in these sites.

As noted previously, the revised Directive has brought about considerable interest in the activities of nonhuman animals around bathing waters—interest that was virtually entirely absent prior to the revisions. This shift is illustrated by Nick Smart, a technical specialist at the Environment Agency, who stated that seagulls are:

> a big, big problem under the new directive. . . . Before, they were more or less background noise. But with these new testing criteria they're going to become a real issue. . . . A seagull eats his fill of chips or sandwich or whatever, and goes and perches on the roof of the pier buildings. . . . He does what he has to do, it rains, and that guano-infested water just runs straight into the sea (Henley 2013).

Whereas in the earlier legislation, water managers generally focused their attention on addressing the most significant sources of faecal contamination, the more stringent standards have encouraged them to explore what might be viewed as more incremental sources. The five most significant sources of intestinal bacteria in bathing waters are widely listed as pollution from sewage; animals and birds on or near beaches; domestic sewage;

water draining from farms and farmland; and water draining from populated areas (LOVEmyBEACH n.d.). The contribution of each category can vary considerably between bathing waters, but the classification of coastal animals as "sources of pollution" (Dunphy 2013, 5) is significant. Whereas birds such as seagulls have regularly been portrayed as a "nuisance" (e.g., Aberdeenshire Council 2015), this has been because of noise, removing litter from bins, or attacking people and their food; their faecal bacteria have rarely been a significant concern. Attempts to quantify the impact of such animals, however, have highlighted the potential contribution of animal activities to poor water quality. A study of two beaches in northwest England, for instance, found that animals on or near the beaches accounted for 10 percent of faecal bacteria, in comparison to 20 percent for domestic sewage (Dunphy 2013, 5).

Through the attempts at quantification that result from the implementation of the new Directive, nonhuman animals have newly been framed by environmental management agencies as threats to human health. Such representations circulate through a variety of contexts. In some cases, the threat is viewed mechanistically and manifests in terms such as "pass" or "fail" under the Directive. An extract from a populist coastal magazine illustrates: "A note to pigeon feeders—go easy on the breadcrumbs this summer. It's worth bearing in mind that in an Olympic-size swimming pool of seawater, just one single dropping from a Canadian Goose will result in a fail by the Environment Agency" (Johnson 2014, 101). While putting this less starkly, similar framings have adopted by government bodies and politicians. For instance, the UK's DEFRA noted: "We are concerned about flocks of birds roosting near the beach, for example breakwaters or piers, which then impact on bathing water quality. We ask that people do not feed these birds" (DEFRA 2014). During UK parliamentary debate, seagulls were similarly labelled as "indiscriminate defecators, with the ability to expel significant quantities of runny faeces on the wing" (Peter Aldous MP in the UK Parliament 2011).

So while the Directive makes no explicit mention of animals, it unwittingly affects the perception and potential treatment of birds such as seagulls and starlings. Although the Directive's implementation is at an early stage, these representations of animals as threats are slowly translating directly into physical management measures. In Blackpool, for instance, which is the UK's most popular seaside holiday resort, it was "proposed that there needed to be improved management of birds as they could have a great impact on water samples. It was advised that netting on piers and discouraging people from feeding seagulls would be considered in the management of this issue" (Blackpool Council 2012, 13).

Such concerns extend beyond birds. It is increasingly common, for instance, for dog walking to be either discouraged or banned on designated bathing waters. Such bans on walking dogs highlight not only the spatiality of the Directive's implementation, where boundaries are drawn around areas within which certain animal activities are permitted, but also its temporality. Dogs are banned from Blackpool Central Beach, for instance, between May 1 and September 30 each year (the beach's legally designated bathing season), because of their potentially polluting behavior. Because waters are not tested outside the season, dogs and their human companions may essentially do as they please from October to April, even though their bacteria are likely to survive longer at that time of year (an issue I return to in the final section) and have a greater impact on anyone willing to brave the cold English winter sea. Animals' enrolment in the assessment of water quality, in other words, varies not only spatially but also temporally and between different species.

In this section, I have shown some of the ways in which the revisions to the Bathing Water Directive have led to changing representations of, and interactions with, particular animals around coasts. In many ways, these reflect Delaney's (2015, 99) characterization of law as producing "territorializations," carving "life-worlds into innumerable boxes and assembl[ing] and reassembl[ing] them in ways that structure experiences." Not only are lines drawn around areas of water, but animals (and their actions) are labelled and categorized in new ways in relation to, and by, various laws. Yet these representations and interactions are uneven spatially and temporally, and vary between species. Whereas some species (such as dogs) are represented as "polluters" only during the summer, others (such as seagulls) might be increasingly discouraged year-round. Animals of the same species, meanwhile, can be treated very differently in close proximity to one another—for instance, where only one of two adjacent bays has been designated as bathing water.

The implications of the Directive extend beyond actors and events within the spatial boundaries of designated bathing waters. Accordingly, the next two sections explore how "traces" of animals come to matter in the Directive's implementation, as they destabilize the Directive's territorializing tendencies and implicate animals in a politics of blame. The next section, therefore, moves away from a focus on physically present animal bodies toward the Directive's concern over the bacteria that are carried and dispersed by these bodies.

Animal Flows and Traces

A number of authors have recently highlighted how animals become present in more-than-human relationships not only through their embodied materiality but also through the "traces" they (and their relationships) leave. These traces have included imprints on the physical environment (such as the otter footprints discussed by Hinchliffe et al. 2005), the physical transformation of bodies by viruses (Greenhough 2012, 292), the contemporary distribution of a species (the "traces of human–elephant companionship" discussed by Lorimer 2010, 497), or the signs of human-animal conflict, such as the "companion planting . . . protective containers [and] pellets" that respond to slug presence in gardens (Ginn 2014, 534). Studying traces offers a route through which animal practices that take place away from direct observation by, or contact with, humans might be acknowledged. The study of traces encourages an exploration of the remnants of embodied relationships, as they continue to be affective and co-constitutive of a place long after the human or animal body has moved on.

The traces I am interested in here often spread across considerable distances, reaching places that the animals themselves may never have encountered. Although environmental managers and politicians are taking an increased interest in certain animals that inhabit, or are in close proximity to, bathing waters, the revised Directive's focus on faecal bacteria has concurrently stimulated heightened interest in what is often labelled "diffuse pollution." The earlier Directive, in relation to animals at least, was most concerned with diffuse pollution in the form of runoff from livestock farming. This makes a highly variable contribution at different bathing waters, but can be significant. For instance, the previously alluded to study of two beaches in northwest England found that water draining from farms and farmland accounted for 55 percent of "pollution" at one beach (Walney) and 25 percent at the other (Morecambe) (Dunphy 2013, 5). In many ways, this pollution can be seen as an issue of farm management—a full discussion of which extends beyond the purposes of this chapter (but see, for instance, Winter et al. 2011). Instead, my interest is more in how animals have come to be made present in bathing waters in spite of their physical (or topographical) distance.

While the Bathing Water Directive itself does not require differentiation between human and animal sources, doing so is increasingly viewed as desirable for two reasons. The first reason such differentiation is considered desirable is that it is perceived as assisting managers in addressing the most serious threats to their "sufficient" water quality classification. The Scottish Environmental Protection Agency notes accordingly that "the recent implementation of the Revised Bathing Water Directive highlights the need for more accurate apportionment of the sources of faecal contamination. If we can identify the sources of potentially harmful bacteria then we can better target investment and remedial work" (2011, 6). Similarly, the Environment Agency notes that, "In order to manage faecal pollution in our bathing waters we need more information on the sources of pollution" (2008, iv). The second reason that the differentiation between sources of faecal bacteria is considered desirable is that management authorities can then highlight the potentially more significant impacts on human health from animal faeces, which "often contain high levels of bacteria (much higher than treated human waste)" (Natural Resources Wales 2014). However, as a report from Scotland suggests, "It is very difficult to distinguish between human and animal sources of contamination" in marine waters (Baxter et al. 2011, 57).

A variety of approaches has been tested with the aim of identifying sources of faecal contamination, including assessment on the basis of known ratios of faecal coliform bacteria to faecal streptococci for different species, "chemical analysis for products related to human activity (i.e. caffeine and detergents et cetera) or for compounds found in faeces such as stanols, sterols and immunoglobins" (Scottish Environmental Protection Agency 2011, 6). However, the approach currently favored in the United Kingdom is microbial source tracking (MST). This form of tracking "uses DNA markers to identify sources of bacterial pollution to determine whether it is derived from sewage, agricultural diffuse pollution (including livestock) or other sources, such as birds or dogs" (DEFRA, quoted in Scarborough Borough Council 2012, 25).

The MST technique can highlight significant variability in the source of bacteria. One study in Scotland, for instance, found that whereas in one July day in 2008, 40 percent of faecal bacteria were derived from humans, with the remainder deriving from ruminant animals, on a day in the following month, 87 percent of faecal bacteria came from humans and only 13 percent from ruminants (Scottish Environmental Protection Agency 2011, 6).

The report also comments that prohibitive costs had prevented the collection of a suitable number of samples, making it inappropriate to classify the water "with such a small amount of data" (Scottish Environmental Protection Agency 2011, 7). Nonetheless, the Environment Agency increasingly uses MST "to investigate sources of pollution at bathing waters which have failed to meet mandatory water quality standards" (quoted in Scarborough Borough Council 2012, 25).

While this technique remains in its infancy—at least in its practical application to bathing waters—its implications for the treatment of animals in relation to the revised Bathing Water Directive are significant for three reasons. First, MST distinguishes between human and nonhuman sources of bacteria. This distinction changes fundamentally the nature of what is being managed, from a broad focus on bacterial concentrations to a system of categorization that enables the construction and targeting of particular groupings of bacteria-dispersers. Second, while too much uncertainty remains in this area at present, the technique is likely to distinguish more clearly in the future between different species of nonhuman animals. While this may be beneficial in targeting key sources of pollution and in moving beyond assumptions, the results may end up demonstrating that animals, once thought to make significant contributions, are insignificant in comparison to other sources. Equally, certain groups could become easy targets: the quick-fix, low-cost route to achieving what the Directive defines as "sufficient" water quality might be to ban dogs on beaches, cull seagulls, or prevent starlings from nesting on piers, although more significant (though potentially harder to eradicate) pollution originates from other sources. Third, animals here are known and managed not through material presence on or near a beach but through DNA and associated bacteria.

The new Directive, therefore, enrols animals as much (if not more) through their bacterial traces as it does through their bodily presence. In one sense, the Directive encourages managers to follow these dispersed animals' trails. In another sense, the actions of animals, embodied in these bacterial traces, themselves disperse the legislation, destabilizing "the territorial rubrics of containment associated with sovereign power" and challenging "regimes of spatial ordering" (Johnson, this volume), thereby extending bathing waters considerably beyond the confines of their legally designated boundaries. While the actions and movements of animals increase the spatial complexity of the Directive's implementation, managers' increasing ability to pinpoint sources of bacteria can lead to the construction of particular animals as polluters.

Fluid Ecologies

Until now I have focused specifically on nonhuman animals. In this final section I attend to the broader lively legalities implied by the Directive. Specifically, I am interested here in how the Directive deals with the fluid materialities it attempts to regulate and how, in turn, water disrupts and confuses the assessment of its own quality. My own work on water has increasingly highlighted its "messiness . . . in terms of both form and flow; it does not neatly conform to abstract models but moves in often unexpected ways with unpredictable consequences" (Bear and Bull 2011, 2262). Jones and Macdonald (2007, 535) similarly describe urban water management as an attempt to "script [the] continued performance" of water as it moves through cities. Elsewhere, I also showed how wind, currents, and the resultant movement of the seabed has led to considerable uncertainty and controversy around the impact of dredging on the sea floor (Bear 2013). In that particular case, the pointillist approach to management referred to earlier struggled to contain or stabilize the nonhuman actants involved—whether fish, water, sand, or dolphins.

Despite its different focus on flows of bacteria into water bodies, the revised Bathing Water Directive raises similar issues. The Directive's approach to monitoring is explicitly pointillist. Article 3.3 states, for example, that:

> The monitoring point shall be the location within the bathing water where:
>
> (a) most bathers are expected; or
> (b) the greatest risk of pollution is expected, according to the bathing water profile.

In other words, water quality is only assessed at a single defined point within any designated site. In addition, the fact that only four samples (or one sample per month—whichever is greater) are required in any one bathing season means that assessments take little account of spatial and temporal differences within bathing water. The only exceptions are "abnormal situations" (e.g., when there is a one-off event, such as a slurry spill, at which point additional samples should be taken).

Water, sunlight, and weather more broadly play important active roles here in determining the impact of bacteria. As DEFRA (2013, 2) notes, "during wet weather, combined sewer overflows operate more frequently; diffuse pollution increases from urban and agricultural sources; and, there is less sunlight to kill off bacteria in water." This combination of events intensifies the potential impact of bacteria. DEFRA's stress on the impact of sunlight considerably complicates any attribution of impact that might be apportioned to animals. This can be seen through more localized examples. Blackpool Council (2012, 11), for instance, comments on how "hotter, drier summers may be beneficial for bathing waters as bacteria in the water would be killed quicker due to the increased sunlight." Indeed, sunlight's role can be significant even on a single day. One microbiologist found that:

> during the bathing season all three of Morecambe's bathing waters failed the Bathing Water Quality Directive when sampled at 7am but passed at 7pm. The difference was attributed to the indicator bacteria surviving in the dark prior to the morning sample and being killed by UVB during daylight prior to the evening sampling. We proposed that all bathing waters throughout the European Union should be sampled in the early morning to allow for the worst case scenario (Jones 2008, 25).

While the focus in the previous examples was on sunlight, other commentators highlight an even greater complexity to the emergence of any quality reading. One environmental management agency comments, for instance, that "sources of bacteria . . . and their distribution relative to the beach, soil conditions, river flows, tidal state, wind speed and direction and solar irradiance could all influence bacteriological quality at the beach sampling location" (Scottish Environmental Protection Agency 2001, 1). Despite their importance, the majority of these factors are rarely discussed in management and policy documents relating to the Directive. Nonetheless, the examples provided in this section demonstrate the contingency of the notion of quality as promoted by the revised Bathing Water Directive.

While animals are constructed as "polluters" on the basis of the bacteria they produce and disperse in their faeces, these bacteria in fact generate highly variable effects that depend not only on their concentrations but also on their subsequent dispersal (in stormy conditions they will disperse in the sea more rapidly, but in the same conditions the bacteria will reach the sea more easily) and their eradication (through sunlight). While approaches such as MST may seem to go some way toward apportioning impact definitively, the occasional nature of the sampling process has the potential to play down the frequent (even diurnal) changes brought about by the materiality of bathing waters. As a result, even employing MST does not work as a significant antidote to some of the more drastic blanket measures introduced in response to the new Directive.

Conclusion: Bacterial Legalities

This chapter has explored ways in which forms of nonhuman life—animals and bacteria—are made visible in the European Union's revised Bathing Water Directive and its implementation. Animals are ostensibly absent from this legislation, which focuses simply on acceptable levels of bacterial pollution and their monitoring and assessment, but the chapter has highlighted two central ways in which animals have nonetheless become visible through the Directive and its implementation.

First, certain animals (such as dogs and seagulls, but potentially encompassing any animal that releases faecal bacteria that reaches a bathing water) have been made visible through their classification as "polluters." This classification sits alongside and overlaps with other representations of the same animals—as species to protect, as nuisances that steal sandwiches, as cherished pets, as significant variables in a healthy ecology, or even as vital subjectivities. The interplay of these multiple enactments extends beyond the confines of this chapter, but could potentially form the focus of future work around the everyday life of law. Here, the central interest has been in the animals' shift from background noise in the previous Directive to their more visible and even lively role in the implementation of the revisions.

The animals' more central role carries potentially significant implications for the creatures concerned. To return to Jane Bennett's (2005, 464) discussion of the politics of blame, the attribution of pollution to nonhuman life acknowledges "the distributive quality of agency"—as there is no *a priori* assumption that pollution relates to human activity. Indeed, the focus of the Directive on bacteria, and its flattening of distinctions between sources, allows the issue of blame to remain open to question. However, nonhuman life does not exist in abstraction from its environment, and the failure of emerging management strategies to engage holistically with the vital materialities of bathing waters—including the interplay of bacteria, sunlight, wind and currents—results in that the blame for pollution has been thus far directed to specific actants. Put simply, for coastal managers who have responsibilities relating to the tourist economy, it might often be more palatable to attempt to control the activities of birds rather than restricting humans' bathing activity in relation to sun, wind, temperature, and currents. This might be interpreted as "a strategic understatement of material agency" (ibid.), focusing on approaches that might have the economically least detrimental impacts yet that could prove detrimental to the lives of nonhuman others (through culling or restrictions on habitat, for instance).

Second, the chapter has shown how animals become visible in the Directive through their movement and dispersal of bacteria. In many ways, the Directive is pointillist and territorializing—bathing water profiles, for example, are built on water quality sampling at fixed locations and focus on designated bounded locations. However, as managers implement the legislation and attempt to reduce flows of faecal bacteria, they are increasingly drawn away from the designated waters, following flows of bacteria to their topographically dispersed and distant sources. In this way, nonhuman life plays an active, if hidden, role in the Directive's implementation, as its unruliness enfolds distant sites and actants into regulatory frameworks.

The spatial extension of the law, which takes it away from the sites to which it was centrally directed, may be driven by the movements and actions of certain animals, but in turn relies on new ways of identifying—incriminating even—those animals. The monitoring of faecal bacteria in bathing waters, therefore, increasingly extends beyond mere levels of concentration and is moving toward the attribution of source to particular species. While animals and their bacteria extend the spatial reach of the law, those implementing the Directive, in other words, search for new ways to render the bacteria (and, as a corollary, the actants who carry and disperse those bacteria) manageable and governable.

The chapter has also hinted at the disruptive—perhaps even transgressive—forces of water, wind and sun. Future research could usefully extend this theme to consider, for instance, how management measures that attempt to restrict the activities of birds may be disrupted by the same creatures, or how bacteria might defy definitive assessment of their origin. Doing so might extend the interpretations of nonhuman resistance, as put forward by Gillespie in this volume. In Gillespie's case, resistance involved cows running away or kicking humans who attempted to control them and confine them, forming "an active form of resistance" (Coppin 2003). Because their control often takes place at a distance and through preventative measures, more "passive" forms of resistance might, therefore, be significant, as birds find alternative nesting sites and bacteria travel along unexpected routes.

Law thus extends beyond the written Directive; its everyday, multiple, and, most importantly, lively implementations allow it to emerge differently in different spatial settings. Such lively legalities render animals both visible and meaningful in new ways, while the animals themselves simultaneously co-author law's implementation through their everyday activities. It is therefore important that the emergent literature on lively legalities does not limit itself to studying explicitly animal-focused legislation. It should instead seek to explore the unintended or unexpected implications and manifestations of regulatory forms for nonhuman others.

Acknowledgments

I am grateful to Irus Braverman for her careful and insightful editing, and to participants at the *More-than-human Legalities* workshop for their helpful comments on an earlier version of this chapter.

Note

1 There are three forms of binding legal act at the level of the European Union. Regulations are applied "in [their] entirety across the EU," while Decisions are addressed to specific parties (such as a country or a company). In contrast, Directives set binding goals that must be met by all EU Member States, but members have discretion over how to meet these goals (see European Union 2014).

References

Aberdeenshire Council. 2015. *Survivor's Guide to Living with Urban Gulls.* Aberdeen: Aberdeenshire Council.

Baxter, John M., Ian L. Boyd, Martin Cox, et al. eds. 2011. *Scotland's Marine Atlas: Information for the National Marine Plan.* Edinburgh: Marine Scotland.

Bear, Christopher. 2013. "Assembling the Sea: Materiality, Movement and Regulatory Practices in the Cardigan Bay Scallop Fishery." *Cultural Geographies* 20 (1): 21–41.

Bear, Christopher and Jacob Bull. 2011. "Water Matters: Agency, Flows, and Frictions." *Environment and Planning A* 43 (10): 2261–6.

Bennett, Jane. 2005. "The Agency of Assemblages and the North American Blackout." *Public Culture* 17 (3): 445–65.

Benson, David and Andrew Jordan. 2014. "Subsidiarity as a 'Scaling Device' in Environmental Governance: The Case of the European Union." In *Multilevel Environmental Governance: Managing Water and Climate Change in Europe and North America.* Edited by Inger Weibust and James Meadowcroft, 39–57. Cheltenham, UK: Edward Elgar Publishing Ltd.

Blackpool Council. 2012. *Bathing Water Quality Scrutiny Review Final Report.* Blackpool: Blackpool Council.

Braverman, Irus. 2015. "More-Than-Human Legalities: Advocating an 'Animal Turn' in Law and Society." In *The Handbook of Law and Society.* Edited by Austin Sarat and Patrcia Ewick, 307–21. Chichester, UK: John Wiley & Sons.

Buller, Henry. 2014. "Animal Geographies I." *Progress in Human Geography* 38 (2): 308–18.

Commission of the European Communities. 2000. *Communication from the Commission to the European Parliament and the Council: Developing a New Bathing Water Policy.* Brussels: Commission of the European Communities.

Coppin, Dawn. 2003. "Foucauldian Hog Futures." *The Sociological Quarterly* 44: 597–616.

DEFRA. 2008. "Bathing Water Directive: History of the Revision Process." http://archive.defra.gov.uk/environment/quality/water/waterquality/bathing/history.htm.

———. 2010. *Guidance for Bathing Water Controllers in England: Provision of Information to the Public.* London: DEFRA.

———. 2012. "Bathing Waters and the Bathing Water Directive." http://archive.defra.gov.uk/environment/quality/water/waterquality/bathing/.

———. 2013. "Statistics on Coastal Bathing Waters—A Five Year Summary of Compliance with Mandatory and UK Guidelines." https://www.gov.uk/government/uploads/system/uploads/attachment_data/file/255063/bathing-water-release-2013.pdf.

———. 2014. "Press Release: Bathing Water Testing Begins in the South West." http://www.government-world.com/press-release-bathing-water-testing-begins-in-the-south-west/.

Delaney, David. 2015. "Legal Geography I: Constitutivities, Complexities, and Contingencies." *Progress in Human Geography* 39 (1): 96–102.

Doel, Marcus. 1999. *Poststructuralist Geographies: The Diabolical Art of Spatial Science.* Lanham, MD: Rowman & Littlefield.

Dunphy, Rob. 2013. *Morecambe Bay Bathing Water Study.* Morecambe: Love My Beach.

Environment Agency. 2008. *Microbial Source-Tracking Project.* Bristol: Environment Agency.

———. n.d. "Fact Sheet: All You Need to Know About the Revised Bathing Water Directive." http://lovemybeach.org/download/1877/.

European Environment Agency. 2014a. *European Bathing Water Quality in 2013.* Luxembourg: European Environment Agency.

———. 2014b. "Percentage of Coastal Bathing Waters in the European Union Per Compliance Category." http://www.eea.europa.eu/data-and-maps/daviz/percentage-of-coastal-bathing-waters#tab-chart_1.

European Union. 2014. "Regulations, Directives and Other Acts." http://europa.eu/eu-law/decision-making/legal-acts/index_en.htm.

Ginn, Franklin. 2014. "Sticky Lives: Slugs, Detachment and More-Than-Human Ethics in the Garden." *Transactions of the Institute of British Geographers* 39 (4): 532–44.

Greenhough, Beth. 2012. "Where Species Meet and Mingle: Endemic Human-Virus Relations, Embodied Communication and More-Than-Human Agency at the Common Cold Unit 1946–1990." *Cultural Geographies* 19 (3): 281–301.

Henley, Jon. 2013. "England's Polluted Beaches: Stop This Tide of Filth." *Guardian.* July 7.

Hinchliffe, Steve, Matthew Kearnes, Monica Degen, and Sarah Whatmore. 2005. "Urban Wild Things: A Cosmopolitical Experiment." *Environment and Planning D: Society and Space* 23 (5): 643–58.

Johnson, Jessica. 2014. "Love My Beach." *Coast.* 98–101.

Jones, Keith. 2008. "Bathing Water Microbiology: Past, Present and Future." *Health Protection Matters* 12: 22–25.

Jones, Phil, and Neil Macdonald. 2007. "Making Space for Unruly Water: Sustainable Drainage Systems and the Disciplining of Surface Runoff." *Geoforum* 38 (3): 534–44.

Kinver, Mark. 2013. "UK Dips Its Toes into Revised Bathing Water Directive." July 6. http://www.bbc.co.uk/news/science-environment-23183751.

Lorimer, Jamie. 2010. "Elephants as Companion Species: The Lively Biogeographies of Asian Elephant Conservation in Sri Lanka." *Transactions of the Institute of British Geographers* 35 (4): 491–506.

LOVEmyBEACH. n.d. "The Challenge." http://lovemybeach.org/the-challenge/.

Margulis, Lynn, and Dorion Sagan. 1986. *Microcosmos: Four Billion Years of Evolution from our Microbial Ancestors*. Los Angeles: University of California.

Marine Conservation Society. 2014. "Good Beach Guide." http://www.goodbeachguide.co.uk/.

Natural Resources Wales. 2014. "Bathing Water Quality." http://naturalresourceswales.gov.uk/marine/bathing-water-quality/?lang=en.

Pilmoor, Ellie. 2013. "Swimming could be banned at Southsea beach." *Portsmouth News* 15 May 2013.

Scarborough Borough Council. 2012. "FOIA2021 Response." http://www.scarborough.gov.uk/pdf/FOIA2021%20redacted%20response.pdf.

Scottish Environmental Protection Agency. 2001. *A Study of Bathing Waters Compliance with EC Directive 76/160/EEC: The Relationship between Exceedence of Standards and Antecedent Rainfall*. Stirling: SEPA.

———. 2011. *Phase One Characterisation Report for the River Ayr Priority Catchment (Part 7: Faecal Contamination)*. Stirling: SEPA.

———. 2014. "River Basin Planning." http://www.sepa.org.uk/water/river_basin_planning.aspx.

Surfers Against Sewage. 2014. "Water Quality—An Environmental Issue." http://www.sas.org.uk/issues/water-quality/.

UK Parliament. 2008. *Explanatory Memorandum to the Bathing Water Regulations 2008*. London: HMSO.

———. 2011. *Seagulls (Coastal Towns)*. London: HMSO.

Winter, Michael, David Oliver, Rob Fish, A. Louise Heathwaite, et al. 2011. "Catchments, Sub-Catchments and Private Spaces: Scale and Process in Managing Microbial Pollution from Source to Sea." *Environmental Science and Policy* 14 (3): 315–26.

Chapter 5

Crow Kill

Adam Reed

Introduction

> A man is observed and recorded entering a cage of twelve crows and rooks and beating seven of the birds to death with a stick, over a period of several minutes. He uses the stick again and again to hit the terrified birds across their bodies as they attempt to flee his attack on them, flapping over him and clinging to the top corners of the wire cage. Several birds are struck hard and for a moment they struggle from the blows, but manage to continue flying. One by one, seven birds eventually fall to the ground injured, where the man continues to beat them until they finally stop moving. Five birds are left, alive and possibly injured, and the man drives away.

This testimony is extracted from the "Investigation" weblog of a leading animal welfare charity in Scotland (the quoted passage is without citation and lightly redacted in order to preserve organizational anonymity). Although written in the third person, the words belong to the charity's field investigations officer, Barry (pseudonym), who personally witnessed the incident described in the post on a remote grouse moor sporting estate in the Highlands. As the extract suggests, he also managed to capture the crow killing on his video camera; crouched low behind gorse bushes overlooking the scene, Barry used the zoom facility to film the action from a safe distance. The assailant, whom he recognized as one of the estate's gamekeepers, employed to manage grouse and other game birds as they are made ready for organized shoots, never saw him.

As the weblog post goes on to explain, the slaughter and injury of the birds took place inside a crow cage, a relatively common form of funnel or ladder trap used on privately owned sporting estates across the United Kingdom.

Crow Kill, illustration by Astrid Jaekel.

Mainly designed to capture corvids (carrion crows, hooded crows, jackdaws and rooks, but also magpies) held responsible for taking young game birds or stealing eggs, these traps deploy a live decoy bird to attract others into the wire enclosure so that they can subsequently be destroyed. Although perfectly legal (licenses permit authorized persons to take or kill certain wild animals to protect grouse and other birds such as pheasants, who are specifically bred and shot for sport), the crow cage must conform to the conditions of the license that govern its use and to the general principles of the wider animal health and welfare legislation. Among other things, this requires that captured wild animals be despatched "humanely" (defined in the relevant license as a "single swift action") and without unnecessary mental or physical suffering. Judging the specific crow kill as constituting a breach of both license and law, Barry reported it. The weblog post states: "I therefore gave my video film of this incident to the police, who referred the case to the procurator fiscal (the formal title for a public prosecutor in Scotland)."

In this chapter, I explore the role of figures such as Barry in the witnessing, detection, prosecution and legal review of wildlife crime. More specifically, I want to focus on the investigative work done in and around the animal control measure of entrapment; the insights are based on fieldwork conducted over the last five years with a particular animal welfare charity in Scotland, which includes material drawn from interviews with staff, participation in all office activities, and from accompanying Barry on his field trips. This ethnographic attention is in part inspired by the call of Valverde (2003) to consider a wider range of "lowly legal actors" operating in the vicinity of the law. The scholarly failure to acknowledge these figures, Valverde suggests, is linked to the tendency to view the law through an opposition between "expertise" and "everyday" knowledge. Valverde highlights that this tendency is typically manifest in the ethnographic focus on the ways "ordinary people" think about law (and justice) and on how they respond to it (2003, 2). Such an emphasis consistently assumes that these kinds of knowledges lie outside the legal process. Traditions in the sociology of law, often focused on truth construction and dispute within legal settings, may be somewhat closer to the approach she advocates, but Valverde states that she wishes to redirect the emphasis to "law in action" (as opposed to a more conventional "law on the books"). This requires an acknowledgment of the "distribution of epistemological authority" between popular, hybrid and expert knowledges (2003, 23), as well as a nod to the distributed nature of evidence gathering and enforcement. "Unlike Law, which hovers beyond the reach of those who act in its name" (2003, 10), these "legal complexes," Valverde asserts, can be studied and described.

However, in considering Barry as one type of lowly legal actor, I am also bound to take seriously his perspective on the relationship between expertise and everyday knowledge, which creates its own boundaries between the inside and outside of legal process. For instance, Barry, like his charity colleagues, is careful to distinguish between knowledge (whether popular, hybrid, or expert) enacted with law in mind and knowledge enlivened by ethical feeling. Even if the latter becomes sometimes entangled with the work of the lowly legal actor, it is crucial for him that it remains experienced as before or outside the law. The hybridity of knowledge in the legal complex, highlighted by Valverde, is therefore not experienced straightforwardly; in particular, there is no necessary undermining of the kind of distinctions that Barry wishes to uphold. It is possible to stress the point by taking a sideways look at the methodological provocation offered by Latour (2010) in his ethnography of the Council of State, the senior body of French administrative law. Sharply directed at what he views as the conventions of legal scholarship in social science, Latour targets the common tendency to reach for an *externalist* position on law, to understand it through "social" explanation (2010, viii). Instead of just "speaking about law," he tells us that he wishes to experiment with "speaking legally" (2010, ix): i.e., reproducing the associations that emerge from the work and practice of the legal argument itself. But in the case of the investigative work that I want to explore it is precisely the temporal shifts between internalist (i.e. moves that attempt to replicate the form of legal work and practice) and externalist accounts of the law that animate engagement. Barry strives hard to act and speak legally; however, there are moments when he and his charity colleagues insist upon speaking *about* the law, adopting a position beyond it whose efficacy precisely lies in the capacity to generate explanation. This is thus also an ethnography of the lived relationship between internalist and externalist moves, of the shifts between those positions that drive at least some lowly legal actors onwards.

So while it may be reasonable for sociolegal scholars to assert that "law is everywhere" (Sarat 1990), an immanent presence in our lives, this is not necessarily a helpful starting point for taking seriously the kind of experience and engagement that subjects want to describe. Of course, externalist moves include moments when subjects imagine themselves adopting a position of critique. Barry and his charity colleagues, for instance, can sometimes figure the law as a power that blocks or impedes improvements in animal welfare, or even actually contributes to the definition of nonhuman animals as exploitable or killable. The observation is important because this kind of critique is also one central strand of what we wish to develop when we evoke the term "Lively Legalities." In her introductory provocations for the volume, Braverman invites us to explore the dimensions of the anthropocentric bias in modern legal systems, the ways in which animality is "deeply embedded in the constitution of law and, reciprocally, how law is acutely relevant for constituting the animal" (page 9). The focus is intended to illuminate both the dimensions of, and conditions for, human-inflicted animal suffering. It includes the suggestion of examining what critique might infer or project into the future: i.e., the contours of law redefined to account for coexistent societies of human and nonhuman creatures. In their own advocacy, members of the Scottish animal welfare charity I have worked with share a version of this ambition, but for them law is a more humdrum, opportunistic instrument for reaching their ends. Along with investigative fieldwork, the charity heavily invests in parliamentary and government lobbying, which includes formal interventions in the process of lawmaking. Legalities may provide a template for change; however, for the charity it is not what initiates or self-evidently begets an animal turn. That always comes from within the individual human subject, as a consequence of ethical feeling (Reed 2015), or from the individual relationship between particular human and nonhuman animals.

Indeed, the charity's attention is more sharply focused on instances of law in action. This involves a strategic assessment but also an attuning to its place within what we might term, following Valverde, different "legal complexes." To the charity, the latter always have a more-than-human dimension. Barry and his colleagues are very much aware of what Braverman describes as the "particular configuration of human–animal relationship" at play in various scenarios of legality (2015, 317). They recognize and act in answer to the "specific temporalities, materialities, and legal protections" manifest by legal category and classification. Barry has an intimate knowledge of the responsibilities that flow from law or license in particular circumstances, about who is obligated to whom and when. This involves not only the human–animal relationships implicated by law but, in addition, those actively generated within the legal complex.

This chapter is not only concerned with birds designated as "wild," but also, crucially, with birds designated as "captive" or trapped. Part of my interest in the particular crow kill incident that I described above is a focus on entrapment itself, an event or moment in the life of the individual wild bird that seems to alter its classificatory status in law and hence its relationship to proximate humans (and animals). Unlike, say, zoo animals (Braverman 2012), crow capture is explicitly temporary or provisional; it is a condition prior to slaughter or the termination of life. The terms of license require gamekeepers to check their funnel traps every 24 hours and to kill trapped animals as soon as possible. Nevertheless, it is for this brief period, between a free or truly *wild* life and "unnatural" killing, that crows and other trapped corvids on shooting estates most fully experience what it means to be governed or subject to the law. Entrapment may involve regulation and lead to untimely death, but, I want to argue, it also opens a space in which the crow, or at least the crow body, takes on the translated or assigned status of another kind of lowly legal actor.

(Un)Witnessed Crime

It is a commonplace observation in government, legislative, and lobbying circles focused on the management of Scottish countryside that particular details are notoriously hard to come by when offences against wildlife occur. Indeed, in a much-repeated phrase, agencies speak of the challenges of policing and prosecuting "unwitnessed crime." In part, this is because incidents often take place in remote and therefore hard-to-reach locales. But it is also because enforcement agencies in this sphere are heavily under-resourced; it is widely accepted that wildlife crime is not a top priority in the determinations of justice ministers or police chiefs. Such incidents, for instance, were only relatively recently made a recordable offence and remain inconsistently documented. More seriously, just 14 staff members across Police Scotland are assigned the role of Wildlife Crime Liaison Officer, and they operate with a mainly responsive rather than investigative brief; unlike their human-crime counterparts, these constables do not patrol the countryside searching for wildlife crime. The issue of tracking unwitnessed incidents can to a certain extent be offset by scientific instruments for modelling the unexplained absence of species across the Scottish landscape. Both government agencies and conservation bodies, for example, rely heavily on consultative academic reports that run experiments to assess the geographic spread and hotspots for crime against wild bird species such as protected raptors, measurements based on the statistical idea of ecological traps. However, these statistical standards cannot act as a legal proof of offence or pinpoint individual culpability.

The perceived problem then is that no one (neither police officers nor members of the public) tends to *see* acts of illegal or inhumane animal control; in this regard, the crow kill observed and recorded by Barry is a rare exception. Knowing or believing that incidents are happening but not being able to observe them lends a strange undertone to discussions about wildlife crime. It is in this environment of the unwitnessed offence that Barry and other field investigators operate (Barry tells me that there are at present seven individuals in the United Kingdom, employed or working by contract for various animal welfare agencies; conservation charities also hire or employ their own field investigators). As actors who are perhaps uniquely available to see wildlife crime, their struggle is often centered on getting others to recognize that they meet the appropriate conditions for witnessing. It is the very dynamics of this looking and seeing in the light of the law that draws out my interest in the lived relationship and conversion between externalist and internalist moves.

As the careful testimony in the weblog post quoted right at the beginning of this chapter emphasizes, Barry, and by extension the charity he works for and its supporters, believe he has been on hand to observe a wildlife crime. After the third person description of the crow killing, the entry switches abruptly to a first person statement that attests that the incident was "accidentally witnessed" during a hike across a sporting estate in the month of May 2011. To the casual reader, the relative specificity of time and place seems appropriate, but the other points of stress appear somewhat less expected. Why *accidentally* witness? And why present himself so specifically in motion, *hiking* across the grouse moor estate? Barry, after all, is the charity's investigations officer, as the weblog post makes clear. Like other field investigators, he is a man employed to conduct both "overt" and "covert" research into standards and abuses of animal welfare in Scotland and further afield. Indeed, the weblog post outlines his specific reason for being on the Highland estate, "to collect video and photographic data of the different ways legal snares are laid to entrap wild animals" (snares, wire loops about the size of a watermelon, are widely laid by gamekeepers to trap predator species such as foxes). Barry, then, is in some ways professionally looking with the intent of becoming a witness to something.

In one obvious sense, Barry's phrasing throws up the traditional dilemma of the private investigator operating as a witness in the legal process: the need to continually demonstrate that his watching or seeing is not unlicensed surveillance and hence inadmissible as evidence in court. Barry is there to document the spread and use of legal snares on that estate, an activity, which he admits, might result in him discovering illegally laid fox traps. But, and this partly explains the emphasis, he was not expecting to be a witness of what he actually saw; in this respect, the crow killing can be said to have genuinely taken him by surprise.

This need to prove that his witnessing was unplanned connects to a broader apprehension of what it means to adopt an internalist form of looking: i.e. to see with the law in mind. As he is fully aware, the statutory public rights of access to private land in Scotland can guarantee Barry's presence on the sporting estate, allowing him and other field investigators to operate without the threat of prosecution for trespass. However, as he well knows, the codification of the freedom to roam does not simply open the countryside to animal welfare investigation (in fact the legislation on this matter makes no mention of such activity); rather, it requires that such investigations strategically take on the form of statutory public rights to land access. Indeed, it is as a member of the public entering private land for the purpose of recreation and exercise (the main rationales for legal access) that Barry principally gains his status as prospective eyewitness of wildlife crime. Although the latter can imply more concentrated forms of seeing or looking *for* something than the idiom of roaming might suggest (Barry highlights the studied vigilance of the bird watcher and also the clause allowing entry for "educational activity," which the charity regularly identifies as the descriptor for his snaring field research), the statutory right implies that access, and hence any witnessing that might flow from it, is predicated on movement across the land. In describing himself on the weblog as a figure in motion—"I was hiking across a sporting estate"—Barry is therefore speaking correctly in the language of the law. To be admissible as a witness, he must ensure that he *comes across* incidents of wildlife crime during the performance of his "educational activity" rather than seeks them out.

This equivocation between accidental witness and professional investigative observer is complicated, as Barry is very conscious of, by the stringent rules of corroboration in criminal cases (often presented as a unique or distinctive feature of Scots Law). They require that each "essential" or "crucial" fact be corroborated by the testimony of at least one other witness; as the definitive Carloway Report states, "Corroboration is about the number of witnesses available to prove facts. It is not about the number of facts available to prove guilt." In other words, Barry constantly worries that his gaze may not be enough; part of his reason for videoing the crow killing was precisely that he understood filmed footage could sometimes constitute such corroboration or active second witnessing. The idea that the camera might provide an independent set of eyes on the same incident is particularly compelling when considering the unwitnessed quality of wildlife crime. However, the choice to film the crow kill risks reintroducing the problem of witnessing that plagues the investigator. Footage may corroborate the facts as Barry saw and recorded them, but as he knows it may also serve to remind the judge of the original witness' status as professional observer, reinforcing the impression that accidental looking is in fact covert surveillance.

Such issues about the quality of witnessing, which includes debates about whether observation exhibits or lacks motivation, define the legal dilemmas of field investigation. But Barry perceives himself as not only a witness in law but also as a public witness of human-inflicted animal suffering. In his perspective, then, the legality or illegality of animal control is somewhat beside the point. For Barry is principally there to look for, document and archive what he and the charity he works for view as unethical and cruel treatment. In this register, the visual emphasis is less on internalist tensions around eyewitnessing—from within the law—and more on the externalist act of "exposure": the deliberate attempt to throw light on the pain and misery that results from legal and illegal human actions. Barry's looking is therefore also always driven by moral outrage and compassion, a feeling that he sometimes identifies with what is just or right and that he consistently locates outside the law, informing strategies for legal engagement and for public campaigning. "I just hate injustice," he once told me. This ethical witnessing is on behalf of nonhuman animals, but equally in some ways placed before them as a new standard of responsiveness, part of the redefined human–animal publics that Barry and the charity wish to support and embrace.

A Forensic Detection

Barry's status as a lowly legal actor is not just confined to the task of eyewitnessing. As usually the only other human subject in the vicinity of an incident, he regularly appears to stray into the domain of formal detection. This includes the acceptance or adoption of a semi-acknowledged position as evidence-gatherer. Such work is conducted on behalf of the charity, in his role as collator of field information to assist with educational research and campaigning; however, in practice, the activity often leads him to cooperate with or assist the official investigations of others. Indeed, in a legal environment in which wildlife crime is not just unwitnessed but, in addition, poorly policed, Barry's findings are sometimes the prompt for the work of Wildlife Crime Liaison Officers and the material basis for any file of evidence finally submitted. So what looks like the non-legal work of overt or covert animal welfare field research must necessarily also always be prototypical evidence gathering for making a case in law. While the dilemma of eyewitnessing is about the tension between happenstance and the intention to look, at times played out in Barry's witness testimony in court, this form of deliberative seeing must precede the law in action (narrowly defined) and ultimately be converted into the looking of another, more formally recognized, agent of detection.

The perceived professionalism of Barry's work in large part centers on the need to make the information and materials he collects meet the standards of legal evidence. Everything he does must anticipate the possibility of making such a contribution. This is reflected in the careful and long preparation for field research. The night before setting out, for instance, Barry lays out and checks all his equipment. This includes several pairs of binoculars, a video camera and stills camera, wire cutters in case he finds himself caught in fencing, a compass and relevant local maps, a mini tape recorder, handheld and head torches for scrambling through dense woodland, rubber gloves for touching decomposed animal corpses, bin bags for bagging any evidence that needs collecting, a tape measure to check that cages and traps conform to legal sizes, and a GPS (Global Positioning System) reader to guarantee he can geographically fix the location of an incident or communicate his often remote location to others. Barry also ensures he has a range of clothing, including wet and cold weather wear for occasions when the exposed moors and upland areas he visits undergo sudden temperature or climatic changes. The latter is essential because his self-assigned evidence-gathering role consists not just in discovering and documenting the incident, but also in calling and directing Wildlife Crime Liaison Officers to the scene. Since these police officers are few in number and the location of incidents out of the way, Barry can be waiting for hours on end.

In this preparatory endeavor, he presents himself as possessing a unique kind of expertise. Indeed, Barry repeatedly told me that police officers tend to rely on his field research knowledge of the wildlife crime scene. He often has to point out to them, for instance, what the evidence for unnecessary suffering looks like on the ground, which license regulations or aspects of animal health and welfare law is being broken, and what they should be recording. Barry explained that while waiting for these officers to arrive, "I would start gathering material for myself, and any evidence that may be needed for the police." While the knowledge that Barry displays is informed by a close reading of relevant legislation and an understanding of what needs to be gathered and recorded for a convincing case to be made in a court of law, it is mostly driven by a skilled interpretation of physical clues. In this regard, it is nearer to a "forensic gaze" or the kind of "low-status" technical knowledge of material signs that Valverde (2003, 63–4; Weizman 2010) describes as increasingly prominent in North American criminal justice as well as in popular film, television and literary depictions of legal detection. Indeed, Barry once told me that his fieldwork is "a bit like a forensic scientist that goes out to a murder, they get to understand the scene and read all the signs and over time I get to read them too." The difference is that this technical knowledge is self-taught, absorbed, and developed by Barry and other animal welfare investigators over the long years of field research.

Although sometimes aligned with or dependent on scientific expertise, the rise of the forensic gaze, Valverde claims, is interesting precisely in the degree to which it deviates from the principles or logic of science (Valverde 2003, 64). In law, the scientist is typically interested in numbers, probabilities or risk factors, and with the predictive question of whether a person is more or less likely to re-offend. Valverde states that, by contrast, the forensic technician remains firmly focused on "particular events, events that are always in the past." The outlook is in this respect more similar to the procedures of criminal law, "though it is distinct from law precisely in being concerned with physical visible traces and bits rather than in abstract, textually mediated concepts, doctrines, and rules" (ibid., 64). Always centered on what is visible as detectable to the eye or to instruments that assist the eye, it is this "epistemology of the clue" (ibid., 63), seeming to conjoin "technological optimism" with "a lingering belief in the detective's intuition" (ibid., 65), that matters most.

In fact, it is only because Barry knows how to look for and intuit clues or physical signs in the landscape that he regularly comes across incidents of wildlife crime worth reporting. He typically starts by searching for "tracks," footmarks made by gamekeepers but also the marks left by their quad bikes and land rovers. He explains that this is because gamekeepers usually lay their crow cage and snare traps a short distance from where they park their vehicle. At other times, Barry detects signs of human interference in the woodland, for example manmade channels where cut-down tree branches wall the path, encouraging wild animals to take a certain trap-lined direction. The same strategy may be deployed using the draw of scent: it is quite common for Barry to smell and then discover "stinkpits" in the woods of sporting estates, deliberate dumps of dead animals, containing the rotting remains of sheep, deer, badgers, foxes, crows, and even sometimes fish. Usually encircled by snares, the stinkpit is intended to attract grouse and pheasant predators, principally foxes, but as Barry points out, it inevitably also attracts and traps other sorts of local creatures.

As well as watching for signs of human movement in the landscape, Barry also looks out for animal tracks or paths. "I mean looking in some woodland," he continued, "it may to everybody else look quite chaotic, just lots of trees, lots of foliage everywhere, but you can see that something's gone through there. I don't know, I just get an eye for it." In addition to crow cages and snares, Barry sometimes catches sight of other traps along these paths. Once, for instance, he found a pine marten, a protected and endangered species from the weasel family, locked in a mammal cage trap under brambles. Alerted by a hissing noise and the sight of horizontal lines through the foliage, Barry zoomed in on the green cage: "I just caught it out of the corner of my eye, and you know you pick these things up as you go along."

In addition to leading Barry to traps and hence to possible incidents of animal suffering or wildlife crime, visual, aural, and olfactory clues can help him interpret the scene of entrapment. He believes, for instance, that he can read the duration of captivity from physical clues of devastation around the area. Bark stripped from adjacent trees tells him that a snared fox was trapped for at least a few days before he or she died (it is commonly known that foxes will start eating tree bark to try and stay alive). Likewise, the size of the circular ditch, or "doughnut," dug by a struggling and snared badger provides evidence that the animal may have been trapped for a week or more. All these clues are diligently recorded by Barry, photographed or videoed with the time, date, and GPS location inscribed on the digital image or footage.

Of course, Barry's forensic gaze is not solely motivated by the technical desire to decipher signs or gather evidence to a legal standard. As with the casual glance of the eyewitness, ethical feeling or the passion to protect wild animals from human-inflicted suffering animates his looking. This leads Barry to view physical clues of trapping and devastation as signs of injustice. The indignation drawn from him by the identification of these signs is what ensures his continued going out onto the land in search of legal and illegal traps. It is what fuels his commitment to the painstaking attention of forensic work and what keeps him there regardless of weather, when perhaps other, officially recognized, agents of the law might have retreated. In addition, it is what makes him stay for long hours besides deceased trapped creatures but especially alongside alive and injured ones, remaining until the police officer or qualified veterinary agent arrives. Barry told me, "I will always wait with the animal, I would never leave it once I have discovered it." For him, this is in part to preserve the crime scene and any evidence he might wish to point out. However, it is more crucially an act of companionship or fellow feeling (Reed 2015), an acknowledgment of the investigator's co-presence (we might even claim co-looking) with the trapped and suffering animal.

The ethical dimension of the forensic gaze is also what places it most at risk. Time and again, Barry warned me that succumbing to those passions, feeling the indignation and injustice of animal suffering, threatens his ability to do his job as evidence-gatherer or as reader of signs. "If you allow your emotions to go too far," he advised, "and get involved in the situation at that time then you'll forget the reasons why you are there, and you are there to obtain evidence only, the facts of the situation." So while being upset by human-inflicted animal suffering is a prerequisite for the investigative task of working with the law in mind, it is also what requires taming in order for the forensic gaze and the monitoring of both legal and licensed obligations to operate effectively. Barry has numerous cautionary tales of botched investigation, examples of where he got emotionally caught up with what he was seeing and consequently forgot to press the play button on his video camera or to measure the size of the illegal cage trap or to bag materials or animal tissues he needed chemically tested. In the end, these ethical responses but evidential failings become another kind of motivation. Barry is further driven by the injustice of the fact that those whose misdeeds he has detected may get away with wildlife crime and animal abuse because of his own lapses into moral care and co-present attention.

While working effectively as a forensic, lowly legal actor necessitates taming his instinctive moral nature and the accompanying desire to recognize or return the gaze of the wild animal, in the legal complexes that Barry describes this does not mean that the trapped creature is entirely without any assigned power. The active looking of the fox caught in a snare or the crow caught in a funnel trap may not register as a form of eyewitness testimony, but there are ways in which these live or dead animals can elicit relations that matter. When considering law in action, it is the object of the gaze and not just the seer (i.e., eyewitness or detective) that generates momentum. In particular, Barry is aware of the degree to which the very physical presence, quality and condition of the trapped animal body really counts, has the capacity to speak back to the law and provoke response.

In this regard, Barry once again remains close to the principle of the forensic gaze. As Weizman (2010, 11) points out, the whole notion of forensics is traditionally focused on the "speech acts" of objects rather than humans, an emphasis that for him is played out today in international humanitarian law where the close study of material remnants from war-damaged buildings has increasingly overridden the classic and previously privileged status of the human witness in war crimes investigations (2010, 10). In this field,

Weizman highlights, expressions such as "the bones/rubble is speaking to us" are commonly uttered (2010, 11). For Barry, the forensic power of the trapped animal body is not only in its embodied species status but also in its status as individual living material or corpse, as emitter of evidential signs. As well as deciphering clues about the scene of devastation, Barry's gaze and other forensic senses rest on a reading of the entrapped and injured body or carcass. The smell or lack of smell given off by a decomposing corpse, for instance, or the extent to which snare wire has cut through tissue and bone, will tell him how long the wild animal has been caught and whether, as a result, there is sufficient evidence of prolonged and unwarranted suffering that might constitute illegal activity. In this regard, we might speak of the body of the fox or the body of the crow as another kind of lowly legal actor.

As Barry is quick to highlight, the process of "evidence gathering" cannot rely on his intuitive skill alone: it is always necessarily shaped by the kind of incidents he comes across and by his reading of the particular implications of embodied contexts. For instance, a dead fox found in a legally-set snare or a dead crow in a legally-prepared funnel trap may simply provoke Barry to record the scene for the charity's records. But if a non-target species such as the body of a deer or badger is found dead in a snare, or a buzzard carcass is discovered in a crow cage, then Barry will record the findings and send them to the local divisional Wildlife Crime Officer to investigate. When a live animal body is found in a trap, a different range of responses, including the introduction of a new range of lowly human legal actors, comes into play. Upon finding a trapped and injured fox or crow, regardless of the legality of the particular trap, Barry knows he should also call in an authorized animal welfare inspector to examine the creature and make a judgement about its continuing health. Far more numerous than Wildlife Crime Officers (there are 62 working for the SSPCA or Scottish Society for the Prevention of Cruelty to Animals), these inspectors, whom one sheriff referred to as "private individuals," formally enjoy limited investigative, enforcement, and deputized reporting powers under the relevant animal health and welfare legislation. SSPCA inspectors will often take on an inquiry after it has passed through the hands of police and the police will take on inquiries initiated by inspectors. However, such deputized powers only extend to wild animals once they have been made captive or caught in a trap and only for so long as they remain alive.

In the crow kill case, Barry called an animal welfare inspector to assess the condition of the surviving, injured birds in the cage. He did so in part because he knew inspectors tend to arrive more quickly than police, and because he judges them to be more sympathetic to the vigorous prosecution of wildlife crime. But for him a further value lies in their simple physical presence as another pair of eyes and as a corroborating witness of the scene. The inspector couldn't provide first-hand testimony of the gamekeeper's actions, however the fact that not all the caged birds were despatched meant that he could formally assess the living ones for signs of stress or neglect.

So, although crows have no particular statutory rights of protection in their natural state as individuals or species, once they are inside the funnel trap, tangible legal protections and obligations do emerge. First and foremost, these birds compel the attention of, and draw out responsibilities from, the trap-setter, usually a gamekeeper, who is yet another lowly legal actor. Indeed, while the man caught on video in the crow kill case might be the accused, he is also, through the instrument of a general license (i.e., one that does not require a formal application but simply compliance with its criteria), a certain kind of self-regulating subject. As Valverde (2003, 178) highlights, when talking about the wider pervasive use of licensing in both North America and the United Kingdom, this legal technology rests on principles of "responsibilization." Indeed, the assumption often exists that licensees are the chief monitor and enforcer of a particular license's terms and conditions. In the case of the "general license to kill or take certain birds," it states that the gamekeeper or licensee is "responsible for the welfare of any bird or other animal under your control" (Scottish Natural Heritage 2014). More specifically, he or she has a duty of care that includes knowing the licensed standards: for example, that decoy birds in a cage must be provided with suitable water, food and shelter and an adequate perch, that injured or deceased birds must be removed, that live traps must be checked once a day and that those not in use must be immobilized. As already indicated, the licensee should also know that captive animals must be "destroyed humanely." By implication, the responsibilities fall not just on the individual gamekeeper but equally upon the whole professional gamekeeping association, which tacitly accepts that its members ought to know their licensed obligations to the welfare of trapped birds.

In this scenario, the same individuals are responsible for administering the licensed trap and for seeing or identifying improper use. Although each crow cage should display a tag listing the phone number of the local Wildlife Crime Officer and the ID number of the trap's owner so that members of the public can report incidents of abuse, the likelihood of anyone else being in the vicinity is remote. Once again, this is where Barry's presence on the sporting estate is crucial: one of the other occasional roles he assigns himself is to watch the response or check the compliance of the licensee.

Epilogue: The Law is an Ass

Despite the obviously dispersed and hybrid nature of detection, evidence gathering and reporting of wildlife crime, once the crow kill case reached court Barry reverts to the singular position of eyewitness, purveyor of what Valverde terms the "little facts" known to a private individual. It is in this capacity that he later received news of the case's dismissal. While no formal justification of the verdict was ever published (there is no such requirement in Scottish law), the charity did succeed in getting a brief two-paragraph e-mail response from the relevant procurator fiscal. The e-mail informed them that it was in fact the contested status of the investigator's observations that ultimately mattered most. Specifically, it stated that Barry's witness testimony could not be heard since he "had no entitlement to investigate potential snaring offences and carry out surveillance on land without permission of the landowner and without a police officer." The cited case law for this decision rested on a judgement from 2004 involving a field investigator for a conservation charity and the reported witnessing of peregrine falcon chick theft from a nest. As the explanatory e-mail implied, the legal precedent here centered once again on the issue of looking with the law in mind. This included the question of whether seeing is intentional (i.e., did the conservation investigator follow the accused onto the shooting estate with the specific purpose of watching him commit this crime) and the question of the location from which witness observations took place. For instance, the sheriff in this quoted case law determined that had the conservation investigator seen the theft from "a vantage point outwith the lands in question" then his testimony might have been admitted and persuasive.

The initial response of Barry and his charity colleagues was to meet this disappointing judgement with a counter legal argument: i.e., to answer by "speaking legally" (Latour 2010, ix) or by finding an internalist rejoinder. Hence, the policy director drafted a letter requesting that the crow kill ruling be reviewed. In it, she proposed various forms of counter-weaving that realigns the legal circumstance of Barry's looking. She pointed out, for instance, that the cited case law predates the codification of the right to roam (legislation which the charity had long taken to legitimate the presence of field investigators on private land). The policy director also worked hard in other ways to demonstrate that Barry's purpose was "not comparable" to the motivations of the conservation field investigator in the cited case law. This involved attempts to deny equivalence on the suggested basis of surveillance, but also to highlight alternative readings of the relationship between witnessing and the act of looking with intent. Unlike the conservation agent, she offered, Barry was not "acting illegally" for the purpose of observing what he actually saw (i.e., a crow kill) but rather for the purpose of observing something else (what the e-mail communication from the procurator fiscal described as "potential snaring offences"). In other words, even under the terms of the cited case law Barry's eyewitnessing was still "fortuitous," a circumstance that is identified as crucially lacking in the observation of the peregrine falcon egg theft.

But the efforts to present causes for review that still maintained precedent-based tendencies, or the internalist momentum to ensure the crow kill case spoke even more like the law, were in the end unsuccessful.

In response to her letter, the policy director received a brief reply from the Lord Advocate's office upholding the inadmissibility of Barry's testimony. By way of conclusion, the response added, "I must advise you therefore that Crown Counsel's decision in this case is final." As both Barry and the policy director fully appreciated, this meant that the particular crow kill litigation was now absolutely closed.

While formal legal actors (judges, lawyers, police officers) might move on to "speaking" the law through other cases (Latour 2010, 103), for the animal welfare charity this was the point at which speaking legally stopped; it was also the moment at which the hybrid knowledge of the investigator bifurcated. For Barry in particular, extra-legal or externalist positions such as moral outrage or ethical feeling, which fuel the work of detection and evidence gathering, also now became a basis for conscious critique of or talk *about* the law. The sense of injustice, of the countryside as a site of traps and human-introduced hazard, could now resurface to explain legal decisions.

Barry, for instance, spoke with renewed force about the law as a prop or support for the landowning class in Scotland. He pointed out that the vast bulk of Wildlife Crime Liaison Officers' time is spent on police work to defend and monitor the interests of shooting and hunting estates rather than the interests of wildlife. For him, this is epitomized in the disproportionate police attention placed on poaching: the illegal hunting, killing and theft of wild animals largely on private land. Unlike raptor poisoning and illegal crow trapping, this offence does not require the usual legal standard of corroboration (poaching offences are singled out in law as prosecutable on single witness evidence, usually that of a gamekeeper or landowner). Seen in this light, the judgement about the inadmissibility of his testimony became an instance of law's corruption, of its collaboration with agents of animal suffering, and hence of its externality from the principles and compassions driving animal protection.

But the bifurcation of justice from legal knowledge is sanctioned in further ways by the charity as a whole. Once the review body finally closed the case, the organization took the decision to publish Barry's video footage online. No longer just a piece of disputed legal evidence, the video became a means of making supporters and the public as a whole into non-legal witnesses of the crow kill and hence participants in a new campaign. The charity invited viewers of the video to corroborate the outrage of Barry and his colleagues at the inhumane actions of the gamekeeper, but also at the injustice of law, evinced for all to see. "The terror and suffering that these poor birds felt is unimaginable," one viewer posted; "It's cruelty at its worst. I feel so sad," responded another. "There is no justice for the innocent in this country," and again, more succinctly, "law is an ass." As well as leaving comments below the streamed footage, the website invited these new witnesses to "take action" by signing an open letter addressed to the Scottish

Minister for the Environment, asking that the government ensure that all wildlife crimes are pursued by the authorities.

The charity also highlighted the case and video footage in order to fundraise: supporters were asked to make a financial contribution to support the field activities of Barry. This latter action suggested a prospective return to an internalist approach, to speaking legally or working with the law in mind. For, like the judges and lawyers described by Latour, Barry knows he must ultimately move on from the crow kill and once again discipline his emotive, ethical self in order to carry on the lowly but, for him, vital responsibilities of both witnessing wildlife crime and its forensic investigation.

Acknowledgments

I would like to thank all the members of the animal welfare charity that I work with. I am especially grateful for the comments of Irus Braverman, and the feedback provided informally by Alain Pottage, Annelise Riles, and Shari Sabeti. As well as the initial project workshop in Buffalo, versions of this chapter were given at the Danish Mega Seminar, the Department Seminar at St. Andrews and the Edinburgh Candlelit Seminar, and I thank all those audiences too.

References

Braverman, Irus. 2012. *Zooland: The Institution of Captivity*. Stanford: Stanford University Press.

———. 2015. "More-than-Human Legalities." In *The Wiley Handbook of Law and Society*. Edited by Patricia Ewick and Austin Sarat, 307–21. West Sussex, UK: Wiley Press.

Latour, Bruno. 2010. *The Making of Law: An Ethnography of the Conseil D'Etat*. Cambridge: Polity Press.

Reed, Adam. 2015. "Snared: Ethics and Nature in Animal Protection." *Ethnos*. DOI: 10.1080/00141844.2015.1028563. Published online: 10 Apr 2015.

Sarat, Austin. 1990. " 'The Law is All Over': Power, Resistance and the Legal Consciousness of the Welfare Poor." *Yale Journal of Law and the Humanities* 2 (2): 343–79.

Scottish Natural Heritage. 2014. General Licence 02/2014: To Kill or Take Certain Birds for the Prevention of Serious Damage to Livestock, Foodstuffs, Crops, Vegetables and Fruit.

Valverde, Marianna. 2003. *Law's Dream of a Common Knowledge*. Princeton: Princeton University Press.

Weizman, Eyal. 2010. "Forensic Architecture: Only the Criminal Can Solve the Crime." *Radical Philosophy* 164: 9–24.

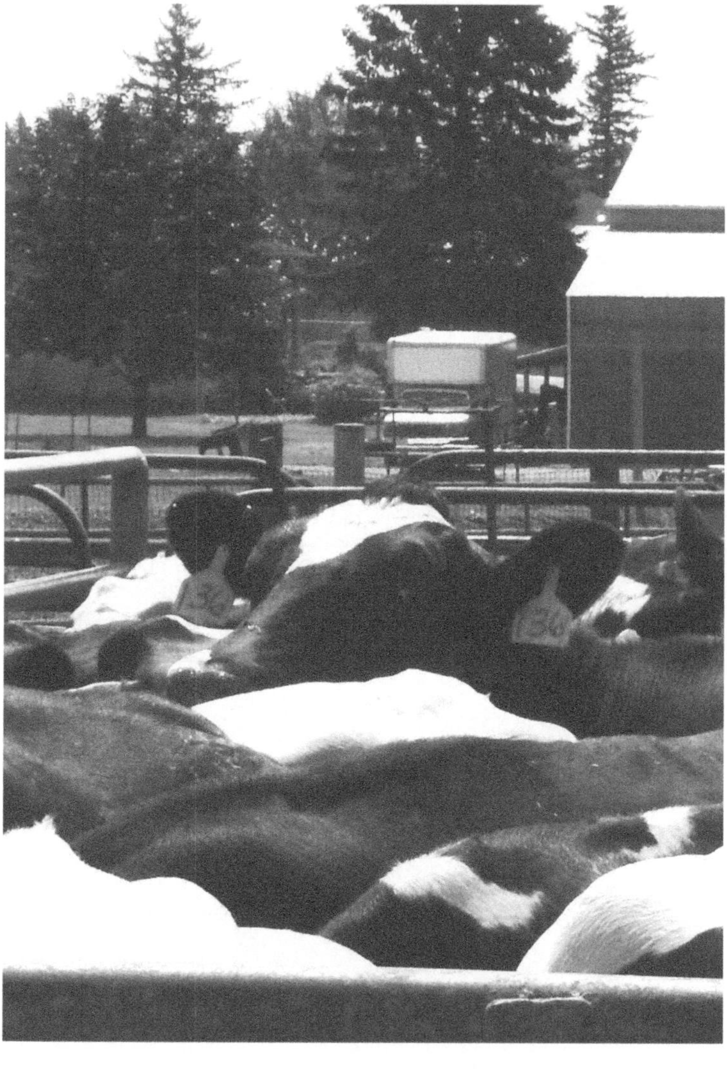

Chapter 6

Nonhuman Animal Resistance and the Improprieties of Live Property

Kathryn Gillespie

I sit in the bleachers at a Washington State auction yard and wait for the dairy market auction to begin. The sale is starting late, and I soon learn that the reason for the delay is an escaped steer who was confined in a holding pen behind the auction yard. He had leapt the six-foot fence and had taken off running down the country highway. A group of auction workers and attendees had jumped into their pickup trucks to go after the steer with rifles. When they finally cornered him on the highway, they shot and killed him. Returning to the auction yard, the men loudly lamented the fact that the steer had escaped because it meant a not-insignificant economic loss. A mother cow and her calf are herded into the auction ring. The calf comes into the ring easily, but the cow resists mightily. She kicks and bellows and repeatedly moves her body in between her calf and the human herder. The herder grows increasingly aggressive in response to the cow's resistance, yelling loudly and hitting her. Finally, exhausted, she comes running into the ring with her calf. At this moment, an audience member sitting next to me comments, "I would have bid on this pair—they're real beauties. But the way that cow is resisting, it's clear she's psychotic."

These stories are not unusual. My notes over nine months of multispecies ethnographic fieldwork on dairy production in the Pacific Northwestern United States are filled with these kinds of incidents: moments of everyday resistance by farmed animals. I did not approach my research with the topic of nonhuman animal resistance in mind; rather, moments of resistance emerged as somewhat of a surprise, populating the spaces and places of farming animals in the dairy industry. As I noticed these acts and recognized them as resistant, I paid more attention to the stories farmers and workers told about nonhuman animal resistance: farmed animals escaping,

---

Waiting in pens at a California auction yard. Photo by Kathryn Gillespie, 2012.

kicking, biting and refusing to eat or work. Farmers, sanctuary workers, industry workers, and agricultural community members shared stories of resistant farmed animals from their own cross-species encounters.

This chapter asks: if we take as a starting point that nonhuman species engage in resistant acts, what might be gained from taking this resistance seriously? How might those of us dedicated to creating more liberatory legal frameworks for nonhuman animals imagine our role as scholars and scholar-activists in *resisting with* animals through first trying to understand their resistance on its own terms? In order to theorize nonhuman animal resistance, it is necessary to move away from the anthropocentric assumption that humans are the only species that resists. Taking nonhuman animal resistance seriously presents an opportunity for reconceptualizing how we think about other animals, how they are positioned in our current legal structures, and how they live and die in service of capital accumulation.

Farmed animals resist from within their legal status as live property. Farmed animals are owned outright, the property of the humans who farm them, and this status creates and maintains certain conditions for them. For example, bovine animals used for dairy are subjected to everyday forms of gendered violence for commodity production (Gillespie 2014): female cows are annually impregnated via artificial insemination and milked intensively for 300 days out of every year until their productivity wanes and they are slaughtered at 3–7 years of age and many male calves are slaughtered at approximately 4–6 months of age for veal. By contrast, the natural lifespan of a dairy-breed cow is more than 20 years. Female calves born into the system are often raised as cows for milk production. A few male adults are kept to produce semen, a process by which they are forcibly ejaculated by human or machine. Since they are of limited use to dairy producers even on small-scale farms, male calves are often either slaughtered for veal or auctioned off at the auction yard for beef. These animals are also subjected to other routine forms of bodily modification and appropriation that signal their status as property: branding, ear-tagging, tail-docking, nose-ringing, castration without anesthetic, and artificial insemination. Their status as property serves as the central physical and legal context for their resistance.

Multispecies ethnography is the primary method I employed in my research on the dairy industry. This is an emerging methodology in anthropology and the social sciences more broadly that is dedicated to recognizing the political and social worlds of many species (Kirksey and Helmreich 2010). In particular, "multispecies ethnography centers on how a multitude of organisms' livelihoods shape and are shaped by political, economic and cultural forces" (ibid., 545). In this vein, I focused on the lived experiences of individual cows in the dairy industry as a way of understanding how economic and political structures shape their lives. The result is a series of narratives and glimpses into the embodied lives of cows at different moments in the commodification process.

This chapter's attention to bovine animals offers up a lens into the intimate worlds of other animals' experiences and corresponds with other multispecies ethnographic approaches in this volume. Elan Abrell's choice to center the effects of captivity on Tony the tiger and Lolita the orca whale and Eben Kirksey's attention to the place of Maui the macaw in the multispecies family structure, for instance, emphasize the productive possibilities of centering partial or full life stories of nonhuman animals in multispecies ethnographies.

This chapter argues for a serious consideration of nonhuman resistance in the context of other-than-human animals' status as live property in order to understand the violence of their property status. I also advocate a new legal standing for nonhuman animals. Whether and how nonhuman species have agency is a topic I will not address in this chapter; scholars elsewhere have dedicated much excellent work to establishing that nonhuman animals have agency and that this agency should be recognized as a starting point for our studies of others (e.g., McFarland and Hediger 2009). To begin, I will review the debate over the category of living property. Next, I will theorize nonhuman animal resistance and draw on examples of real, embodied bovine animals who are resisting their conditions to understand what this resistance looks like and how it can be understood. Finally, I will suggest pathways forward for responding to nonhuman animal resistance, with a particular attention to what this means for "more-than-human legalities" (Braverman 2015).

Animals as Live Property

The debate over nonhuman animals' status as property is varied and nuanced, a spectrum that includes those who have no problem with maintaining these nonhuman animals' property status, those who suggest modest reforms, and those who advocate the abolition of property status altogether. Legal scholars David Favre and Gary Francione both find the current property status of other species to be problematic, but their proposed solutions are fundamentally opposed: Favre (2011) advocates the creation of a new category of property—"living property"—for other species; Francione (2000; 2004; 2008) argues for the abolition of other animals' status as property and advocates for animal rights under the law. Following the abolitionist approach, my research leads me to believe that violence against cows is enabled in important ways by their status as property. However, I depart from the abolitionist approach where rights are concerned, as a rights framework is deeply anthropocentric and tied to the anthropocentric institution of human law.

Much of the conversation around animals-as-property creates a dichotomy within a liberal rights framework: property versus persons. Within this context, Francione and other animal rights advocates identify the moral issues with the legal status of property. Steven Wise (1996) argues that "there are significant moral issues" with assigning animals what he terms, "legal thinghood" rather than "legal personhood"—namely, that being categorized as "things" denies animals basic rights that are reserved for only those who have been granted "personhood." Further, he traces the history of the "legal thinghood" of animals, rooting this conception in ancient hierarchies of anthropocentrism (1996). It is precisely this deep-rooted anthropocentrism that reserves "personhood" only for members of the human species, Wise argues.

Indeed, as Maneesha Deckha teaches us, law is a fundamentally anthropocentric institution: "the product of human actors, it entrenches the interests of humans [and human-populated corporate entities] over virtually all others" (2013, 742). The reservation of personhood for only members of the human species is certainly one manifestation of this anthropocentrism, but we see anthropocentric priorities even in projects like Steven Wise's Nonhuman Rights Project (2015), which work to extend legal rights and personhood to certain other-than-human species: great apes, elephants, and dolphins. Wise's project aims to obtain the right to bodily liberty for these particular species precisely because they possess cognitive and emotional capacities that are similar to humans. The anthropocentric hierarchy that positions humans as the standard against which all other species are measured will, of course, prioritize those species who are more similar to humans. But what of the snail or chicken whose way of being in the world may be very different from a human's? Will they eventually be granted personhood, too, or will they be relegated to a lesser legal status because they do not share enough similarity with the human species?

We even see this anthropocentrism in the current legal overtures, which have been made in the form of welfare and humane treatment laws to try to discourage cruelty and regulate the treatment of other species by humans. For example, the United States' animal welfare and protection laws cover some species—namely, those that are closer in cognitive/emotional capacity to humans and who are more charismatic. Even when a particular species is legally protected, animal cruelty cases require proof of intent for cruelty to the animal and this must be proven beyond a reasonable doubt, which rarely happens (Francione 2004). Indeed, those legal protections that do exist for nonhuman animals remain notoriously lax and insufficiently enforced (e.g., Wolfson 1996; Wolfson and Sullivan 2004). Importantly, such laws entirely fail to cover certain less human-like species (poultry, rats, mice, fish, rabbits, etc.). In the context of agriculture, unsatisfactory welfare legislation also occurs because of legal exemptions at the state level, called "common or customary farming exemptions" (CFEs). These allow animal farming enterprises to engage in practices that would otherwise be considered cruel (e.g. tail-docking, beak-trimming, and castration without anesthesia, etc.) because they are "customary" in the industry (Wolfson and

Sullivan 2004). Drawing on my experience of researching cows used for dairy, I am convinced that, despite the strides that welfare legislators try to make, so long as some species are categorized as property (living or otherwise), their interests will frequently be compromised to the various interests of human "owners."

The Animal-as-Commodity

Not all nonhuman animals are constituted as property in the same way that farmed animals are. The legal status of "wild" or "free-roaming animals" is theorized in different ways that are beyond the scope of this chapter (Braverman 2013). Although it is not a condition that all species experience, animals-as-property is a legal and material framework that reproduces a hierarchy of humans over other species. That a human can own a cow is a mode that enables the making of the cow as a "thing"—a thing to be commodified, reproduced, and eventually killed. But harm to the cow also relies, more generally, on her objectification—a point that is relevant also to the management of "wild" species. In other words, an animal does not have to be property to be the subject of violence and bodily appropriation, nor does a body have to be property in order to be commodified. Property, then, does not explain all conditions under which animals suffer and are commodified. However, that many of the nonhuman species with whom we are intimately connected suffer bodily violence and premature death–through human consumption of their bodies as food, clothing, or other commodity products—and that this is enabled, at least in part, by their property status—is an important insight for my argument here. The status of animals as property arguably makes it easier to objectify and commodify the cow and many other species for everyday use by humans and capital accumulation.

Indeed, if we look at the lived experience of nonhuman animals under capitalism—in the food system, in entertainment, in experimentation, and in fashion—we can see that economic interests often dictate their lives and, even more often, their deaths. Within capitalist regimes, the cow used for dairy, the hen raised for eggs, and the chickens, pigs and steers raised for meat are commodities in life and in death. Animals are also commodifiable in wildlife trade and entertainment industries, where their liveliness, "wildness," and encounterability are prized (Collard forthcoming; Collard 2012; Whatmore and Thorne 1998), making the animal a "lively commodity" whose value emerges from their status as a living being (Collard and Dempsey 2013). Similarly, other industries, too, commodify nonhuman species to advance human interests: biomedical research and product testing use animal lives and bodies in service of scientific experimentation and new biomedical technologies (Collard and Gillespie 2015; Haraway 1989). Animal bodies used in the fashion industry are another site of animal use that has yet to be explored by academics. Animals are widely wild-caught and captive-bred for fur, leather, feathers, wool, and silk around the world (Collard and Gillespie 2015). Together with an anthropocentric legal structure that subordinates nonhuman species through their property status, the drive for capital accumulation under capitalism creates conditions whereby animal bodies and lives are commodified.

In the livestock auction yard, the relationship between the cow's property status and commodification becomes evident in spectacular detail. Nonhuman animals are literally bought and sold in this space. Certain qualities make them more or less sellable for different purposes: their skin is marked with various neon symbols to identify certain qualities important to buyers (e.g., whether they have been castrated, whether they were born sterile, etc.). Additionally, depending on the condition of the animal, they are either sold "per head" or "per pound." "Per pound" animals are generally destined directly for slaughter. The commodification of the cow's body at the auction is intimately intertwined with her status as property. The commodity form is reliant on an object or thing being ownable in order for it to be exchanged for money in a capitalist system of trade. Although property status does not guarantee violent treatment, in order to be bought and sold and subjected to the conditions of violence that this commodity status enables, she must be ownable in the first place.

When Animals Resist

Resistance by animals laboring in the service of humans comes in many forms. As the property of farmers and/or food corporations, cows on dairy farms are a somewhat unique group because of the way their bodies' productive and reproductive capacities are used while they are alive (i.e., through milk, semen, and reproduction) and then commodified again in death (when they are slaughtered for meat). The cows' commodification in death relies on an additional form of objectification beyond being "mere" property. Although the cow is long dead, her property status lives on and enables further violence and abuse through the efficient dismemberment and the packaging of her body into tidy pieces of "meat" for sale and then through rendering what is left after the slaughterhouse into other new commodities.

Violence against the farmed animal body is not limited to industrial- and large-scale production practices. My fieldwork exploring various scales of production revealed that, while the industrial nature of contemporary production practices intensifies the effects on the cow's body, the appropriation of her life and body and everyday forms of violence occur even on small farms where her property status is maintained. Thus, my primary concern with the effects on animals of commodity production lies not with the scale of production, but with the violence that is enacted on their bodies *because they are ownable.* New insights for legal scholars, critical animal studies scholars, activists, and others concerned with the legal and moral status of nonhuman animals might be gained from interrogating more closely the effects of property status of animals on the animals themselves. One way of exploring these effects is by looking at the trend of animal resistance—in other words, the way in which animals themselves oppose the conditions that their property status dictates.

Chris Philo (1995) argues that it is possible for nonhuman animals to transgress human social worlds and orders. He is cautious about projecting human notions of resistance onto animals—an anxiety I share, not because humans are the only species that resists, but because assuming that animal resistance takes a similar form as human resistance prevents us from potentially learning about the possibilities and potentialities emerging from acts of animal resistance. Chris Wilbert (2000) theorizes animal resistance in relation to intentionality, arguing against the problematic understandings of animal resistance that emerge from an assumption of the animals' "conscious intentionality" (Cresswell 1996) in acts of resistance. Instead, Wilbert suggests that we recognize these as intentional *acts*: "forms of resistance to human ordering" (Wilbert 2000, 250). Following Wilbert, I do not pretend to know whether animals demonstrate conscious intentionality when they resist and I do not use animals' resistant behaviors as metaphor; instead, I recognize the way other species act in response to conditions created by the uneven hierarchies of power between humans and animals. In particular, I focus on animal actions in the context of their commodification by humans, and humans' responses to them. What are the boundaries of such resistant acts? Without the need for intentionality, resistance could be defined more broadly than these individual acts: resistance *could* be theorized in terms of species going extinct as a result of anthropogenic climate change, or bacteria mutating as a result of heavy antibiotic use. However, in the context of my argument here, I have focused on a particular form of animal resistance: individual animals who physically struggle against their conditions through fighting back or escaping their captivity—acts that we can understand as resistant if we attempt to read nonhuman animals' own life-worlds.

In 2011, news broke about a six-year-old cow named Yvonne who escaped from a dairy farm in Germany. Just before Yvonne was to be collected and sent to slaughter, she broke through an electric fence and fled the farm where she was being kept. She hid in the forest and eluded capture for several months before she was caught and returned to the farm. During her period of freedom, she had become a national icon and the public travelled across the country to try to spot a glimpse of her living in the forest. Yvonne was labeled by media sources as a "freedom fighter for the animal-loving republic," "an incandescent symbol of freedom and animal dignity" (Chappell 2011). In the end, the public rallied to save her from slaughter and an animal sanctuary purchased her for 600 euros so that she could live out her days at the sanctuary.

A similar news story had broken in the United States more than a decade earlier when Emily, a three-year-old cow, had escaped from a slaughterhouse in Massachusetts. She evaded capture for 40 days and, in that time, drew national attention as a "folk hero" and a symbol of animal resistance against oppression (Hribal 2007). Due to the outpouring of support for her resistance, Emily was sold by the slaughterhouse to an abbey for 1 dollar, where, upon her capture, she was allowed to live out her days in sanctuary. When she died in 2004, the abbey buried her onsite and erected a bronze statue of her to sit atop her grave (Roadside America 2014).

Human recognition of the resistance of other species extends to spaces of enclosure and captivity beyond the farm. For example, the documentary film *Blackfish* (2013) swept mainstream media with its exposé of the plight of marine mammals in captivity. In particular, the film tells the story of Tilikum, a captive orca at SeaWorld who killed trainers on three separate occasions. Tilikum's story, and the film in general, illustrate the emotional and psychological consequences of captivity for orcas. The public response to *Blackfish* has been significant, with dozens of musicians canceling shows scheduled at SeaWorld, various boycotts and targeted actions taken against the park, and revenues being impacted by the film (Zimmerman 2014). Individuals who saw the film connected with the story of Tilikum and the fact that baby orcas are frequently captured from the wild to live lives of service in marine parks around the world (Blackfish 2013).

On this subject of animal use in spaces of entertainment, Jason Hribal, in his book *Fear of the Animal Planet* (2010), documents individual acts of resistance by animals used in entertainment (zoos, circuses, marine parks). Tatiana, a Siberian tiger at the San Francisco Zoo, escaped her enclosure and passed by numerous bystanders to kill and maim three teenagers who had teased, taunted, and thrown things at her. She was hunted, shot, and killed by park security. Janet, an elephant at the Great American Circus, chased down and tried to injure abusive circus employees while she had a group of children riding on her back. In the middle of the chaos, she stopped, let someone remove the children safely from her back, and then continued to chase the employees. She grabbed the bullhook which they had often used to beat her, and smashed it repeatedly against a wall. A group of baboons in Northern Africa resisted the slaughter and capture of members of their community by chasing a group of animal traders all the way to the train station. They launched raids on the train cars to try to free the captured baboons. These are just a few examples of individual and collective acts of resistance by animals used by humans.

Hribal's (2010) aim is to show that acts of animal resistance are numerous and varied. In his work on the labor history of animals (2003), he writes:

> Most owners, managers, or observers of laboring animals—whether through their written word or through their counteractions—fully admitted to the presence of such resistance. These acts could be maliciously violent in form. Horses "bucked." Cattle "charged." Cows "kicked." Pigs "bit." Chickens "pecked"—all with the recognized intent that is recognized by the employers themselves, to harm or kill the employers. Or it could be nonviolent in form, such as refusing to work or, at least, work hard. . . . As the exploitation increased, so did the resistance to it—both by laboring animals and concerned humans (2003, 449; 452).

The media coverage and public relations discourse present various acts of resistance as isolated incidents, as "animals gone wild," as individual animals being a "bad seed," or simply as accidents (Hribal 2010). Hribal presents these stories in a different light—if looked at not as isolated incidents but as a rich and varied history of animals resisting their conditions, these individual and collective actions can be read as a new kind of social movement. He writes, "Captive animals escaped their cages. They attacked their keepers. They demanded more food. They refused to perform. They refused to reproduce. The resistance itself could be organized. Indeed, not only did the animals have a history, they were making history. For their resistance led directly to historical change" (29). Only a fraction of these kinds of stories make it into public view, and yet those that do often motivate reflections on issues relating to agency, welfare, captivity and domestication, as in the case of *Blackfish*.

Unlike the steer, cow, and calf from the auction yard mentioned at the beginning of this chapter, Yvonne and Emily became symbols of resistance: stories of extraordinary individuals with a will to live and the ingenuity to escape their impending slaughter. The telling and retelling of Yvonne's and Emily's stories in the media perpetuated the notion that they were exceptional and encouraged the public to rally around them.[1] Even as the public continues to believe that farmed animal resistance is infrequent and unique to a few individuals, many workers I encountered in animal agriculture know that instances of animal resistance happen frequently and become part of routine material human-animal encounters on the farm.

Unlike Yvonne and Emily, most cases do not end in animal celebrity and sanctuary. More typically, animal resistance is met with repression. Indeed, the majority of animals who resist are not granted sanctuary or freedom from captivity. Spaces of animal use, like the farmed animal auction yard, are designed to subdue animal resistance: the pens and chutes are constructed to move animals easily through the space with as little opportunity for resistance as possible. The auction also facilitates the efficient commodification (through sale) of the animal and reproduces the status of animals as property to be bought and sold in the process. At the auction, animal resistance is also violently repressed. During the course of my fieldwork, I observed animals being beaten, yelled at, kicked, shocked and crushed against the wall or floor for trying to escape or fight back against humans who were herding them through the space. I saw piglets body-slammed against the wall, cows beaten repeatedly on the head with steel rods, and bulls shocked with electric prods. In the most extreme cases, like the steer who escaped the auction yard, animals are killed for their resistance.

Resistance is a highly undesirable trait in farmed animals. As a result, farmed animal management practices aim to anticipate and quell resistant behaviors *before* they happen. Even at the point of breeding and birth, farmers try to manage and prevent resistance. Breeding practices on the farm have long sought to breed resistant qualities out of animals: dairy breeds are bred for docility and even temperament, in addition to prolific milk production, milk taste and quality. Nose ringing is a practice used to dominate the bull's body (nose rings allow for significant control of the bull in that the farmer can lead the animal around using the sensitivity of the bull's nose; nose rings are also primary tools of discipline for the bull). Bulls, along with other animals who resist on the farm (especially those who resist on multiple occasions), are routinely killed because they are perceived as dangerous or as simply too much trouble. One motivation for "culling" cows used for dairy, for instance, is that their dispositions have worsened after the repeated seizure of their calves away from them. Recall the cow at the auction yard who was conceptualized as "psychotic" for attempting to protect her calf: the woman in the audience defined the cow's desire to protect her offspring as a psychological disorder and dismissed it as such. Finally, some spaces of slaughter have famously been redesigned by animal scientist Temple Grandin to improve animals' experience of the slaughterhouse leading up to their deaths. While these new slaughterhouse designs have been developed around responses to the things cows fear (e.g., certain lighting, movements or sounds), they can also be read as efforts to prevent moments of resistance (e.g., a cow trying to escape, refusing to move forward, or kicking) and are touted as ways to help the slaughterhouse operate more efficiently.

Because these moments of resistance are seen as threats to the efficient accumulation of capital, they become practical problems to be prevented or mitigated through breeding and spatial or bodily management. It is partly this inability to see acts of nonhuman resistance as an agential rejection of the legal and economic structural conditions that make them first ownable and then commodifiable. And it is their property status, and the ability to profit from their commodification, that obscures human recognition of their resistance as more than isolated incidents of psychosis or bad temperament. In fact, in order for their resistance to be successful, Yvonne's and Emily's freedom from commodity production and slaughter had to be bought (Yvonne for 600 euros and Emily for a symbolic one dollar)—a point that illustrates both the property status of farmed animals and the limits to their resistance. Farmed animals are so thoroughly dominated by humans that even their most direct forms of resistance (escapes, attacks, etc.) often go unremarked, and are repressed through mundane, everyday acts of violence (beating, shocking, killing, etc.). Even as they embody significant modes of appropriating and managing animal life, the everyday practices in industries such as the dairy industry are rarely seen as violence against the animals (Gillespie 2014). This "making mundane" is central to the continued commodification of animals and the hegemony of animal use. Acknowledging acts of animal resistance *as resistance*, however, creates fissures in the dominant order of human–animal relations and urges us to respond.

Responding to Animal Resistance

The public outcry around Yvonne's and Emily's escapes, the woman's response to the cow protecting her calf at the auction, the auction workers' beating, kicking, shocking and yelling at animals moving (or refusing to move) through the auction yard, the breeding of resistant traits out of future animals—all are different responses to animal resistance. The public responded with concern and respect to Yvonne and Emily, who had the will to survive, and advocated for their pardon from slaughter. Embedded in the social and cultural conditions of animal commodification, the woman at the auction found the cow's resistance to be an undesirable trait and decided not to bid on the pair, although they were quickly bought by another audience member. The workers responded to animal resistances at auctions as actions that must be overcome and managed in order to facilitate the political–economic efficiency of dairy and animal agriculture. Seen as a problem to be fixed by genetic selection, resistant traits are attempted to be bred out of future cows, impacting breeding practices in the industry. Although such acts of resistance are dismissed or repressed, cows still resist and fight back against their conditions.

In the face of such resistances, I argue, it is our responsibility as scholars and activists to respond. In spite of and, indeed, perhaps *because of* the uneven hierarchies of power between human and nonhuman animals, we have the opportunity to do what we can to recognize, acknowledge, and change our behaviors in response to the unique features of animal resistance. Animal resistance is a grossly understudied subject in scholarship on human–animal relations, a trend that may be exacerbated by a perpetual fear of anthropomorphism. In spite of these fears, careful, critical empirical and theoretical studies of animal resistance are needed. Acts of animal resistance may not mean or be the same as human acts of resistance—and we should not assume that they are. We have the potential to learn from the way animals resist *on animals' own terms.* This chapter makes a call for rigorous and thoughtful engagement with the subject of animal resistance, for further studies that take animal resistance seriously and explore what can be made of these acts of resistance for animals' lives and for humans' relationship with them.

Concluding Thoughts

How might scholars interested in lively legalities respond to nonhuman animal resistance? Animal resistance has discursive, and potentially political, power as we consider the ways in which this resistance challenges animals' positioning as ownable bodies. I suggest here that confronting the legal implications of animal resistance means rethinking animals' legal status as property. That animals have agency and interests, and that these matter—that animals resist conditions that violate their bodies and interests—calls into question whether animals, as living, resistant beings who suffer as a result of their commodification should be owned. Jeffrey St. Clair writes, "Each trampling of a brutal handler with a bull-hook, each mauling of a taunting visitor, each drowning of a tormenting trainer is a crack in the old order that treats animals as property, as engines of profit, as mindless objects of exploitation and abuse" (2010, 16). The only adequate response by law, geography, anthropology, and other scholars to animal resistance would be to boldly advocate for the abolition of their property status. This would go a long way to challenging the political economic order that commodifies animals in the first place.

If animals were no longer property, how should they be categorized under the law? As I alluded to earlier, and as Elan Abrell explores (in this volume), the anthropocentrism of the law makes the property/persons dichotomy a problematic way forward because of the countless species who will be excluded from the category of personhood. At the same time, for those species who *are* granted personhood, their lives will likely change dramatically as they will experience increased bodily liberty and autonomy. These insights—the potential and problems associated with granting other species nonhuman personhood and the anthropocentrism of current legal structures—are instructive for how we think about the role of animals in law. As we imagine and present possibilities for more inclusive, less anthropocentric legal institutions that take seriously nonhuman life and body, eliminating the current frameworks that work efficiently to dominate other, as well as our own, species (e.g., the animals-as-property legal regime) is a critical first step in creating livelier legalities. This chapter has focused on animal resistance to illuminate the violence of animals-as-property and make a call for new legal regimes that would take seriously animal agency and autonomy that is made visible in their efforts to resist. This would entail greater attention to the alterity of species and a deeper respect for, and attention to, what is meaningful and central to each species' flourishing at the scale of the embodied animal. Recognizing and responding to resistance can be a first step in building less anthropocentric legal regimes dedicated to rejecting law that reinforces the primacy of the human and advancement of human interests, and instead transforming law into a more fundamentally multispecies project.

But what of animals who do not resist? Does a lack of visibility of animal resistance mean that those animals are content and it is acceptable to commodify them? Animals may not resist for many reasons. For instance, resistant qualities may have been bred out of animals or animals may just have "given up." A dairy farmer informed me that some cows on his farm had resisted and become depressed initially after the removal of their first calf or two, but that once they realized this was a regular occurrence, they seemed to have "just given up." This is one site where animal resistance as a guiding frame has its limits. I would argue that we cannot use animal resistance as the *only* measure for the wellbeing and welfare of animals living, laboring and dying in service to capital accumulation. This is where multispecies ethnographic research is particularly useful in documenting the variability of animals' responses to captivity. Some animals resist to the point where they are killed for it, some resist a little but give up when they learn that their resistance does not improve their conditions, and some never resist. Just as humans respond with frequently radical variability in response to oppression or violence against our bodies, animals too respond in a variety of ways.

That some—no, *many*—animals do resist their commodification enabled by their property status, though, is important to note for the intellectual inquiry to move forward. Animal resistance reveals that there are conditions against which to resist; these instances show that animals may not want to be commodified or owned and that they have the agency to reject these structures of power and hierarchy. Animal resistance is thus a viable framework for enriching the scholarly understanding of nonhuman lives and lively legalities, and also offers another lens through which to understand the ethical and political dimensions of commodifying nonhuman life. Rather than seeing it as a potential measure of the legal and moral status of animals that replace other ethical measures, theorizing animal resistance would be most useful in conjunction with other ways of thinking about our effects on the intimate experiences of other animals. For instance, ethical considerations of the *suffering* of animals, championed by Jeremy Bentham and Peter Singer, correspond with documenting and responding to animal resistance. Thus, animal resistance can be productively read alongside other ethical measures of how other animals live and die in a multispecies world.

Finally, I would like to offer a speculative call for exploration going forward. What does animal resistance mean for thinking about social movements, becoming allies with animals, and activism and education geared toward greater care in our relationships with other animals? Disrupting the status quo for how animals are, and should be, treated may suggest new ways of understanding the role of animals in social movements. Animal advocacy movements tend to frame their work for animals as "working on behalf of animals," "speaking for those who cannot speak for themselves," and "saving" or "rescuing" animals. But these are anthropocentric notions of advocacy, whereby humans remain in positions of power atop hierarchies of species ordering. Certainly there are ways in which farmed animals' ability to resist (and for this resistance to result in more liberatory conditions) is limited by their captivity and subordinate position to humans on the farm. Yet, rather than construct animals as "victims" in need of rescue, recognizing animals' efforts to resist opens the opportunity to view animals as more autonomous subjects in a movement for social change. Thus, animal resistance urges us to *resist with* animals, rather than *resist for* them. What possibilities emerge for interspecies social movements that address intersections of human and animal oppression? What might we learn from taking seriously this resistance on the animals' own terms? And what might these movements of (and with) animal resistance look like?

Acknowledgments

Special thanks to Irus Braverman for her keen editorial feedback and organizational role in this book project and to the participants in the *More-than-Human Legalities* workshop at the Baldy Center for Law & Social Policy at SUNY Buffalo in September 2014. Thanks especially to Christopher Bear and Peter Gillespie for their productive feedback and thoughtful suggestions on how to improve this chapter.

Note

1 Importantly, the notion that Emily and Yvonne were extraordinary (and that their resistance was exceptional) allowed the public to call for their pardon while simultaneously continuing to support industries that appropriate the bodies and lives of seemingly not-so-resistant individuals (other cows, pigs and chickens in the food system). This reflects what Francione terms our "moral schizophrenia" toward animals, whereby we can extend our moral circle to include some animals (in this case, those animals who are plucky enough to make national news with their resistance) while excluding others.

References

Blackfish. 2013. Documentary. Directed by Gabriela Cowperthwaite. US: Magnolia Pictures.

Braverman, Irus. 2013. "Animal Mobilegalities: The Regulation of Animal Movement in the American City." *Humanimalia* 5 (1): 104–35.

———. 2015. "More-than-Human Legalities." In *The Wiley Handbook of Law and Society*. Edited by Patricia Ewick and Austin Sarat, 307–21. Chichester, UK: John Wiley & Sons.
Chappell, Bill. 2011. "Yvonne, A Cow Wrapped in a Mystery Inside a Forest." *National Public Radio*. August 15. http://www.npr.org/blogs/thetwo-way/2011/08/15/139648411/yvonne-a-cow-wrapped-in-a-mystery-inside-a-forest.
Collard, Rosemary-Claire. 2012. "Cougar-Human Entanglements and the Biopolitical Un/Making of Safe Space." *Environment and Planning D: Society and Space* 30 (1): 23–42.
———. 2014. "Putting Animals Back Together, Taking Commodities Apart." *Annals of the Association of American Geographers* 104 (1): 151–65.
———. 2015. *Animal Traffic*. Durham: Duke University Press.
Collard, Rosemary-Claire and Jessica Dempsey. 2013. "Life for Sale? The Politics of Lively Commodities." *Environment and Planning A* 45 (11): 2682–99.
Collard, Rosemary-Claire and Kathryn Gillespie. 2015. "Doing Critical Animal Geographies: Future Directions." In *Critical Animal Geographies: Politics, Intersections, and Hierarchies in a Multispecies World*. Edited by Kathryn Gillespie and Rosemary-Claire Collard, 203–12. New York: Routledge.
Cresswell, Tim. 1996. *In Place/ Out of Place*. London: University of Minnesota Press.
Favre, David. 2011. "Living Property: A New Status for Animals Within the Legal System." *Marquette Law Review* 93 (3): 1021–70.
Francione, Gary. 2000. *Introduction to Animal Rights: Your Child or the Dog?* Philadelphia: Temple University Press.
———. 2004. "Animals—Property or Persons?" *Rutgers Law School: Faculty Papers*, Paper 21.
———. 2008. *Animals as Persons: Essays on the Abolition of Animal Exploitation*. New York: Columbia University Press.
Gillespie, Kathryn. 2014. "Sexualized Violence and the Gendered Commodification of the Animal Body in Pacific Northwest U.S. Dairy Production." *Gender, Place and Culture* 21 (10): 1321–37.
Haraway, Donna Jeanne. 1989. *Primate Visions: Gender, Race, and Nature in the World of Modern Science*. New York: Routledge.
Hribal, Jason. 2003. "'Animals are Part of the Working Class': A Challenge to Labor History." *Labor History* 44 (3): 435–53.
———. 2007. "Resistance is Never Futile." *Counterpunch*, April 17. http://www.counterpunch.org/2007/04/17/resistance-is-never-futile/.
———. 2010. *Fear of the Animal Planet: The Hidden History of Animal Resistance*. Petrolia and Oakland, CA: Counterpunch and AK Press.
Joy, Melanie. 2009. *Why We Love Dogs, Eat Pigs and Wear Cows: An Introduction to Carnism*. San Francisco: Conari Press.
Kirksey, Eben and Stefan Helmreich. 2010. "The Emergence of Multispecies Ethnography." *Cultural Anthropology* 25 (4): 545–76.
McFarland, Sarah and Ryan Hediger. 2009. *Animals and Agency*. Leiden, the Netherlands: Brill Academic Publisher.
Nonhuman Rights Project. 2015. "Home." http://www.nonhumanrights.org/.
Philo, Chris. 1995. "Animals, Geography and the City: Notes on Inclusions and Exclusions." *Environment and Planning D: Society and Space* 13 (6): 655–81.

Roadside America. 2014. "Emily the Cow, Vegetarian Activist." http://www.roadsideamerica.com/story/11766.

St. Clair, Jeffrey. 2010. "Prologue." In Jason Hribal, *Fear of the Animal Planet: The Hidden History of Animal Resistance*. Petrolia and Oakland, CA: Counterpunch and AK Press, 1–20.

Whatmore, Sarah. 2002. "From Farming to Agribusiness: The Global Agro-Food System." In *Geographies of Global Change*. 2nd edition. Edited by R.J. Johnston, Peter Taylor and Michael Watts, 57–67. Oxford: Blackwell.

Whatmore, Sarah, and Lorraine Thorne. 1998. "Wild(er)ness: Reconfiguring the Geographies of Wildlife." *Transactions of the Institute of British Geographers* 23 (4): 435–54.

Wilbert, Chris. 2000. "Anti-this—Against-that: Resistances Along a Human—Non-Human Axis." In *Entanglements of Power: Geographies of Domination/Resistance*. Edited by Joanne Sharp, Paul Routledge, Chris Philo and Ronan Paddison. 238–55. London: Routledge.

Wise, Steven. 1996. "The Legal Thinghood of Nonhuman Animals." http://lawdigitalcommons.bc.edu/ealr/vol23/iss3/2.

Wolfson, David. 1996. "Beyond the Law: Agribusiness and the Systemic Abuse of Animals Raised for Food or Food Production." *Lewis and Clark Animal Law* 2: 123–54.

Wolfson, David and Mariann Sullivan. 2004. "Foxes in the Hen House: Animals, Agribusiness, and the Law: A Modern American Fable." In *Animal Rights: Current Debates and New Directions*. Edited by Cass R. Sunstein and Martha C. Nussbaum, 205–33. Oxford: Oxford University Press.

Zimmerman, Tim. 2014. "First Person: How Far will the Blackfish Effect Go?" *National Geographic*. January 13. http://news.nationalgeographic.com/news/2014/01/140113-blackfish-seaworld-killer-whale-orcas/.

Chapter 7

Lively Sanctuaries: A Shabbat of *Animal Sacer*

Elan Abrell

Tony the tiger, a 14-year-old Siberian-Bengal hybrid, has spent over a decade of his life living in a cage next to US Interstate Highway 10 at the Tiger Truck Stop, a gas station in Grosse Tête, Louisiana. For the last three years, he has been the focus of an international campaign opposing his confinement. This chapter exemplifies the legal struggles currently waged in the arena of administrative law between private owners of exotic animals and the activists and animal welfare lawyers who seek to have them relocated to sanctuaries where, in the words of an animal welfare attorney with whom I spoke, "animals can live out their lives to be who they are and not have any obligations." Although much attention is paid to the questions of rights and legal personhood for other-than-human animals (e.g., Siebert 2014), these quiet battles over interpretation and enforcement of regulatory norms for the housing and care of various animal species are actively transforming the lives of individual animals and humans at local, state, and national scales. While such legal strategies eschew rights-based language for the more obtainable welfare-oriented goals of regulatory enforcement afforded by administrative law, they still often focus on animals as individuals rather than as entities within larger collective populations—an inversion of the balancing scheme employed by conservation projects (Braverman 2013, 22).

This chapter is based on two years of multispecies ethnography fieldwork conducted at multiple animal sanctuaries in Texas, Hawaii, Florida, and New York. In addition to conducting interviews with sanctuary caregivers, volunteers, and visitors as well as animal law attorneys, I collected data through participant observations as a sanctuary volunteer, observing daily practices of care and human–animal interactions at each site. Drawing on this research, I will explore the ethical and political implications of using

---

administrative law—under which animals ultimately remain within the status of property—to "save" animal individuals from conditions of confinement. Arguably, through these legal contestations, animals like Tony cross over from the realm of *zoë* to the realm of *bios*, gaining recognizably biographical and political lives (Kirksey and Helmreich 2010, 545; cf. Agamben 1998). How do those lives change as animal advocates replace one form of captivity with another? Despite the paradoxes of sanctuary life—mainly, the fact that the benefits of care necessarily come with limits on animal autonomy—this chapter argues that human and nonhuman animals form multispecies assemblages that—rather than comforming to the "given prescriptions of legality"—generate their own kinds of lively legality in which oppositions like human/animal and freedom/captivity are reconfigured (Philippopoulos-Mihalopoulos 2013, 161).

Tony

Litigation over Tony's captivity has been ongoing since April 2011, when the Animal Legal Defense Fund filed a lawsuit against the Louisiana Department of Wildlife and Fisheries. While the focus of the Animal Legal Defense Fund's legal strategy has been the administrative enforcement of permitting regulations, their goal has been to improve Tony's general quality of life by having him relocated to a "reputable, accredited sanctuary where he can live out the rest of his life in an environment that caters to his needs rather than one that exploits him as a profitable spectacle" (Liebman 2012). The Fund's website describes the conditions from which they have been hoping to save him:

> Tony is . . . frequently harassed and taunted by visitors at the truck stop. His enclosure is devoid of adequate enrichment, such as logs, trees, or complex vegetation that would allow him to engage in natural tiger behaviors. He has no pool of water large enough to allow him to submerge himself to cool off in the blazing heat of the summer. As a result of the stress of his confinement, Tony constantly paces on the hard concrete surface of his enclosure, putting him at risk for dangerous and painful veterinary conditions. . . . Year after year of living at the Tiger Truck Stop have taken their toll on Tony's health. The ambient noise from the nearby freeway and the idling trucks, their diesel engines spewing noxious fumes directly into his enclosure, is painful and obtrusive to an animal with such sensitive hearing and an acute sense of smell (Animal Legal Defense Fund 2011).

I initially came across Tony's case by chance after stopping for gas in Grosse Tête in 2011. What I witnessed of his living conditions was consistent with the Animal Legal Defense Fund's description. Cars and trucks had to drive right by his cage to access the gas pumps. The cage itself was made from metal bars, cinder blocks, and concrete. Tiger feces and piles of fly-infested, ground meat were scattered around the concrete floor, rotting in the hot and humid Louisiana weather. Gasoline fumes hung heavily in the air. Noise from the passing vehicles on the adjacent highway drowned out the shouts of children trying to catch Tony's attention as he sat in his cage, swishing his tail languorously back and forth and staring off into space. It was indeed difficult to imagine a more incongruous environment for a tiger than this small, industrialized patch of former swampland.

In their lawsuit, the Animal Legal Defense Fund argued that the Louisiana Department of Wildlife and Fisheries violated state law by granting a permit allowing Tony's owner, Michael Sandlin, to exhibit him at the Tiger Truck Stop (Animal Legal Defense Fund 2011). The Louisiana Department of Wildlife and Fisheries had enacted regulations that prohibited citizens from "keeping a tiger as a pet or exhibiting a tiger in the state" because possession of such animals "poses significant hazards to public safety and health and is detrimental to the welfare of the animals" (ibid.). However, a grandfather provision in the regulations granted an exception to individuals who legally owned large cats prior to August 15, 2006, requiring them to apply for an annual permit from the department (ibid.). Although Sandlin received one of these permits, the Animal Legal Defense Fund argued that he did not qualify for the exception since he did not have legal possession of Tony prior to the grandfathering date. They based their argument on a 1993 ordinance passed in Iberville Parish, where Tony resides, which made it "illegal for anyone to keep a tiger or other large exotic cat on his or her premises for exhibition" (ibid.). The lawsuit against the Louisiana Department of Wildlife and Fisheries thus sought the invalidation of Sandlin's permit. In November 2011, a judge ruled for the Animal Legal Defense Fund, holding that Sandlin was ineligible for a permit under the state regulations, and ordered the department "to revoke Sandlin's permit and not issue any new permits" (Liebman 2012). Sandlin appealed to the Louisiana Court of Appeal, and in 2013 this court, too, ruled in the Animal Legal Defense Fund's favor. Following this decision, Sandlin appealed to the Supreme Court of Louisiana, but the court denied his appeal.

At that point, the Louisiana State Senate passed Senate Bill 250, brought on Sandlin's behalf by Senator Rick Ward. The bill created an exemption to the 2006 state law that banned private ownership of large exotic cats for people who have continuously possessed their cats since August 15, 2006. Since no other citizens of Louisiana had continuously possessed a big cat after that date, the bill essentially created a special exemption just for Sandlin. On June 20, 2014, Governor Bobby Jindal signed the bill into law despite a major publicity campaign and petitions urging him to veto it. In the most recent turn in Tony's ongoing legal saga, on June 24, 2014, the Animal Legal Defense Fund filed a new lawsuit against Sandlin, the

State of Louisiana, and various state agencies "for violating the Louisiana Constitution by passing a law that exempts a single individual—Michael Sandlin—from existing state public safety and animal welfare laws" (Animal Legal Defense Fund 2014a). At the time of writing, this lawsuit is still pending.

Lolita

In a case similar to Tony's, animal advocates have been waging a struggle on behalf of Lolita, an orca in her mid- to late-40s who has resided at the Miami Seaquarium for 44 years. This approximately 6,000 pound, 20-foot-long whale has spent most of her life in a tank that measures 60-by-80 feet with a depth of 20 feet. She was captured in a mass whale hunt along with dozens of other whales in Penn Cove, Whidbey Island in the Puget Sound.[1] In his book *Deeper Water*, cetacean advocate Len Varley describes Lolita's life in captivity:

> Lolita arrived at Miami Seaquarium on September 24, 1970. She was kept several hundred feet from her future tank-mate orca Hugo until June 2, 1971. During that time they called to one another incessantly across the park. They performed together for 9 years, until Hugo's death, 30 years ago in 1980, after repeatedly bashing his head into the walls and windows of the pool, in what many believe to be an act of suicide after 12 years in captivity. Lolita has been alone (aside from a few dolphins) for almost 30 years, performing two shows a day for tourists. Since 1970 Lolita has resided in what is the smallest and oldest orca tank in North America (2012, 96).

Animal advocates have filed two separate lawsuits against Lolita's confinement at the Seaquarium. On August 22, 2012, the People for the Ethical Treatment of Animals (PETA) Foundation, along with the Animal Legal Defense Fund, the Orca Network, and private citizens filed a lawsuit against the United States Department of Agriculture (USDA) challenging its renewal of the Seaquarium's federal Animal Welfare Act license (Animal Legal Defense Fund 2012). The Animal Welfare Act, which the USDA is responsible for enforcing, "prohibits licensing a facility that is out of compliance with the act" (ibid.). The lawsuit argues that Lolita's confinement violates the Animal Welfare Act's mandated protection from weather and direct sunlight (her tank has none); its space requirements for orcas (her pool is 3.4 feet less than the required tank dimensions for a marine mammal her size); and its standards for housing with compatible animals (she has not been in the company of another orca since 1980 despite the fact that orcas are highly social and often maintain close familial relationships for decades in the wild; Varley 2012, 96).

That these organizations found it necessary to sue the USDA to enforce the regulations by which it is bound is indicative of why legal interventions on behalf of captive animals in the administrative arena are both possible and necessary. As PETA Foundation Director of Captive Law Enforcement Delcianna Winders observed, "It shouldn't take a lawsuit to force the USDA to stop handing out permits to the smallest orca tank on the continent" (Animal Legal Defense Fund 2012). Nonetheless, the US District Court for the Southern District of Florida dismissed the case on March 18, 2014, ruling that since Congress did not directly address license renewals when adopting the Animal Welfare Act, the USDA can "rubber-stamp" license-renewal applications (Animal Legal Defense Fund 2014b). Under this ruling, the agency can grant a permit "even if it knows that the applicant is violating the [Animal Welfare Act] and that the applicant's certification of compliance with the [act] is false" (ibid.). Animal Legal Defense Fund Executive Director Stephen Wells has argued that through this failure to administer the law, "the USDA sentences Lolita to another year of solitary confinement each time it renews Miami Seaquarium's license" (ibid.). On June 15, 2015, the United States Court of Appeals for the Eleventh Circuit affirmed the lower court's ruling.

Lolita's advocates hope to retire Lolita to a transitional coastal sanctuary sea pen in Kanaka Bay, Washington state (Clark 2014). Accordingly, the Orca Network and the Center for Whale Research have devised a detailed retirement plan:

> The primary goal of the Lolita Retirement Plan is to relocate Lolita to a rehabilitation/ retirement facility in an ocean water sea-pen in a protected cove in her native habitat in Washington State. . . . Throughout the transport and relocation, and as long as she remains in human care, she will continue to receive high quality food and medical care. The rehabilitation phase will be considered accomplished when Lolita demonstrates satisfactory metabolic strength and medical parameters, including a healthy diet, longer dive times and sustained power swims. . . . The secondary goal is to train Lolita for gradual open water exercises with progressively longer boat-follow training . . . to further build her strength to eventually approximate the physical condition of her family pod members. Control by training staff will continue to be exerted throughout this phase of the project (Center for Whale Research 1995).

Lolita's advocates acknowledge that after living in captivity for so long, Lolita may never be ready to be released back to the wild. Still, they believe these plans for an open-water net pen far larger than her current tank would be a vast improvement over her current living conditions (Welch 2014). This plan exemplifies the tension between the two predominant perspectives regarding the legal treatment of animals: animal welfare and animal rights. Whereas welfarists advocate an incremental improvement in the treatment of animals through legislation and policy reform, animal rights advocates seek an end to the instrumental use of all animals through an extension of basic rights to certain animals, especially rights to a life free from harm. Within the animal rights approach, abolitionists extend this logic even further, advocating the complete abolition of the property status of animals (Francione and Garner 2010). Mirroring the dilemma faced by Lolita's advocates, philosopher Tom Regan summarizes the difference between the rights and the welfare approach: "Empty cages, not larger cages" (Regan 2004, 78). While the ideal goal of Lolita's welfare advocates would have been the elimination of Lolita's cage altogether, her inability to survive in the wild may require them to settle for the larger cage of an open-water net pen.

Animal Sacer

What motivates these efforts to save Tony and Lolita from the deprivations of captivity is the recognition and valuing of their subjectivity as individuals and their unique qualities of liveliness (see Philippopoulos-Mihalopoulos, this volume). As Animal Legal Defense Fund's executive director Stephen Wells explains, "Freeing Tony would mean sending him to a . . . sanctuary, where he can finally have some peace in his lifetime and live like a tiger" (2014). This sentiment mirrors the motivation expressed by the animal welfare attorney quoted in the introduction—the desire to help make it possible for animals to "live out their lives to be who they are and not have any obligations" to humans.

Despite this recognition of other-than-human subjectivity by animal advocates, animals remain legal property without having rights as legal persons. As Irus Braverman notes, "courts have established that 'wild animals reduced from the wild state in compliance with applicable law become property of an individual' " (2013, 152, citing *Animal Protection, Education, and Information Foundation v. Friends of the Zoo for Springfield, Missouri, Inc.*). David Favre points out that as "living property," animals do in fact possess limited basic rights under anti-cruelty statutes, specifically the right to be free from pain and the right to have their basic sustenance needs met (Favre 2010, 1033; Gillespie in this volume examines the political and ethical problems with the "living property" concept).[2] Nonetheless, as legal theorist Maneesha Deckha observes, law as an anthropocentric institution instantiates the property status of animals: "Statutes that purport to protect animals are limited in their effect since they are founded on and interpreted through anthropocentric assumptions about animal inferiority and reside in an overall legal framework that subordinates animals through their property classification" (2013, 813). The property status of animals like Tony and

Lolita thus renders them vulnerable to the biopolitical effects of the law (see Bear and Lorimer's chapters in this volume for examinations of other legal mechanisms and processes through which animals are biopolitically governed).

Foucault theorizes biopolitics as an historical shift in modes of power, from "the ancient right to take life or let live" associated with sovereign power to the "power to foster life or disallow it to the point of death" associated with the modern state (Foucault 1978, 138). Giorgio Agamben sees more of a continuity between these two historical modes of power. He conceptualizes *homo sacer*, a human who "may be killed but not sacrificed," as the "state of exception" upon which sovereignty defines itself through the biopolitical power to determine who can be brought from the realm of *zoë*, bare life, into the realm of *bios*, political existence (1998, 8). In his book *The Open: Man and Animal*, Agamben further links this biopolitical distinction to the categories of human and animal, arguing that "the decisive political conflict, which governs every other conflict, is that between the animality and the humanity of man. That is to say, in its origin Western politics is also biopolitics" (2004, 80). The opposition between man/animal and human/inhuman, in both its modern and earlier forms, is defined by Agamben as the "anthropological machine":

> If, in the machine of the moderns, the outside is produced through the exclusion of an inside and the inhuman produced by animalizing the human, [in the earlier version] the inside is obtained through the inclusion of an outside, and the non-man is produced by the humanization of an animal: the man-ape, the enfant sauvage or Homo ferus, but also and above all the slave, the barbarian, and the foreigner, as figures of an animal in human form. Both machines are able to function only by establishing a zone of indifference at their centers, within which . . . the articulation between human and animal, man and nonman, speaking being and living being, must take place. . . . What would thus be obtained, however, is neither an animal life nor a human life, but only a life that is separated and excluded from itself—only a bare life (37–8).

Agamben's *homo sacer*, the embodiment of this bare life, is a useful theoretical lens for understanding the status of animals-as-property in the context of nonhuman animals in the United States. Though animals are protected by anti-cruelty laws, humans have the right to kill—albeit humanely—even a perfectly healthy animal as long as she is their property, with the possible exception of animals who are covered by the Endangered Species Act. Firmly in the realm of *zoë*, the animal-as-property is perhaps the ultimate embodiment of the state of exception: *animal sacer*.

Building on Agamben's understanding of biopolitics, Dinesh Wadiwel sees democratic politics as the process of admitting animal life into the political sphere (2008, 23). He argues that it is this biopolitical distinction that marks "the struggle over the definition of . . . the fully formed human subject," which is reflected in "democratic struggles over the last two hundred years: for example slaves, women, savages, queers and children" (29). The realm of *animal sacer* thus comprises the alterity that defines and makes possible the liberal subject—it is precisely what the human person is not. But while *homo sacer* has historically been a porous category from which certain groups of humans have been able to escape even as others have replaced them, the status of fully formed liberal subjects has historically remained off limits to other-than-human animals (but see Braverman, this volume, for a description of the political lives of endangered species produced through the technology of the list). Within the zone of exception at the center of the anthropological machine, bare life recursively fractures into the same man/animal, human/inhuman oppositions it produces: *homo sacer/animal sacer*. The question arises: if *homo sacer* has been porous to certain groups of humans, then could animals perhaps escape the bounds of *animal sacer*?

While the traditional legal conception of animal-as-property has and continues to treat animals as grounded in the realm of *zoë*, practices of relating to and presenting animals as individual thinking subjects with personal interests in life, rather than as generic members of a collectively suffering population, increasingly afford these animals access to the realm of *bios*. For example, Eben Kirksey, in this volume, provides an ethnographic analysis of other multispecies entanglements in which animals are gaining similar status. Such subject-making practices are reflected in the efforts of animal advocates to make legal interventions on behalf of animals like Tony and Lolita. Advocates' legal strategies employ administrative regulations in efforts to limit animals' property status enough that advocates can at least shield them from the deprivations of *animal sacer*, if not render them full legal subjects. Perhaps more importantly, advocates' efforts to relocate these animals to sanctuaries where they can have more freedom to live lives for themselves (rather than for humans) promote greater recognition of and concern with these animals as individual subjects with their own other-than-human interests (but see Gillespie, this volume, for a critique of how framing animals as victims to be rescued can also reinforce hierarchies of species ordering).

The various legal interventions described above foster an increased recognition of the animals' vulnerability and subjectivity as nonhuman individuals. Deckha sees such a recognition as an important step in changing how the law treats animals. In an illuminating analysis of Chief Justice of the Alberta Court of Appeal Catherine Fraser's dissent in the case *Reece v. Edmonton (City of)*, Deckha describes how the judge's decision contributes in a small but significant way toward such a change (2013, 793). Similar to the cases of Lolita and Tony, this case involved an effort to improve the living conditions of a 36-year-old Asian elephant named Lucy, who lived in an enclosure by herself at Edmonton's Valley Zoo. Animal advocates applied for a declaration that the City of Edmonton had "breached Alberta's Animal Protection Act" (ibid.). The majority decision of the court upheld a lower court dismissal of the application on the grounds that it "constituted an abuse of process" (794). By contrast, Judge Fraser's dissent valued Lucy "as a being in her own right rather than for her instrumental value to her owners" (813). In Judge Fraser's words:

> Animals over whom humans exercise dominion and control are a highly vulnerable group. They cannot talk—or at least in a language we can readily understand. They have no capacity to consent to what we do to them. Just as one measure of society is how it protects disadvantaged groups, so too another valid measure is how it chooses to treat the vulnerable animals that citizens own and control (*Reece* at para. 88, quoted in Deckha, 802).

In Deckha's view, Fraser represents "animals as beings made vulnerable by their property status whose lives hold value independent of their usefulness to humans" (813). Like Fraser's dissent, animal advocate interventions in the arena of administrative law foster recognition of the vulnerability and subjectivity of other-than-human animals. And through such efforts, these advocates are responding to the biopolitical power exerted over captive animals with care and compassion.

Pastoral Power

Care-based interventions take multiple and at times conflicting forms, all of which resonate with yet another form of power theorized by Foucault: pastoral power. In her book *Zooland: The Institution of Captivity*, Irus Braverman draws on this concept—which Foucault develops in his collection of lectures *Security, Territory, Population* (2009)—to analyze interrelated technologies of animal governance within zoos (Braverman 2013, 34). Specifically, Braverman focuses on three elements of pastoral power as it relates to zoos. First, as Foucault claims, "pastoral power is fundamentally a beneficent power" (Foucault 2009, 171): "In fact the essential objective of pastoral power is the salvation . . . of the flock" (172). It is for this reason that pastoral power can be understood as a power of care: "It looks after the flock, it looks after the individuals of the flock, it sees to it that the sheep do not suffer, it goes in search of those that have strayed off course, and it treats those that are injured" (ibid.). In this sense, as Braverman argues, the modern Western manifestations of zoos "as institutions that practice control through care . . . are uniquely grounded in the Western pastoral tradition that Foucault explores" (Braverman 2013, 36). The "zoo's governance of animal populations in the name of conservation, stewardship, and care"[3] is a form of power that functions as an exercise of care (35). Interestingly, when it comes to the application of this power, Foucault distinguishes between two types of actors: "The bad shepherd only thinks of good pasture for his own profit, for fattening the flock that he will be able to sell and scatter, whereas the good shepherd thinks only of his flock and of nothing else. He does not even consider his own advantage in the well-being of his flock" (Foucault 2009, 172). Seen from their perspective, accredited North American zoos fall into the latter category. Although it may be impossible to care for animals under the current regime of globalized capitalism without at least some concern for financial resources, Braverman makes it clear that for contemporary accredited zoos, their "extensive power to govern zoo animals is driven by a desire to care for and save animals" (35).

The second element of pastoral power is a power over a non-territorialized multiplicity of beings: "The shepherd's power is not exercised over a territory but, by definition, over a flock, and more exactly, over the flock in its movement from one place to another. . . . So, in contrast with the power exercised on the unity of a territory, pastoral power is exercised on a multiplicity on the move" (Foucault 2009, 171). Contemporary species management practices that often entail the transfer or loan of individual animals between various zoos reflect this element of pastoral power, which is enacted upon aterritorial, mobile populations of animals: "Much like a gigantic Noah's Ark, animals are constantly in motion—here, transferred from zoo to zoo—to conserve their population according to reproductive needs" (Braverman 2013, 37). Zoo animals are thus mobilized and de-territorialized in a double sense: they are simultaneously "dislocated from their territorial habitats" as well as "constantly on the move between institutions" (ibid.)

Finally, "pastoral power is an individualizing power" (Foucault 2009, 173). Although the shepherd directs the whole flock, Foucault argues that "he can only really direct it insofar as not a single sheep escapes him" (ibid.). The shepherd "does everything for the totality of his flock, but he does everything also for each sheep of the flock," looking "after each of them individually" (ibid.). This, however, creates a paradox for the shepherd. By simultaneously looking out for all animals and each individual animal, the shepherd creates a potential dilemma in which it may be necessary to consider the sacrifice of the whole of the flock—"since he must save each of the sheep, will he not find himself in a situation in which he has to neglect the whole of the flock in order to save a single sheep?" (ibid.).

For zoos, this pastoral paradox "manifests in the various everyday conflicts between the zoo's concerns for the individual captive animal vis-à-vis its concerns for the collective population" (Braverman 2013, 36). However, Braverman notes that in the zoo context, "it seems that zoos more readily sacrifice the individual animal for the benefit of the flock, rather than the other way around" (ibid.). She also notes that, like the lawyers and animal advocates making interventions on behalf of animals in the arena of administrative law, "animal activists . . . offer a different balancing scheme, based on the assumption that the individual animal should not be sacrificed in the name of its species" (ibid.). Foucault, she explains, "frames this contention between various groups—each claiming to be the exclusive caregiver for the animal and its only shepherd—the 'great battle of pastorship' " (ibid.; also see Foucault 2009, 149).

As the cases outlined here illustrate, there are in fact many conflagrations within the "great battle of pastorship." It is true that the animal welfare advocates attempting to help animals through administrative law interventions differ from zoos in how they perform the elements of pastoral power outlined above. These advocates also attempt to exert a beneficent power of care in the goal of salvation, and they endeavor to exert it over animals that, like zoo animals, are de-territorialized from wild habitats. Unlike zoos, however, the advocates' ultimate goal is to permanently remove these animals from "circulation" as commodities, and from the possibility of any future circulation. They wish to relocate them in one final move that will end in the sanctuary, or, in the rare cases of animals like Lolita, possibly even in their repatriation to wild habitats. Although animal welfare advocates often oppose the actions of zoos (see, for example, the cases of Lucy the elephant above, or Timmy the gorilla in Braverman 2013, 16–39; 207–9), they also may have more in common with accredited zoos than with some of the other animal owners with whom they find themselves in conflict. Since both animal welfare activists and zoos actually share the desire to help animals—even while conceptualizing their salvation quite differently—they reflect differing views of what it means to be a "good shepherd." On the other hand, institutions like the Miami Seaquarium and the Tiger Truck Stop arguably align more clearly with Foucault's "bad shepherds," who place profit above the well-being of their flocks.

The biggest difference between the sanctuary and conservation approaches to "good" pastorship, however, is in how they balance the individual and the flock in navigating the paradox of pastoral power. The type of administrative law cases described here use legal tools designed to benefit multiplicities of animals in order to benefit specific individuals. At times this may even lead to potential risk to the flock, such as the dilemma described by Braverman in the case of Timmy the gorilla, whom activists wanted to remain at the Cleveland Metroparks Zoo with his infertile companion Kate. At the same time, "concern for the collective zoo gorilla population dictated and justified the zoo's decision to move Timmy to the Bronx Zoo, with its fertile female gorillas" (2013, 37). The individualizing aspect of pastoral power is an important element in advocates' efforts to foster the recognition of the vulnerability and subjectivity of animals necessary to afford those animals access to the realm of *bios*. By valuing animals as individuals, these advocates counter the kind of "species-thinking" (Chrulew

2011) that justifies privileging the well-being of a collective species over that of its individual members. Animals' interests as individuals are thus invested with a legal weight they did not previously possess, rendering them subjects of value in their own right irrespective of their importance to the preservation of their species. Although not necessarily contributing to (or potentially even disrupting) species protection goals, this individualizing aspect helps animals gain the sort of political lives that allow them to move beyond the category of *animal sacer*, even while, legally, remaining property.

The Sanctuary Paradox

As many advocates have realized, sanctuaries are not a solution to the problems of captivity. Feminist philosopher and ethicist Lori Gruen describes captivity as "a condition in which a being is confined and controlled and is reliant on those in control to satisfy her basic needs"[4] (2011, 133). Sanctuaries, although ideally focused on meeting the needs of the animals in their care, still fit this definition of captivity. As Gruen notes, the "goals of true sanctuaries are to rehabilitate abused animals, nurture orphaned animals, provide companionship and enriched environments in which animals can express species-typical behavior, and to respect each animal" (159), but sometimes expressing species-typical behavior conflicts with the other goals of the sanctuary. For example, sanctuaries are usually opposed to breeding. The idea behind this is that allowing captive breeding would subject future generations of animals to the same restrictions on their freedom that their parents already face (160). Gruen observes:

> [T]he freedom to reproduce and to care for young is central in the development of important affiliative social skills that are necessary to build meaningful binds with conspecifics and to enhance group stability. Denying captive animals the possibility to reproduce strips them of the chance to engage fully in species-typical behaviors, and this is particularly detrimental to females who are, in most species, primarily responsible for rearing young. Having infants born in captivity allows individuals to experience a full range of social relations, and it serves as enrichment for captive groups. Yet, allowing captive breeding perpetuates the wrongs that captivity poses (ibid.).

Consider Tony the tiger. Typical behavior for a tiger would include the hunting, killing, and eating of prey. Even if Tony could be afforded a large enough space to hunt prey, and even if he could learn how to do it after a lifetime living by himself in a small cage, it would be necessary to provide him with other live animals whose own vulnerability and subjective interests would, under the principles being applied to Tony, demand equal consideration to his.[5] This concern with freedom and species-typical behavior also

Figure 7.1 A captive macaque at the Buffalo Zoo. Photo by Ariel Braverman, July 8, 2015. Used with permission.

leads to broader questions about animal agency (for divergent perspectives on nonhuman agency see Gillespie and Philippopoulos-Mihalopoulos, this volume).

Miriam Jones, cofounder of VINE Animal Sanctuary, a farmed animal sanctuary in Vermont, directly addresses the problem of freedom in the sanctuary setting. Humans at VINE use the term "as free as possible" to describe the conditions of the animals who live there, "as fences, enforced routines, involuntary medical procedures and regimes (including everything from forced sterilization to forced feeding), and other impositions certainly do not comprise a free state of being for those on the receiving end" (2014, 91). Such choices regarding care in the sanctuary setting are made, however, with the understanding that humans "live in a world that requires the rescue of members of certain species because other members of our own species will hurt and kill them if we don't" and that for many of those animals, "survival on their own is an impossible goal" (92). Thus, Jones explains, "we do what we need to do, as ethically as possible, within the context of that reality" (ibid.). This understanding is common among many sanctuary workers I've interviewed. As one caretaker at an exotic sanctuary where several monkeys lived told me: "There is no cage in the world big enough for a monkey (see Figure 7.1 for illustration), but they can't survive on their own. And as long they have to live here, we're going to give them as big and nice a space as we can." In other words, as long as sanctuaries are the best living conditions humans can offer such animals, they will continue to be subjected to the power of care exercised by humans.

Conclusion: "Shabbat of Animal and Man"

Describing the pastoral battle between "the two groups that claim to be the sole expert authorities on the captive animal's well-being: zoo people and animal protection activists," Braverman states that this war can be boiled down to the following questions: Who cares more, and more properly, about animals? Who is the better pastor?" (2013, 203; 38). In examining administrative interventions on behalf of animals (and their ultimate goal of relocating these animals to sanctuaries), I would like to offer a more specific variation on these questions: As good shepherds, how can activists help animals in captivity gain access to the best conditions under which they can live lives for themselves in accordance with their unique qualities of liveliness and free from the instrumentalization of humans, if not completely free of the bounds of captivity? As many sanctuary advocates see it, one important part of the answer is fostering a greater recognition of and concern for animals as vulnerable, relational subjects rather than as *animal sacer*.

If "good shepherds" wish to truly move beyond an anthropocentric legal relationship with animals (and if such a goal is even possible), they must confront a final paradox. In addition to sacrificing the flock for the individual, Foucault also claims that another "form taken by the paradox of the shepherd is the problem of the sacrifice of the shepherd for his flock" (2009, 173). Foucault meant that the shepherd's dedication to care is so absolute that even self-sacrifice is possible in service to the flock. If we follow the logic of pastoralism to its endpoint—assuming that sanctuary institutions operate as shepherds—it could result in the abolition of sanctuaries. Indeed, if the ideal goal for sanctuaries is the complete liberation of animals, then might they, as "good shepherds," need to ultimately sacrifice themselves? To be truly free, must animals be liberated from all forms of control, including the power of care?[6]

As outlined above, pastoral governance in perpetuity must be weighed here against its stark alternative: the withholding of such interventions, as some abolitionists and other animal rights proponents would advocate, even if refraining from providing care or otherwise interacting with these animals ultimately results in their deaths. Many sanctuary activists are acutely aware of the concerns underlying these questions. In the words of one sanctuary founder, "My ultimate goal is for this place not to exist." "But," she adds, "until the world changes, it has to" (see Braveman 2015 for a similar perspective on the necessity of intense conservation management). Aside from the current impossibility of an absolute freedom that would not lead to death for these animals, these questions also assume the same totalizing scheme of human–animal incommensurability at the heart of Agamben's anthropological machine—namely, of two opposing sides, whereby one must be sacrificed for the other to thrive.

In his reading of the literal pastoral relationship between shepherds and their flocks in Valentina de Marchi's 2009 ethnography *Hunger for Grass*, Andreas Philippopoulos-Mihalopoulos presents an alternative to this bifurcated approach. Rather than the unbridgeable divide between human and animal produced by the anthropological machine, the flock–shepherd relationship is an assemblage: the shepherd "becomes his beast more and more, never totally one or the other, and his becoming never following one or the other direction only. The sheep becomes human as much as the human becomes sheep" (2013, 162). This becoming generates its own animal law, "a law that does not subscribe to the given prescriptions of legality, but withdraws from it, creating its own atmosphere of legality" (161).

Human and nonhuman animals in sanctuaries form similar multispecies assemblages through which they share intersubjective experiences with each other, generating their own atmospheres of animal legality in which oppositions between human/animal, freedom/captivity, care/control, and subject/property are both challenged and reconfigured. These alternate zones of exception in which animals *do* have political lives disrupt the operations of the anthropological machine, achieving a temporary "suspension of the suspension, Shabbat of both animal and man" (Agamben 2004, 151).

Achieving a broader, permanent suspension may not be possible at this particular historical moment. Until it is, however, humans can continue to work toward a sociolegal system in which other animals' vulnerability and relational subjectivity are valued in ways that make treating them as *animal sacer* impossible.

Acknowledgments

I am grateful to my fellow participants in the *More-than-Human Legalities* workshop at the Baldy Center for Law & Social Policy as well as my fellow participants in the 2014 ASI-WAS Human-Animal Studies fellowship for sharing their helpful insights on the ideas explored here. This material is based upon work supported by the National Science Foundation under Grant Number 1322203. Any opinions, findings, and conclusions or recommendations expressed in this material are those of the author and do not necessarily reflect the views of the National Science Foundation.

Notes

1 "At least 13 members of her family were killed during the brutal captures" (Varley 2012, 95–6). The violence of these operations, sometimes entailing the use of explosives to herd mothers and their young into position for capture, is vividly described by a tearful hunt participant in the film *Blackfish* (2013).
2 This does not apply to wild animals, or *ferae naturae*, to whom nobody has a legal obligation to provide basic sustenance.
3 Braverman sketches the historical development of zoos as they transformed from exhibitionary institutions to educational institutions and finally to conservation-oriented institutions (2013, 40–65).
4 Gruen clarifies that this definition fits "normally functioning adult beings" such as people incarcerated in prisons, but dependent children, for example, would not generally be thought of as captives (Gruen 2011, 133–4).
5 Of course, a similar ethical dilemma arises in feeding Tony meat from slaughtered animals, whose interests were of equal importance. This is a dilemma that any sanctuary housing carnivores must contend with, while balancing the interests between two live animals in the sanctuary raises even more direct challenges to the exercise of pastoral power in the sanctuary.
6 This question follows from the premise that animals want to be free and that this would be the ideal conditions for them, which is the assumption of many animal rights advocates, but not of many conservation advocates (see Braverman 2015).

References

Agamben, Giorgio. 1998. *Homo Sacer: Sovereign Power and Bare Life.* Translated by Daniel Heller-Roazen. Stanford: Stanford University Press.

——. 2004. *The Open: Man and Animal.* Translated by Kevin Attell. Stanford: Stanford University Press.

Animal Legal Defense Fund. 2011. "ALDF Files Suit to Free Tony the Truck Stop Tiger." *Animal Legal Defense Fund*. http://aldf.org/press-room/press-releases/aldf-files-suit-to-free-tony-the-truck-stop-tiger/.

———. 2012. "ALDF, PETA Sue USDA For Renewing Miami Seaquarium's Federal License." *Animal Legal Defense Fund*. http://aldf.org/press-room/press-releases/aldf-peta-sue-usda-for-renewing-miami-seaquariums-federal-license/.

———. 2014a. "Tony, the Truck Stop Tiger Update." *Animal Legal Defense Fund*. http://aldf.org/cases-campaigns/features/tony-the-truck-stop-tiger/.

———. 2014b. "Judge's Refusal to Review Seaquarium's Violations of Law Prompts Court Appeal." *Animal Legal Defense Fund*. http://aldf.org/press-room/press-releases/judges-refusal-to-review-seaquariums-violations-of-law-prompts-court-appeal/.

Animal Protection, Education, and Information Foundation v. Friends of the Zoo for Springfield, Missouri, Inc., 891 S.W.2d 177 (Mo. Ct. App. 1995).

Blackfish. 2013. Documentary. Directed by Gabriela Cowperthwaite. US: Magnolia Pictures.

Braverman, Irus. 2013. *Zooland: The Institution of Captivity*. Stanford: Stanford University Press.

———. 2015. *Wild Life: The Institution of Nature*. Stanford: Stanford University Press.

Center for Whale Research. 1995. "Proposal to Retire the Orca Known as Lolita to Her Native Habitat in the Pacific Northwest." *Orca Network*. http://www.orcanetwork.org/Main/index.php?categories_file=Retirement.

Chrulew, Matthew. 2011. "Managing Love and Death at the Zoo: The Biopolitics of Endangered Species Preservation." *Australian Humanities Review* 50. http://www.australianhumanitiesreview.org/archive/Issue-May-2011/chrulew.html.

Clark, Cammy. 2014. "Killer Whale Activists Try Again to Free Lolita after 43 Years at Miami Seaquarium. *Miami Herald*. February 1. http://www.miamiherald.com/2014/02/01/3907229/killer-whale-activists-try-again.html.

Decka, Maneesha. 2013. "Initiating a Non-Anthropocentric Jurisprudence: The Rule of Law and Animal Vulnerability Under a Property Paradigm." *Alberta Law Review* 50 (4): 783–814.

Favre, David. 2010. "Living Property: A New Status for Animals Within the Legal System." *Marquette Law Review* 93 (3): 1021–71.

Foucault, Michel. 1978. *The History of Sexuality, Volume I: An Introduction*. Translated by Robert Hurley. New York: Vintage Books.

———. 2009. *Security, Territory Population: Lectures at the Collège de France, 1977–78*. Edited by Michel Senellart. Translated by Graham Burchell. New York: Picador/Palgrave Macmillan.

Francione, Gary and Robert Garner. 2010. *The Animal Rights Debate: Abolition or Regulation*. New York, NY: Columbia University Press.

Gruen, Lori. 2011. *Ethics and Animals: An Introduction*. Cambridge: Cambridge University Press.

Jones, Miriam. 2014. "Captivity in the Context of a Sanctuary for Formerly Farmed Animals." In *The Ethics of Captivity*. Edited by Lori Gruen, 90–101. Oxford: Oxford University Press.

Kirksey, Eben and Stefan Helmreich. 2010. "The Emergence of Multispecies Ethnography." *Cultural Anthropology* 24 (4): 545–76.

Liebman, Matthew. 2012. "Making Sense of the Current Status of the Tony the Tiger Cases." *Animal Legal Defense Fund.* http://aldf.org/blog/making-sense-of-the-current-status-of-the-tony-the-tiger-cases/.

Philippopoulos-Mihalopoulos, Andreas. 2013. "The Normativity of an Animal Atmosphere." In *Law and the Question of the Animal: A Critical Jurisprudence.* Edited by Yoriko Otomo and Ed Mussawir, 149–64. New York: Routledge.

Reece v. Edmonton (City of). 2011. ABCA 238 (CanLII).

Regan, Tom. 2004. *Empty Cages: Facing the Challenge of Animal Rights.* Oxford: Rowman and Littlefield Publishers, Inc.

Siebert, Charles. 2014. "Should a Chimp Be Able to Sue Its Owner?" *New York Times Magazine.* April 27. http://www.nytimes.com/2014/04/27/magazine/the-rights-of-man-and-beast.html.

Varley, Len. 2012. *Deeper Water.* Bloomington, IN: Balboa Press.

Wadiwel, Dinesh. 2008. "Three Fragments from a Biopolitical History of Animals: Questions of Body, Soul, and the Body Politic in Homer, Plato, and Aristotle." *Journal for Critical Animal Studies* 7 (1): 17–31.

Welch, Craig. 2014. "Feds Want Endangered Status for Captive Orca Lolita." *The Seattle Times.* January 24. http://seattletimes.com/html/localnews/2022749958_lolitaxml.html.

Wells, Stephen. 2014. "Legally Brief: ALDF's Case to Free Tony the Tiger." http://aldf.org/blog/legally-brief-aldfs-case-to-free-tony-the-tiger/.

Chapter 8

Multispecies Families, Capitalism, and the Law

Eben Kirksey

Consumer values ascribing worth to novelty result in the importation of several million animals each year to the United States (Herrel and van der Meijden 2014, 106). The spirit of capital and the popular desire for the exotic have together generated *laissez-faire* policies in Florida, a state that has become home to over 500 species of "introduced" animals and 1,180 kinds of "alien" plants. In Florida, exotic animals generally stand not "before the law," as Cary Wolfe has it (2013, 9–10) but *beside the law* in the moral milieu of the human home. Multispecies families, with diverse kinds of critters regarding each other as kin, have formed amid the play of capitalism and the law. These households often involve queer sensibilities, in the sense that they are often based on relationships involving choice and love, rather than fixed relations of biological descent. According to Kath Weston's book *Families We Choose*, biological ties are often decentered in gay and lesbian notions of kinship (Weston 1991, 25–6). However, choice in multispecies families is typically asymmetrical, with humans keeping other species in conditions of captivity. Within human households, exotic pets are less regarded as "co-citizens," but treated as liminal beings who can suddenly be demoted to the status of commodities or things (Shir-Vertesh 2012). Even still, critters that are folded into human families often choose to reciprocate by returning the love, affection, and social advances of other household members.

Influential environmental organizations that advocate for more regulation of the wildlife trade largely focus on the relationship between capitalism and death. Under pictures of tiger rugs and elephant skulls, a WWF webpage reports: "Illegal wildlife trade is driven by high profit margins and, in many cases, the high prices paid for rare species. Vulnerable wild animals are pushed further to the edge of extinction when nature can't replenish

---

Many kinds of birds, like macaws, readily form social bonds with humans. Credit: Nachosuch, Thinkstock.

their stocks to keep up with the rate of human consumption" (World Wildlife Fund n.d.). Making similar critical observations, Nicole Shukin argues that global capitalist markets "fetishize animal alterity" and keep creatures in a perennially undead state of "interminable survival" (2009, 225–6). Exploring the marketplace for exotic life within Florida, an economic sphere focused on homegrown animals rather than wild-caught creatures, I studied the political economy of life and death as an ethnographer. While international wildlife trade networks generated mass-death, and indeed even pushed some species toward the brink of extinction, other articulations of capital and life generated promising futures. Committed breeders, often working out of their own homes, generated capital while animating rare forms of life—giving intergenerational gifts to species they loved.[1]

While interviewing people who have formed multispecies families in Florida and other parts of the United States, I found a large network of people caring for tropical birds, endangered frogs, venomous snakes, and lizards in their own homes. Providing entertainment, love, and affection for these animals involves difficult daily labor. Specialized shelters, veterinary care, and food can also prove costly. Some people are committed to care for exotic animals in their own homes even though they are unlikely to get any economic returns on the time and money they devote to their animals. Others are using their multispecies households to generate what Donna Haraway calls *lively capital*—a force that produces hopeful coalescences where "commerce and consciousness, evolution and bioengineering, and ethics and utilities are all at play" (2008, 45–7). A multitude of entrepreneurs are channeling their love and passion for particular species into moneymaking ventures. Spectacular life forms are multiplying in garages, studios, and basements—producing emergent ecological communities within human dominated landscapes (see also Kirksey 2015).

Non-Native Amnesty Day

Florida's permissive laws enable ordinary citizens to bring a diversity of creatures into their familial spheres, provided that adequate documentation is provided about caging and wildlife care experience. Cassowaries (genus *Casuarius*), giraffes and okapi (family Giraffidae), proboscis monkeys (genus *Nasalis*), and wolverines (*Gulo gulo*) are all listed as requiring Class II permits as creatures that pose "some danger to humans." Cheetahs (*Acinonyx jabatus*), komodo dragons (*Varanus komodoensis*), rhinoceros (family Rhinocerotidae), and gorillas (genus *Gorilla*) cannot be kept as pets and established zoos must obtain Class I permits since they "pose a significant danger to people" (My FWC n.d.). Breeding, selling, or keeping other kinds of wildlife, like frogs, snakes, turtles, exotic birds, spider monkeys, capuchin monkeys, and woolly monkeys only requires that applicants be at least 16 years old and apply for a 50 dollar Class III permit. Keeping primates requires more paperwork: two letters of reference, only one of which can be from a relative. "We allow just about anything as a pet as long as the owner obtains a proper license and proper cages," said Jenny Novak, a biologist who was the Exotic Species Special Projects Leader for Florida's Fish and Wildlife Conservation Commission. "Our agency is not against exotic animals. We support responsible ownership. And we are simply not going to spend billions to kill everything that escapes."

Although permits can be obtained through a straightforward process, many people in Florida told me that they do not bother with this bureaucracy after acquiring animals through quasi-legal networks (flea markets, friends, or the internet), or buying them illegally on the black market. Captain Linda Harrison, a senior officer with the Florida's Fish and Wildlife Commission in Tallahassee, told me about how she once worked as a rookie inspector in the Miami airport, screening incoming shipments. Every day, all year round, crates of wildlife came into Miami that were the size of her desk. Captain Harrison remembers one shipment in particular with nothing but hundreds of tiny little chameleons, each packed in a toilet paper roll. Seeing the volume of imports made her wonder about the countries where these animals were coming from and about the impact of the pet trade on wild animal populations. But, she said, these countries were outside her jurisdiction. Captain Harrison also told me "war stories" from her beat as an officer tasked with visiting squalid roadside zoos and backyard animal menageries that had fallen into disrepair. These stories revealed that she was making careful calculations about how to apply the law in situations where the rights of property owners were at odds with ethical and political concerns of the state. Captain Harrison was acutely aware that making new laws, or applying statues already on the books, can have unintended consequences. "We don't want to see exotic wildlife banned," she told me, explaining: "banning the pet trade would push everything underground." When a law was passed in Florida banning the sale of Burmese pythons, for instance, people began abandoning pythons and boas on roadsides by the hundreds.

In 2006, the State of Florida started an amnesty program for illegal alien animals. Officials wanted to protect animal welfare and reduce the frequency of exotic pet releases into the wild. Rather than attempt to eradicate all alien animals, Florida state officials made creative use of their sovereign authority. Rather than simply render exotic organisms killable, state agents began working to foster continuity of care for non-native animals who have been orphaned by economic systems. "The Exotic Pet Amnesty event gives people with unlicensed animals, or even something like a tiger acquired on the black market, the opportunity to surrender their animals with no questions asked," said Jenny Novak, who organized this event for many years. A frequently asked question on Florida's Amnesty Day website is: "What will happen to my pet if I surrender it?" The website, in response, assures potential donors that healthy pets will not be euthanized. The program promises to place all animals in the hands of capable "pre-qualified adopters" with specialized knowledge of birds, amphibians, or reptiles (My FWC n.d.b.).

Gatorland, near Disney World in Orlando, hosted an Amnesty Day in May 2012. Many of the participants seemed to be relieved to give up their pets, and told stories about changing family circumstances. One grandmother handed in two obese sugar gliders, marsupials from New Guinea that can fly through the air. She could no longer afford to pay for their PediaSure vitamins and no longer had the energy to clean their cages. These two animals had been left behind by her daughter-in-law 11 years ago. Other animals were handed in because their temperaments did not fit with the rest of the household. A mother abandoned a green iguana because it liked to bite. A reporter with the *Tampa Bay Times* described one family that decided to not give up their pet at the last minute: "At the edge of the parking lot, a woman stood surrounded by her husband and three children, cradling a sand-colored bearded dragon. She kept shaking her head. She wasn't ready to get in that line. Not yet. She stroked the reptile's spiky head, tears trickling beneath her sunglasses" (DeGregory 2012). Despite such intense feelings of attachment, by mid-2014 the Exotic Pet Amnesty Program had found new homes for a total of 1,947 animals (My FWC n.d.c.).

Animals that have been acquired from illegal wildlife smuggling rings, or that "retire" after spending a lifetime on display in a zoo or circus, are also sometimes placed in homes through the amnesty program. These animals often need physical and mental rehabilitation as they move to new circumstances of captivity with greater freedoms. Providing entertainment, love, and affection for orphaned animals involves difficult daily labor (Collard 2014, 152–3). While programs for rehabilitating native animals are often oriented toward preparing them for release into the wild, the creatures that feature in Florida's Exotic Pet Amnesty program are destined to live forever within human households. The home economics of multispecies families in Florida are calculated against the backdrop of fickle market forces. High unemployment and low property values following the 2008 housing market crash have led many entrepreneurs to breed animals and trade them through informal economic networks. Flexible strategies for accumulating and selling valuable animals have helped countless Floridians adapt to sweeping changes in political and economic landscapes. Garages, studios, and basements have become makeshift laboratories where hobbyists conduct Do-It-Yourself (DIY) breeding experiments with their multispecies families—using Mendel's principles of genetics and emergent DNA testing technologies to create new forms of life. I began to explore multispecies family values as household members were swept up in moneymaking dreams and schemes (see also Cheah 1999; Shukin 2009).

Designer Babies

After meeting people who participated in the Exotic Pet Amnesty events, I followed them back to breeding facilities in their own homes. Caroline Elliot, a retiree who lives in the Orlando area, walked away with a blue and yellow macaw worth around 2,000 dollars from an Amnesty Day event in Tampa.[2] Ever since, Caroline has been calling up Florida's exotic pet rescue hotline every few months, asking: "Got anything for me?" When I visited Orlando in April 2009, Caroline introduced me to her "babies," birds who live in a makeshift aviary on the back porch of her double-wide mobile home in assorted cages strewn through her backyard amidst a collection of salvaged lawnmowers, motorcycles, and golf carts. One of her favorite babies, Maui, a Hahns macaw (*Diopsittaca nobilis*), readily engages in mimetic play.

Caroline: Maui, Wanna grape?
Maui: Kuluroraow
Caroline: No, not cold, it's warm out.
Wanna: sing like Nanna? Sing! Ah, ah, a a aaaah! Sing Maui."
Maui: Kuluroraow
Caroline: Nah.
Maui: Ah ah, a a aaaah! Wanna apple?
Caroline: [Laughs] Give Nanna a kiss.

After kissing Maui, Caroline explained that birds learn to make a little noise when we pucker, "Mwah," since they carefully listen to people. "Right before they get to your mouth, they'll open their beak and just kind of push your lip," she explained.

Caroline and Maui arguably share a social sphere, a bubble of happiness. Friends and family call her the "bird whisperer" because of her ability to work with animals who others regard as mean or intractable. Since injuring her back and being forced into early retirement, Caroline has sustained her household by buying, breeding, and selling birds. Part of her work involves scouring flea markets and Craigslist for animals who are available for below-market prices or for free to a good home. Caroline works with animals who like to bite, teaching them how to be members of human households—with appreciation for human rules about politeness, touch, regard, and response. By transforming her "babies" into social beings, who are attentive to human needs and desires, she adds to their value as commodities on the open market. Caroline routinely sells these family members on the internet.

Some bird species are more flexible as "persons" than others. The notion of *flexible personhood* refers to how animals are often temporarily incorporated into the familial sphere, folded into relationships involving love and care, only to be abandoned amid major life changes. Dafna Shir-Vertesh, who studies human–dog relationships in Israel, coined this term to understand how animals are shuttled among moral spheres where they enjoy different rights and privileges. Pets are often loved, incorporated into human lives, and addressed with kinship terms. But they can be demoted at any moment, moved outside the home and the family, as household income or personal circumstances shift (see also Herzog 2010; Mullin 1999). "Particularly the birth of a human child," writes Shir-Vertesh, "challenges the pet-as-baby human–animal bond and may render void the animal's loving presence as prechild, semichild, or child substitute" (2012, 425).

As I talked with Caroline, someone who decided to never have human children, it became clear that strong affective attachments with some of her babies granted them long-term rights and privileges in her household. While Caroline described her practices of buying and selling family members on the internet, a small bird—an Australian budgie named Peeps—flew out of nowhere and landed on her hand. As Caroline continued to gush about her favorite babies, I considered the serious possibility that she was simply making anthropocentric projections by addressing nonhuman animals as kin. Studies of kinship by anthropologists have historically projected ethnocentric and Eurocentric assumptions onto the social life of others in Asia, Africa, and the Americas (Franklin 2001, 305). As Peeps and Caroline playfully interacted—as he lightly pecked at her fingernails and rapidly rubbed his tail feathers over the knuckle of her thumb—I suddenly realized that this small bird was projecting his species' norms about sociability and sexuality onto a human. When Peeps finished and fluttered off he left a small droplet of semen on Caroline's hand. Wiping her hands on a nearby towel, letting this kinky moment pass without comment, Caroline did not miss a beat and continued to tell me about her flexible strategies for accumulating and selling birds.

Later I found an online discussion group, www.parrotforums.com, where users were swapping tales about the proclivity of their birds to mate with humans. "Last night Bullwinkle (a rescued rose-breasted cockatoo) sat on me and started to rub himself on my arm," wrote Rocky, a user in Pennsylvania. "Then he started swishing his tale back and forth and really humping with his wings open! He started panting and my sleeve was wet! I didn't even know parrots did this, especially not this time of year. Is there anything I can do??" Revealing his own queer attachments with birds, and asserting that parrots should be able to choose their own multispecies families, another user described a female African grey parrot who became attached to his human friend, a person named Mary: "She just loved Mary from the minute she met her, which is why I gave her away. It was a match made in heaven. Birds really don't care if you are male or female."[3]

Thom van Dooren has written about the ethics of imprinting—a psychological process of attachment to a parent that happens early in the life of many birds and some mammals. "Imprinting is not like many other human–bird interactions," writes van Dooren. "It is not about the formation of a relationship between two subjects, who—however unequally positioned—already have a significantly well-formed way of life, a way of being in the world produced through particular biosocial inheritances and individual experiences. Rather, imprinting enters into and disrupts some of these modes of inheritance, taking advantage of an ontological openness to produce an altered way of life (2014, 101–2). The species being of macaws, budgies, and parrots has been altered, or *torqued*, by people like Caroline who are avian aficionados (cf. Bowker and Star 1999, 27). These birds are effectively twisted into a mode of sociability that is friendly to humans. But the flip side is also true: Caroline's own existence has also been torqued by the multitude of birds in her care, who make daily demands on her time and money. Despite the asymmetrical structure of Caroline's multispecies family, I found ample evidence of happy interactions characterized by kinky sex, improvisation, and play (cf. Clifford 1997, 204; Haraway 2008, 134).

Caroline also introduced me to Dale, a rubino bourke, who is one of her other friendliest babies. As Dale flew around the back porch, comfortably perching on my shoulder, Caroline revealed that some of her improvisation and play involved tinkering with the genetic building blocks of life. "Dale is a good boy. But, birds like him don't exist in the wild—bourkes are normally all blue, not like this rubino's striking red and yellow." Caroline showed me the Bourke Genetic Calculator, an online tool for do-it- ourself (DIY) geneticists, which features a photographic "Mutation Gallery" illustrating the effects of different dominant and recessive genes. The calculator enables users to enter the genetic characteristics of the parents—like the recessive genes *cin* for cinnamon, or *fd* for faded, as well as dominant genes like *V* for violet, or *D* for dark. After entering in the genetic information for the breeding pair, the calculate button predicts what the designer baby will look like. Caroline showed me the pedigrees, which looked like human family trees, that she uses to keep track of these dominant and recessive genes. Following time-tested principals of Mendelian genetics, Caroline knows that if she seeks babies with a certain trait—like *cin* for cinnamon—she needs to breed two adults who both carry the recessive version of the gene.[4]

Makeshift family laboratories have been created beyond the reach of human legal institutions. But purists in the pet trade are worried that tinkerers like Caroline are violating the laws of nature. At the same time that Caroline appeals to claims of authority with direct access to the science of genetics, some of her breeding experiments are also undermining the authority of taxonomic scientists (cf. Marks 2001, 335). Caroline told me about her intention to cross a nanday conure with a sun conure to produce a hybrid: a creature called a Sunday conure in the pet trade (*Aratinga nenday* x *Aratinga solstitialis*). These breeding experiments are taking place largely outside formal legal frameworks. Indeed, norms about mating members of different species are only informally policed in the marketplace—where private pet owners and dealers discuss the merits of buying and selling "hybrids" and "wild types" on internet forums, at flea markets, and in commercial establishments.

While some people in online avian chat rooms defend the sanctity of species boundaries, colorful hybrids continue to fetch top dollars in a speculative economy that values novel and rare forms of life. Caroline takes pleasure in her power to confuse certain species boundaries, while also making arguments for responsibly maintaining other distinctions.[5] Ethical commitments centered on the welfare of individual animals, rather than an absolute defense of all predetermined species boundaries, guide Caroline as she pairs her babies together. Caroline's story of rescuing April, a hybrid pairing of a sun conure and a peach-fronted conure (*Aratinga solstitialis* x *Aratinga aurea*), illustrates the embodied problems that emerge when certain species boundaries are irresponsibly crossed. "The guy who gave me April said that the parents pushed her out of the nest and messed up her hip. But, I found out through investigation on google that almost all of the sun/peach-fronted hybrids come out with that same hip deformity. It's a genetic thing." Caroline would never try to repeat such a mistake. While no formal laws govern her DIY genetic experiments, she would never deliberately create a bird with known genetic problems.

As I experienced the full tour of Caroline's double-wide mobile home, I noted that some species of birds—the macaws, African greys, bourkes, and conures—were more flexible, as persons, than others. Some individual birds—like Maui, with her ready ability to mimic human speech and respond socially to cues—were simply more personable than others. To play with my own queer jargon, these animals were social amphibians, able to intra-act with other beings in multiple worlds (Kirksey 2015; Barad 2014). By comparison, her gouldian finches, diamond doves, parakeets, and cockatiels were less easily socialized—less attentive to Caroline's desires for touch, interaction, response, and regard. Caroline told me that she is attached to some of her babies more than others. Even so, in tough economic times, she could not always ignore the exchange value of some of her most treasured loved ones. She cried when she told me about selling Randy, a 5,000 dollar talking Catalina macaw, to pay an overdue medical bill. Many other bird enthusiasts whom I interviewed in Florida shared similar sentiments—they were attached to the animals and saw them as part of their family. Their own feelings of well-being had become contingent on the well-being of the creatures in their care. When circumstances beyond their control resulted in the death of a loved bird, their care takers often experience intense emotional distress (cf. Berlant 2011, 48). Some pet owners, who we not involved in breeding, expressed horror at the thought of selling their flighty companions on the open market. Still, everyone I talked with understood that the nonhuman animals in their families could become vulnerable if major life events suddenly impacted the humans in the household. With a death, a divorce, a lost job, or a child headed for college, the status of prized birds could suddenly be demoted—presenting an opportunity for someone like Caroline who was always on the lookout for valuable orphans.

Happy Bubbles

While some kinds of birds can be flexibly incorporated into human families, like the dogs Shir-Vertesh describes in Israel, other kinds of critters in Florida resist attempts to make them into persons. Issues of legal personhood have been explored by Colin Dayan, who considers how beings and things are transformed as they are shuttled between categories—bearing the status of rights-bearing subjects or as property. "Only with dogs before us and beside us can we understand the making or unmaking of the idea of persons," argues Dayan. "At what point are dogs legally recognizable," she asks, "and when do they cease to count?" (Dayan 2011, 209; 213). As I ventured further into the realm of diverse multispecies families, I became convinced that personhood (or lack thereof) is better understood with the figure of another animal: the snake. While many bird species share social characteristics that readily correspond with panhuman, panprimate, and panmammalian tendencies (cf. Siskind 1978, 860), snakes are not usually personable. Affects often also quickly oscillate around snakes—high excitement about an exotic and potentially dangerous animal can rapidly turn into fear and anxiety with a lightning-fast strike. Snakes living in multispecies families can suddenly become vulnerable, when explosive affects generate sudden state changes (cf. Parrenas 2012; Shir-Vertesh 2012). When a snake bites a human, the animal risks being destroyed.

Zeb Carruthers, a snake enthusiast who got his start with pit vipers, told me that his wife forced him to make a difficult choice when his son was born: either get rid of the venomous snakes, or lose her and the baby.[6] Certain animals, his wife vehemently maintained, are not good for people to live with.[7] After selling his pit vipers, Zeb gradually convinced his wife to accept another species of snake in the house: *Chondropython viridis*, or chondros, for short.[8] But, these new snakes also had problems assimilating to his family. This time, the problem was the snakes, rather than Zeb's wife. The chondros often became agitated when Zeb entered their room, sometimes striking out and hitting the glass of their enclosures. More importantly, these snakes defied Zeb in one of the only real ways open to them: they lost their will to live. After they gradually stopped eating, Zeb's three chondros—each worth 300 dollars – died, one after the other.

Chondros are known to be persnickety eaters. A book by Greg Maxwell, *The Complete Chondro Python*, describes a technique for forcing these snakes to eat, which he euphemistically calls "assist feeding." This involves taking a dead baby mouse or rat (called a "pinkie"), moistening it with water, and then forcing it down the snake's throat. After grabbing the snake by the back of the head the pinkie is pushed into its mouth with a pair of blunt-tipped steel forceps. "Carefully push [the pinkie] past the rear jaw line and into the throat," Maxwell advises. If the snake spits the pinkie out, then the process begins again. "I have a rule when I assist-feed: 'Greg always wins.' Babies hate being assist fed and will resist vigorously" (2005, 4762). Making these unhappy animals live, Greg Maxwell has learned to apply Michel Foucault's core principals of biopolitics—using power over life to deny the right of death (Foucault 1984). "Capturing, restraining, and forcing food down their gullets does expose them to risk of damage," Maxwell continues, but "I assist-feed to save them" (Maxwell 2005, 4739–73). Incidentally, chondros are very valuable on the open market, and so their death is also a financial loss. Indeed these snakes that are made to live have added value because they are very difficult to raise.

At the Daytona Beach National Reptile Breeders' Expo, one of the largest and oldest gatherings of its kind hosted annually in Florida's spring break vacation destination, a dedicated community of chondro enthusiasts intermingled with breeders of bigger snakes like ball pythons and boa constrictors. At the expo I heard about the legendary Trooper Walsh, who used inbreeding to produce one of the very first strains of designer chondros, the Blue Line, in the 1980s. Walsh's snakes caused a sensation. One sold for 100,000 dollars. Chondros were new on the market in the 1980s, freshly imported from West Papua, a territory under Indonesian military occupation where few foreigners were allowed to venture.[9]

Enthusiasts invest in snakes with the promise of generating colorful surprises. Baby *Chondrophythons* are generally more colorful than fully developed adults. Young snakes are either dark red or bright yellow, with distinct black and white stripes. As babies become adults they usually become green, the color of most wild-caught snakes that is not valued in the North American marketplace. Sometimes adult chondros morph into novel patterns of color as adults. The indeterminacy of color patterns in adult chondros prompts speculative investments. The promise of unexpected becomings in future generations of snakes must also be figured into these gambles. A gregarious clean-cut 15-year-old, Sam Reynolds, told me about his collection of eight chondros back in New York City. Sam was the proud owner of a riotous assemblage of color genes with material from most of the major designer lines. In addition to snakes whose lineage he traces to Trooper Walsh's Blue Line, his animals have genes from Greg Maxwell's Calico Project (established in 1993), Damon Salceis' albino python (produced in 2002), and the Lemontree Project, a venture whose tangled genealogical roots are lost in the mists of chondro mythos. Through the pedigrees of these snakes, Sam has established his own ties with a distinguished and distributed kinship network.[10] Sam told me he was attracted to chondros because "they are really expensive, they are hard to find, hard to breed, and have the coolest color patterns of any snake in the world."

In total, Sam has already invested 10,000 dollars in purchasing snakes—not to mention the money he spends feeding, housing, and caring for his animals. Mixing and mating snakes from distinct lines, Sam hopes to make his investment back with a single clutch of eggs. Chondros can lay up to about 20 eggs. Each neonate from designer lines can easily fetch over 1,000 dollars. Sam talked excitedly about snakes as commodities—valued only for the price they might command. Indeed, rather than value animals who might be good to live with, like Caroline Edwards who trains birds to flexibly become social persons, at the Daytona Expo I found breeders whose primary interest in snakes was their exchange value in the market place or their use value as breeding stock. Chasing after elusive genes that encode for pixilated color-breaks and dreamy calico patterns, these breeders dreamed of producing ever more spectacular animals.

A bubble of happiness and speculation was growing in Daytona's Convention Center (Kirksey 2015, 59–60). But the objects at the center of these feelings of excitement, the snakes, were what Sara Ahmed terms "affect aliens" (2010, 42). The sense of alienation experienced by reptiles who were out of sync with the happy feelings of humans looming around them is perhaps best illustrated by the bodily comportment of ball pythons (*Python regius*), a distant relative of chondros from Africa. "Ball pythons" are named for their tendency to curl up into a ball when stressed or frightened (Ball-Pythons.net n.d.). One ball python breeder, whom I asked about the pricing rationale for his 65,000-dollar snake, told me that "it's as complicated as the stock market." This speculative economy, in the words of another high-end ball python breeder, was all about "fun and anticipation of new color morphs." Ball python morphs have names that evoke their colors and patterns: I encountered bananas, pin stripes, deserts, spiders, spinners, mystics, and phantoms. Most of the chondros, like their distant kin from Africa, were curled up on their perches, apparently trying to ignore the chaos as hundreds of noisy humans crowded around them at the Daytona Expo.

Few formal legal regulations are reigning in the wild play of capitalism on the bodies of frightened snakes. In Florida, no special permits are required to own or breed chondros or ball pythons, though other snakes—like the green anaconda, the reticulated python, and the infamous Burmese python—are listed as "conditional reptiles," meaning that they cannot be acquired for personal possession (Myfwc.com 2015). In the absence of formal regulations, and in the face of a dominant culture of snake breeding that seems tone-deaf to issues of animal welfare, a small minority of snake lovers are mindful of both commerce and animal consciousness, working through ethical issues as they engineer novel forms of life (Haraway 2008, 45–7). Lively forms of capital are emerging on the margins of the speculative economy that has emerged around frightened and diseased snakes.

One established chondro breeder, Anne Alison from Minnesota, told me that she is critical of her colleagues who place making money above the welfare of their animals. "These breeders will do anything to keep high-end designer snakes alive," Anne told me. They like to "pip" their precious eggs, to cut open the shells before the snakes hatch. "I refuse to do this," said Anne. Baby snakes usually have an "egg tooth," a pointy protrusion at the end of their snout that enables them to break open eggs. "If a snake is born without an egg tooth, and we help it survive, then we are introducing things into the pet trade that can't survive on their own." Anne told me that designer snakes are vulnerable. Created by humans, these life forms have come to be dependent upon us for their very survival (Bureaud 2002, 39; Zurr 2004, 402). People who inbreed their snakes, or promote genes associated with health problems, are creating sick animals that will suffer their whole lifetime, she said.

Anne developed ethical sensibilities similar to those of Caroline Elliot, who was attentive to the welfare of her hybrid and mutant avian babies. While both parrots and chondros live in human households where few legal regulations about caging or care apply, ethical issues are more central to the concerns of the people who I interviewed in bird worlds. Anne was exceptional in the world of designer snakes for choosing to not focus her efforts on creating inbred animals with colorful patters. Instead, she was envisioning future generations of chondros who would feel comfortable living in captivity. Corn snakes once fetched high prices because they were hard to breed, she said. Now this species is a common pet. Breeders created lines of corn snakes that flourish in human-built life-support technologies. Green tree pythons will never be corn snakes—Anne has lost more chondros than any other snake. But she still hopes to create futures that are easier to live with. "No snake in the world is used to seeing these big primates hovering over them all the time," Anne said. "They don't like to live in tiny see-through rectangular boxes, to eat thawed rats." By breeding only healthy chondros, Anne is attempting to increase the viability of this species in ecosystems that have been created in human homes. Snakes, in contrast to many birds, mammals, or insects, do not generally have prolonged social relationships. "Snakes are usually solitary creatures and are not comforted by interaction with their owners or even other snakes," according to one popular website, acreptiles.com. "When they encounter another animal in the wild, they're either thinking about eating it or being eaten by it—or breeding it :-)" (Anthony Caponetto Reptiles n.d.).[11]

As Anne Alison dreamed of a better future for chondros in captivity, other snakes had already learned to live more or less happily alongside humans. Wayne Smith (pseudonym), a plumber who had tattoos down the length of his arms, showed me his snake and gave me a window into his queer multispecies family. Wayne's chondro, a light green animal with subtle yellow hues and speckled blue mites, was out of its cage, gently and comfortably curled around his arm. Wayne took relish in telling me a story about sex and snakes. He recounted calling up his boss one day to say he would not be coming in to work. A pair of his chondros had been locked together for several days while breeding—the larger female was dragging a smaller male around the cage, who simply refused to let go of her cloaca with his penis. By the time Wayne was able to separate the pair, the male's penis was inflamed, in need of urgent veterinary attention from a specialist doctor who lived out of town. "Let me get this straight," Wayne mimed his boss in a thick Southern accent. "Are you telling me that you can't come to work today because your green tree viper has an infected penis?" Wayne's boss let him miss work and probably enjoyed retelling the story to his own friends. "Most of my neighbors in Northern Florida think that I am a pee-drinking, Satan-worshiping freak," Wayne added.

Under a veneer of bravado, Wayne revealed deep feelings and affection for his snake. Clearly, he was skilled at caring for chondros and was attentive to the needs of the snakes living with him in a common household. Part of what made the snake valuable to Wayne was its ability to respond to human desires for touch and contact, like Caroline Elliot's birds. Care and love was central to Wayne's relationship with his snake, even though

Figure 8.1 The chondros of Wayne Smith have learned how to interact with him, to respond to human desires for touch. Photo by Eben Kirksey.

he was not sure that these feelings were reciprocated. Wayne was not convinced that his snake recognized him as a person, as a social being, or even a living creature. This uncertainty about his own status in the snake's eyes was part of what led Wayne to give it up for sale. Wayne told me about his plans for an epic motorcycle journey with friends, something that would simply not be possible with snakes in his life. Following the logic of Haraway's lively capital, the capacity of Wayne's snake to tolerate human touch, its encounter value, should have increased its exchange value. But, a small sign at his Daytona Reptile Expo stand indicated that he was having trouble making a deal. The sign read: "Sale, Sale, Sale. Everything must go!!! Any reasonable offer will be considered." Instead of lively capital—with commerce and consciousness, ethics and utility all at play—the dominant value system at the Daytona Expo was fixated on novel snake-skin color patterns and underlying genetic codes (Haraway 2008, 45–7). Capital exhibited a fickle spirit at this trade expo—possessing, and then abandoning, the bodies of vulnerable animals (cf. Kirksey 2015, 180).

Conclusion

The lucrative transnational marketplace for exotic animals continues to generate mass death and contribute to the extinction of some species (Herrel and van der Meijden 2014, 106). Almost all of the animals I encountered in Florida—at trade expos and in people's private homes—were captive bred. Rather than generate mass death, these breeders were trying to generate life. At the intersection of competing value systems, as oblique powers transform social, ecological, and familial worlds, some breeders are making ethical interventions. These key players are serving as organic intellectuals—making contingent and piecemeal changes to the hegemonic values of the pet industry (cf. Gramsci 1971). They are working to reclaim the generative possibilities of interspecies love against the backdrop of a marketplace that is producing vulnerable animals, such as sick hybrid birds with deformed hips and colorful baby snakes unable to break open their own eggshells.

Creatures caught in the wild and then adopted into human homes as pets are often out of sync with the social expectations of their new families (Collard 2014). Even if captive-bred animals are socialized to live in human households from birth, some species, like chondros or ball pythons, cannot easily be made into social persons. Others, like parrots and dogs, have flexible personhood and readily form multispecies families with humans. These adaptable creatures are finding opportunities for themselves amid fickle human whims and life-changing events—divorces, marriages, births, and high school graduations (Shir-Vertesh 2012). Carefully guiding the creation of new multispecies families, some exotic animal breeders are patiently giving new households the necessary knowledge and biotechnical tools to care for rare forms of life.

The spirit of capital, and the popular desire for the exotic, has generated novel niches in landscapes that have been transformed by agriculture, extractive industry, and pollution. Animals are invading and occupying bubbles of comfort created by humans, generating lively futures in homes with air-conditioned living rooms, basements, and bedrooms. Florida has become home to diverse kinds of critters. A swarming multitude is proliferating in domestic spaces that are largely beyond the reach of the law. Novel kinds of wild life in Florida are evidence of the leaky nature of the prevailing legal system as well as the challenges faced by law enforcement. Multispecies foraging flocks comprised of different kinds of parrots and parakeets are now a common sight in Florida. Wild pythons with unusual color patterns are also turning up in unexpected spaces. The fickle play of human desires and capital has produced emergent ecological communities that are flourishing beyond regimes of management and control.

Acknowledgments

An earlier version of this chapter was published in *Emergent Ecologies* by Duke University Press, 2015.

Notes

1 Here I am in dialog with Deborah Bird Rose's notion of "double death" (Rose 2011).

2 Caroline Elliot is a pseudonym and a composite personality. I visited half a dozen households in central and south Florida that had received animals from the Amnesty Day program.

3 Quotes and usernames have been modified from the originals on www.parrotforums.com to preserve anonymity. Species-specific identifiers of birds have been preserved.

4 Even when an organism only has one copy of a dominant gene the physical characteristic (or phenotype) is expressed, according to Mendelian principles; recessive genes are only expressed when two copies are present.

5 Cyborgs also "take pleasure in the confusion of boundaries" and make arguments "for responsibility in their construction" (Haraway 1985, 118).

6 Zeb Carruthers is a pseudonym. Details have been changed to preserve his anonymity.

7 Donna Haraway has argued that some animals are not just "good to think with" or "good to eat" but are also beings that are good "to live with" (Haraway 2008; see also Kirksey et al. 2014, 3).

8 In 1993, Kluge rechristened this species as *Morelia viridis*. Since hobbyists who keep these snakes still refer to them as "Chondros," I have used this older species name throughout.

9 For a book-length account of this military occupation, see Kirksey 2012.

10 Sarah Franklin insists that we understand kinship as a technology that activates reproductive substance, controlling and redirecting possible biological

relations. By creatively mixing and matching distinct pedigrees, Sam was pushing biological potentials for reproduction in new directions. Producing successful offspring would be the marker of success—transforming Sam from someone who was embedded within a distinguished kinship network, to a patrilineal progenitor with the power to establish his own lines (Franklin 2013, 152–3).

11 Many skilled breeders and hobbyists who care for snakes in their own homes arguably better understand aspects of reptilian sociality and subjectivity when compared with scientists.

References

Agamben, Giorgio. 1998. *Homo Sacer: Sovereign Power and Bare Life.* Translated by Daniel Heller-Roazen. Stanford: Stanford University Press.

Ahmed, Sara. 2010. *The Promise of Happiness.* Durham, NC: Duke University Press.

Anthony Caponetto Reptiles. n.d. "Ball Python Care Sheet." http://www.acreptiles.com/main/index.php?option=com_content&view=article&id=140&Itemid=312.

Avian Web. n.d. "Hahn's, Noble or Red-shouldered (Mini) Macaws." http://beautyofbirds.com/hahnsmacaw.html.

Ball-Pythons.net. n.d. "Ball Python Care Sheet" http://ball-pythons.net/forums/showthread.php?127203-Ball-Python-(Python-regius)-Caresheet.

Barad, Karen. 2014. "Invertebrate Visions: Diffractions of the Brittlestar." In *The Multispecies Salon.* Edited by Eben Kirksey, 221–41. Durham: Duke University Press.

Berlant, Lauren Gail. 2011. *Cruel Optimism.* Durham: Duke University Press.

Bowker, Geoffrey C., and Susan Leigh Star. 1999. *Sorting Things Out: Classification and its Consequences.* Cambridge: The MIT Press.

Braverman, Irus. 2015. "More-than-Human Legalities" In *The Wiley Handbook of Law and Society.* Edited by Patricia Ewick and Austin Sarat. Chichester, UK: John Wiley & Sons.

Bureaud, Annick. 2002. "The Ethics and Aesthetics of Biological Art." *Art Press* 276: 38–9.

Cheah, Pheng. 1999. "Spectral Nationality: The Living On (*sur-vie*) of the Postcolonial Nation in Neocolonial Globalization." *Boundary 2* 26 (3): 225–52.

Clifford, James. 1997. *Routes: Travel and Translation in the Late Twentieth Century.* Cambridge: Harvard University Press.

Collard, Rosemary-Claire. 2014. "Putting Animals Back Together, Taking Commodities Apart." *Annals of the Association of American Geographers* 104 (1): 151–65.

Dayan, Colin. 2011. *Law is a White Dog: How Legal Rituals Make and Unmake Persons.* Princeton: Princeton University Press.

DeGregory, Lane. 2012. "For Exotic Animals Surrendered On Pet Amnesty Day, It's Not Goodbye, Just Farewell." *Tampa Bay Times.* May 25. http://www.tampabay.com/features/humaninterest/for-exotic-animals-surrendered-on-pet-amnesty-day-its-not-goodbye-just/1232003.

Donaldson, Sue, and Will Kymlicka. 2011. *Zoopolis: A Political Theory of Animal Rights.* Oxford: Oxford University Press.

EcoHealth Alliance. n.d. "Stopping Illegal Wildlife Trade." http://www.ecohealthalliance.org/programs/30stopping_illegal_wildlife_trade.

Feeley-Harnik, Gillian. 2001. "The Ethnography of Creation: Lewis Henry Morgan and the American Beaver." In *Relative Values: Reconfiguring Kinship Studies.* Edited by Sarah Franklin and Susan McKinnon, 54–84. Durham: Duke University Press.

Florida Fish and Wildlife Conservation Commission. n.d. "Captive Wildlife Licenses & Permits." http://myfwc.com/license/captive-wildlife/.
———. n.d.a. "Nonnatives Birds." http://myfwc.com/wildlifehabitats/nonnatives/birds/.
———. n.d.b. "Exotic Pet Amnesty Day Events." http://myfwc.com/wildlifehabitats/nonnatives/amnesty-program/events/.
———. n.d.c. "Exotic Pet Amnesty Program." http://myfwc.com/wildlifehabitats/nonnatives/amnesty-program/.
Foucault, Michel. 1984. "Right of Death and Power over Life." In *The Foucault Reader*. Edited by Paul Rabinow, 258–72. New York: Random House.
Franklin, Sarah. 2001. "Biologization Revisited: Kinship Theory in the Context of the New Biologies." *Relative Values: Reconfiguring Kinship Studies*. Edited by Sarah Franklin and Susan McKinnon, 302–328. Durham: Duke University Press.
———. 2013. *Biological Relatives: IVF, Stem Cells, and the Future of Kinship*. Durham: Duke University Press.
Gramsci, Antonio. 1971. *Selections from the Prison Notebooks of Antonio Gramsci*. Translated by Quentin Hoare and Geoffrey Nowell-Smith. London: Lawrence & Wishart.
Haraway, Donna. 1985. "Manifesto for Cyborgs: Science, Technology, and Socialist Feminism in the 1980s." *Socialist Review* 80: 65–108.
———. 1989. *Primate Visions: Gender, Race, and Nature in the World of Modern Science*. New York: Routledge.
———. 2008. *When Species Meet*. Minneapolis: University of Minnesota Press.
Harvey, David. 1990. "Flexible Accumulation through Urbanization Reflections on 'Post-Modernism' in the American City." *Perspecta* 26: 251–72.
Helmreich, Stefan. 2003. "Trees and Seas of Information: Alien Kinship and the Biopolitics of Gene Transfer in Marine Biology and Biotechnology." *American Ethnologist* 30 (3): 341–59.
Herzog, Hal. 2010. *Some We Love, Some We Hate, Some We Eat: Why It's So Hard to Think Straight About Animals*. New York: HarperCollins.
Herrel, Anthony and Arie van der Meijden. 2014. "An Analysis of the Live Reptile and Amphibian Trade in the USA Compared to the Global Trade in Endangered Species." *Herpetological Journal* 24: 103–10.
Jaclin, David. 2013. "In The (Bleary) Eye of the Tiger: An Anthropological Journey into Jungle Backyards." *Social Science Information Sur Les Sciences Sociales* 52 (2): 257–71.
Kirksey, Eben. 2012. *Freedom in Entangled Worlds: West Papua and the Architecture of Global Power*. Durham: Duke University Press.
———. 2015. *Emergent Ecologies*. Durham: Duke University Press.
Kirksey, Eben and Stefan Helmreich. 2010. "The Emergence of Multispecies Ethnography." *Cultural Anthropology* 25 (4): 545–76.
Kirksey, Eben, Craig Schuetze and Stefan Helmreich. 2014. "Introduction: Tactics of Multispecies Ethnography." In *The Multispecies Salon: Gleanings from a Para-Site*. Edited by Eben Kirksey, 1–24. Durham: Duke University Press.
Marks, Jonathan. 2001. " 'We're Going to Tell These People Who They Really Are': Science and Relatedness." In *Relative Values: Reconfiguring Kinship Studies*. Edited by Sarah Franklin and Susan McKinnon, 355–83. Durham: Duke University Press.
Maxwell, Greg. 2005. *The More Complete Chondro: The Bestselling Manual for all Green Tree Python Keepers*. Rodeo, NM: ECO Herpetological Publishing and Distribution. Kindle edition.

Mullin, Molly. 1999. "Mirrors and Windows: Sociocultural Studies of Human-Animal Relationships." *Annual Review of Anthropology* 28: 201–24.

MyFWC. n.d. "Conditional Snakes and Lizards." http://myfwc.com/wildlifehabitats/nonnatives/regulations/snakes-and-lizards.

Parrenas, Rheana S. 2012. "Producing Affect: Transnational Volunteerism in a Malaysian Orangutan Rehabilitation Center." *American Ethnologist* 39 (4): 673–87.

Rose, Deborah Bird. 2011. *Wild Dog Dreaming: Love and Extinction.* Charlottesville: University of Virginia Press.

Schneider, David Murray. 1984. *A Critique of the Study of Kinship.* Ann Arbor: University of Michigan Press.

Shir-Vertesh, Dafna. 2012. "'Flexible Personhood': Loving Animals as Family Members in Israel." *American Anthropologist* 114 (3): 420–32.

Shukin, Nicole. 2009. *Animal Capital: Rendering Life in Biopolitical Times.* Minneapolis: University of Minnesota Press.

Siskind, Janet. 1978. "Kinship and Mode of Production." *American Anthropologist* 80 (4): 860–72.

Standish, Rachel J., Allen Thompson, Eric Higgs and Stephen D. Murphy. 2013. "Concerns about Novel Ecosystems." In *Novel Ecosystems: Intervening in the New Ecological World Order.* Edited by Richard Hobbs, Eric Higgs, and Carol Hall, 296–309. Chichester, UK: John Wiley & Sons.

Sundberg, Juanita. 2006. "Conservation Encounters: Transculturation in the 'Contact Zones' of Empire." *Cultural Geography* 13 (2): 239–65.

van Dooren, Thom. 2014. *Flight Ways: Life at the Edge of Extinction.* New York: Columbia University Press.

Weston, Kath. 1991. *Families We Choose: Lesbians, Gays, Kinship.* New York: Columbia University Press.

Wikipedia. 2015. "Python Regius." http://en.wikipedia.org/wiki/Python_regius.

World Wildlife Fund. n.d. "Illegal Wildlife Trade." www.worldwildlife.org/threats/illegal-wildlife-trade.

———. n.d.a. "Unsustainable and Illegal Wildlife Trade." http://wwf.panda.org/about_our_earth/species/problems/illegal_trade/.

Zurr, Ionat. 2004. "Complicating Notions of Life: Semi-Living Entities." In *Biomediale: Contemporary Society and Genomic Culture.* Edited by Dmitry Bulatov, 402–11. Kaliningrad, Russia: The National Center for Contemporary Arts.

Chapter 9

The Conflict of Human and Nonhuman Laws

Richard Janda and Richard Lehun

Introduction

Natural science has long sought to identify nonhuman legality. It has done so by finding mathematical formulations that can be used to predict the outcomes of experiments. There is continuing debate among philosophers of science as to whether the laws thus identified are regularities observable with statistical certainty or rather reflect the best approximations we have for identifying physically necessary truths (Swartz 1985). However, the notion "physical law" remains unavoidable on either of these accounts. Thus, for example, the first chapter of Stephen Hawking and Leonard Mlodinow's *The Grand Design*, entitled, "The Mystery of Being," sets out what prompts the inquiries of physics, with the second chapter, in response, entitled "The Rule of Law" (2010). Indeed, they come to defend what they call the "strong anthropic principle" that "the fact we exist imposes constraints not just upon our *environment* but on the possible *form and content of the laws of nature* themselves" (155). This is how they characterize those laws of nature:

> The emergence of the complex systems capable of supporting intelligent observers seems to be very fragile. The laws of nature form a system that is extremely fine-tuned, and very little in physical law can be altered without destroying the possibility of the development of life as we know it. Were it not for a series of startling coincidences in the precise detail of physical law, it seems that humans and similar life-forms would never have come into being. . . . Our universe and its laws appear to have a design that is both tailor-made to support us and, if we are to exist, leaves little room for alteration (161–2).

A view of Earth rising above the lunar horizon photographed from the Apollo 10 Lunar Module, looking west in the direction of travel. NASA, Public Domain. https://commons.wikimedia.org/wiki/File:Apollo_10_earthrise.jpg.

For the jurist, the vast array of this complex system of nonhuman laws is bewildering, covering physical constants, quantum mechanics, relativity, electromagnetism, thermodynamics, chemistry, geophysics and even the building blocks of biology. So disparate and apparently unrelated to human law are these nonhuman laws that the jurist is sorely tempted to treat the word "law" when used by scientists as a mere homonym for the juristic use of this word.

And yet we should recall that not only did scientists borrow the word 'law' from jurists, but that it was a jurist, Francis Bacon, who sought to extend a certain conception of law to the natural world when laying the foundations of the scientific method (Bacon 1620; 1627). For Bacon, since human perception and passions were fragile and utterly unreliable in detecting the operation of nonhuman laws, they had to be constrained and restricted to a rigorous empirical method that would allow general axioms to be induced from data. Even if Bacon was not perfectly accurate in his anticipation of scientific method, the effort to decode natural law by fencing off the intrusion of all-too-human sensibilities remains to this day.

Thus, we could begin a discussion of the relation between human and nonhuman legalities by noting that nonhuman legality is already constructed as exceeding the feeble reach of human legality, susceptible as it is to our fragile perceptions and desires. At the same time, contemporary physicists perceive in nonhuman legality its own fragility: this, in light of the fact that nonhuman legality enables intelligent life capable of observing it. Unobservable laws would be no laws at all. How do these opposing fragilities coexist?

The contemporary scientist may not acknowledge it, but her search for scientific law is still part of Bacon's project to extend human dominion over nature, which Bacon in fact took to be a Christian inheritance extending back to God's grant of creation to us. Human dominion could not be extended if we did not come to know its laws. It is by knowing how nature is governed that we could come to govern it for our own purposes (Merchant 1980). Thus, the acknowledgment of nonhuman legality given to and imposed upon the world within which human beings find themselves has become the key to human mastery. The fragility of human law, indeed its subjugation to unreliable perceptions and desires, was a burden that Bacon believed humans could overcome if we learned to attune ourselves to nonhuman law. Embedded in scientific discovery of nature's laws is the effort to use those laws to pursue our own desires, rather than to learn how to be well-governed according to nonhuman law or indeed to celebrate the possibilities to which it gives rise. The antinomy of overcoming our desires so as to pursue them haunts the scientific project.

And yet, it is increasingly the contemporary scientist, rather than the jurist, who will voice the concern that we are failing to be well-governed according to nonhuman law (Latour 2013a, 3–27; 2013b, 129–35). This is because the scientist can now readily detect the ways in which the pursuit of human desires—including the desires to appropriate, reproduce, and consume—are reaching the boundary conditions for maintaining human life within the operation of nonhuman laws governing the biosphere. We are now in the Anthropocene—an epoch of geological time characterized by significant human impacts on global ecosystems, and indeed characterized as a geological epoch because of changes in physical sedimentation across the planet—compared with the prior epoch, the Holocene (see also this volume, Chapters 3 and 10).[1] The emergence of the Anthropocene or, more precisely, of our recognition that we are in it and producing it, is how the opposing fragilities of human and nonhuman law coexist.

Thus, that we find ourselves in the Anthropocene provides the strong basis for the claim that we are failing adequately to acknowledge nonhuman legality. The first part of this chapter will explore this claim. The second part will propose that the relationship between human and nonhuman law should be understood as giving rise to a new and previously unacknowledged class of what jurists call "conflict of laws" problems, which in turn require a normative framework for their resolution. The third and main part will then sketch how humans can fail to address the conflict of laws if we simply embrace nonhuman law without acknowledging our antinomical burden within the conflict between human and nonhuman law. In particular, we will review four variants of the effort to embrace nonhuman law through our relationship with animals: (1) projection of the human self upon the nonhuman other; (2) recognition of mutuality with the nonhuman other; (3) acknowledgment of the inherent value of the nonhuman other; and (4) affirmation of transhuman justice. The idea of conflict of laws is premised upon the coexistence of sovereigns. It entails that we discover techniques for recognizing overlapping norms and disentangling their contradictions. This chapter seeks to show that the conflict between human and nonhuman law cannot be overcome by substituting for human law an embrace of the nonhuman or transhuman. Not only must the conflict of laws be recognized, but effort must be invested in producing a capacity within human law to respond to signals of that conflict. The conclusion of the chapter will thus summarize how placing ourselves "before the conflict of laws" (drawing on Cary Wolfe's use of "before the law," 2012) is a prerequisite for addressing the antinomical burdens of the Anthropocene.

Acknowledging More-than-Human Legalities in the Anthropocene

That we are in the Anthropocene means that human impacts are now a significant factor in planetary biogeophysical changes. When Bacon envisaged the scientific project, he imagined harnessing and controlling biogeophysical phenomena. He imagined as well that the entirety of the world could ultimately be discovered. But he did not imagine that our science and expanded population would bring about the transformation of planetary systems. For human beings to have become, collectively, capable of perturbing planetary systems is indeed of epochal significance (Rockström et al. 2009). However, one might argue that this in itself does not suggest any conflict with nonhuman laws. It could even represent the triumph of human ambition for dominion and thus the command of human law over nonhuman law.

Yet such a view would fail to take the Anthropocene seriously. If our ability to affect planetary systems did not put in jeopardy the prospects for life, we could simply hail the Anthropocene as the forward march of human progress. Instead, what we discover is that nonhuman laws can readily function without us and absorb our impacts by displacing the relatively narrow felicity conditions that had allowed our species to emerge in the Holocene (Weisman 2007). As Bruno Latour has expressed it, Gaia is ticklish and is responding to us (2014, 3). We are witnessing the eventuality that the Anthropocene itself could become an infinitesimal footnote to the geological record of time.

It is in this sense that the acknowledgment of nonhuman legality becomes critical. Indeed, if human laws, especially those governing the economy, place the prospects of life in jeopardy, nonhuman law, in so far as it conflicts with human law, could be seen as the only true lively legality—the one that is seeking to constrain and transform human law so as to maintain the prospects of life. Human legality thus confronts the possibility that it cannot persist as it is in the face of the operation of a nonhuman law. This is what we mean by direct conflict of laws.

The Conflict of Human and Nonhuman Laws

A brief summary of the legal nature of a standard conflict of laws problem is in order here. When we deal with a conflict of human laws, we have a forum before which the conflicting matter is brought that will govern at least the relevant procedural issues (e.g., time delays, rules of evidence, and forms of pleading) as well as the laws of another jurisdiction that are to be taken into account by the judge. A conflict of laws problem arises when there are some factors tying the matter to another jurisdiction, such as the domicile of a party, the place where a transaction was concluded, the location of property, or the site where relevant acts occurred. The main task of the judge is to determine the proper law governing the matter given a range of factors that connect it to a particular jurisdiction. In principle, there is a legal solution to the problem of finding the "proper" law.

In contrast to the standard conflict of laws problem, there is no convenient forum for the resolution of the conflict between human and nonhuman law. There is no instance to which we can appeal, although we do know in advance that the verdict will be rendered according to nonhuman law if the conditions of life cannot be sustained. If we insist that our human law establishes the forum in which factors connecting us to nonhuman law will be assessed, we face a great difficulty. What connects us to nonhuman law is incommensurable with what connects us to human law. We cannot ask, for example, whether an act of pollution is more properly governed under human law or nonhuman law. We know that even if human law seeks to govern it by requiring the mitigation of impacts, in the end the effects that will be caused by the act will be governed by nonhuman laws: how ecosystems and the forms of life within them respond to deleterious substances.

In light of these considerations, the task of a conflict of laws regime regulating the relationship between human and nonhuman laws is not to decide when to apply nonhuman laws; they always apply. Rather, it is to gather information about how the biosphere responds to the norms governing human behavior and to reorient that behavior when the response to it tends to undermine the conditions for life: the earlier the detection of that response, the greater the prospects of reorienting our behavior successfully.

We have of course long believed that the world is indifferent to our norms. To place in peril the conditions of life has itself been understood as a characteristic of human life, with its violence and struggle. There is even a sense in which we have been able to believe that the majesty of human life and the foundation of its laws come through the wars we wage.[2] We have thought of the world as a stage on which a war of all against all unfolds, rather than as itself being composed of actants that respond to our doings. True, we have held in our imaginations the religious account that our actions in the world can unfold toward apocalypse and a final judgment according to nonhuman laws. But through modernity we have steadfastly isolated the domain of our laws from the operation of nonhuman laws:[3] one operates in the realm of our values, the other operates in the realm of brute facts. This way, we have been able to persuade ourselves that a regime of conflict of human and nonhuman laws would mix incommensurable categories.

It is for this reason that one must emphasize how a conflict of laws regime aligning human and nonhuman laws remains an exercise of our will, and arguably its most challenging exercise. Can we will our norms of behavior to produce a collective response to nonhuman law that allows for the continued existence of the conditions of human life and, more ambitiously still, of the felicitous conditions for all life? That is surely the most significant question that can be put forth at this moment in our history (Christian, Brown and Benjamin 2013).

When the question is put this way it also sheds light on what is meant by the notion of human law. If our challenge is to produce norms of collective human behavior that respond reflexively to results of the application of nonhuman law, an important problem of characterization of law presents itself. What is the relevant, proper human law that governs our collective behavior? It cannot be the law of any specific jurisdiction alone, since the collective impacts of our behavior upon the biosphere are not attributable to any single jurisdiction. Nor can it really be international law, which does not purport to engage in the general governance of collective behavior. Rather, the relevant form of law has to do with how we govern the *oikos* collectively through economics, notably by use of the price signal. Thus, the best we can do as jurists is to assemble the signals that come from our impacts on planetary systems, which are indicators of our continued ability to function within the bounds of nonhuman law, and generate norms that respond to those signals. Human interactions with the biosphere generate signals—notably bioindicators—of our impacts (Holt and Miller 2010). As we gather these signals, we are increasingly able to perform lifecycle assessment of all human health and environmental impacts (USEPA 2006). The task of a normative framework governing the conflict of human and nonhuman law should therefore be to detect and respond to the signals that indicate when collective human impacts take us past planetary boundaries. This is precisely what we have been unable to do adequately as regards climate change, despite having received and gathered clear signals that we are crossing planetary boundaries (Bergoglio 2015, 39).

The jurist will speak of a choice of laws, which means to pick one applicable law and in this sense to avoid the conflict of laws. However, there are no circumstances in which we can make the choice not to apply nonhuman laws. Thus, for example, we might prefer to live in a world in which perpetual motion machines are possible. But the laws of physics apply despite our preferences and will continue to operate even if our personal choices encounter inexorably the point at which they come into conflict with those laws, for example when the positive radiative forcing produced by our greenhouse gas emissions leads to catastrophic climate change. When human laws are in conflict, the prescribed norms produce different outcomes for behavior. When we are in conflict with nonhuman laws, it is the possibility of continued choice or behavior that is in question. In a sense, there is never a violation of one norm by following another. There is only the possible eradication of human normativity.

In short, we have an enormously difficult and unprecedented conflict of laws problem to resolve. How do we master our own capacity for mastering nonhuman laws so as to ensure that by virtue of this mastery we will not put an end to our existence under these laws? Both the conflict of laws outside us and the conflict of laws within us give rise to forms of master–slave struggle for control over the authority of law. Yet the effort to achieve emancipation from this struggle by acknowledging and embracing what is nonhuman law can in fact lead to failure. This problem, which we shall turn to next, is the main idea we seek to highlight in this chapter.

Emancipatory Failures of Embracing Nonhuman Law

We can conceive of the conflict of human and nonhuman law as involving the need for human law to embrace nonhuman law. This might be done in the name of all the others—living and non-living—who are not recognized by human law and deserve its recognition (Latour 1993, 142–5). Yet there is a naturalistic fallacy in the assumption that increasing the recognition of others within our normative frame will be good for them. If we make their natural existence visible to and part of our normativity, so goes the fallacy, we will be able to see nonhuman others as capable of agency with, for, and against us. However, by seeing the other in this way we can also depart from the responsibility toward the question of otherness that was intrinsic to their lived and living experience. Instead, we posit that they are another form of us: equal and belonging. We are beholden to them to the extent that they take a form that we can mirror.

Undoubtedly, such an attempt to embrace otherness can force us to find ways to relate the experience of the nonhuman other to our own. This can take on four broad forms, each of which emerges from the effort to reconceive our legal relationship to other forms of life. We set out these four variants of the effort to embrace nonhuman law in brief compass and then proceed to analyse each more closely in turn.

First, we can find an overlap of experience by imputing a shared perspective to other forms of life. Thus, we can attribute personhood to animals and affirm that they value their own lives, and the right to live them, with as little suffering as possible. Let us call this "projection of the human self upon the nonhuman other." Gary Francione's *Animals as Persons* (2008) exemplifies this position.

In the alternative, we could look to other forms of life to discover anthropomorphic characteristics with which we can identify. Animals that display complex social behavior can prompt us to see claims comparable to our own. For example, the complex social contextualization of higher primates allows us to imagine that human law could be extended to recognize their collective rights, and their rights as individuals. Let us call this "recognition of mutuality with the nonhuman other." Susan Donaldson and Will Kymlicka's *Zoopolis* (2011) exemplifies this position.

The third variant assigns anthropomorphic normative claims to other species or even to non-living things as a counter-factual extension of our ethics and norms. Living things deserve equality or supremacy and even sovereignty, and non-living things deserve recognition and respect because of the ethical demands we place on ourselves. Non-anthropocentric environmentalism and deep ecology can embrace all living things as fundamentally equal or even superior in significance to human life and non-living things as worthy of reverence, concern and aesthetic investment. Let us call this "acknowledgment of the inherent value of the nonhuman other." Roberto Esposito's *Biopolitics and Philosophy* (2008) exemplifies this position.

A fourth variant involves finding the source of nonhuman law in the limit point of human conceptions of justice. In this way, what we term justice alterity is posited as the expression of the antinomies produced upon close and critical reading of what we render through human justice. Let us call this last variant "affirmation of transhuman justice." Cary Wolfe's *Before the Law: Humans and other Animals in a Biopolitical Frame* (2012) exemplifies this position.

In examining each of these variants in turn, the point we wish to explore is the inadequacy of simply finding a relationship between emancipatory justice claims and nonhuman law; we must also be enabled to bear the antinomical burdens of the conflict between human and nonhuman laws.

Projection of Self upon the Nonhuman Other

In our first variant, projection of self upon the nonhuman other, there is indeed a separation and conflict between human and nonhuman law, but only *de minimis* recognition of countervailing emancipatory claims or antinomies to be negotiated. We simply elide ourselves into the other and presuppose that their claims are ours. Gary Francione has extensively explored how our thinking disables us from recognizing the intrinsic value and distinct value of nonhumans:

> To the extent that nonhumans have an interest in their lives, our use of them in situations where we would use no humans necessarily denies them equal consideration for this interest. Moreover, even if it is plausible to maintain that nonhumans do not have an interest in continued existence, application of the principle of equal consideration to animal interests in not suffering—already difficult to do because of the need to make interspecies comparisons—becomes even more complicated when animals are viewed as human property. The property status of animals serves as what I have discussed elsewhere as a "two-edged sword wielded against their interests." Property status stops us from perceiving animal interests as similar to ours in the first instance and subordinates animal interests to human interests even when human and animal interests are recognized as similar because the property status of animals is always a good reason to refuse them similar treatment (2008, 140).

Francione illuminates the inadequacy of human law in dealing with other sentient beings. However, his approach does not seek to address the full range of possible justice claims arising from nonhuman law, let alone to address their contradictions with human law, because it seeks to uncover "animal interests similar to ours." As appropriate (or necessary) as this form of projection might be in advancing the recognition of nonhuman legality, it does not adequately advance our understanding of the alterity of nonhuman justice.

Thus, for example, prohibitions against violations of the protection of habitat will have relatively little weight, since according to this position nonhumans gain agency through the intervention of humans prepared to acknowledge the similarity of animal interests. Animal habitat can be judged insufficiently similar to human property interests. Furthermore, even the instrumental use of nonhumans as property, resources, or ecosystem services can readily trump protection of their habitat based on a cost–benefit analysis. That is, while Francione makes the countervailing ethic very clear, there is no reason that other considerations do not triumph as the similarity of our interests diverge or as human interests gather around other goals.

Nonetheless, it should be acknowledged that this first variant is least susceptible to incidental totalitarianism. There is no appeal to legitimacy extending beyond conventional norms. The dysfunction of human law is not in fact uprooted since it is simply extended indirectly to nonhuman claimants.

Recognition of Mutuality with the Nonhuman Other

In our second variant, recognition of mutuality with the nonhuman other, we aspire to find elements of human law that appear commensurable with nonhuman law and invite nonhuman subjects to share rights. Here, the role of emancipatory claims and antinomical negotiation is ambivalent. We can only imagine what actors in a nonhuman frame are to themselves or us. This does not mean that they are more or less than us. Nor do we necessarily prioritize the justice claims that are conceivable to us, or even simply affirm the emancipatory potential of the generic alterity of nonhuman claims. However, in this variant we are taking as *prima facie* legitimate those claims that overlap with or most resemble claims of our own. In *Zoopolis*, Sue Donaldson and Will Kymlicka discuss the possibility of according citizenship status to nonhumans:

> Many people assume that animals cannot be citizens because (a) citizenship is about the exercise of political agency; and (b) political agency requires cognitively sophisticated capacities for public reason and deliberation. Neither claim is correct, even for human beings. Citizenship is about more than political agency, and political agency takes forms other than public reason. Citizenship has multiple functions, and all of them are, in principle, applicable to animals. Citizenship operates to allocate individuals to territories; to allocate membership

> in sovereign peoples; and to enable diverse forms of political agency (including assisted and dependent agency). Not only is it conceptually coherent to apply all three citizenship functions to animals, but we argue in the remaining chapters that it is the only coherent way to make sense of our moral obligations (2011, 61).

The attempt to discern how our justice conceptions resemble those of nonhuman law risks over-affirming incidental human emancipatory claims buried within this resemblance (e.g., those derived from analogous human marginalization). It also creates a degree of immunity from critical analysis, since any questioning of the nonhuman claim will be excluded as an illegitimate failure to acknowledge resemblance. Such normative decontextualization can also undermine the legitimacy of conventional law by stretching it well beyond its own internally coherent bounds. At the same time, it coopts the complex negotiation of antinomies necessary to align both exoteric (human) and esoteric (nonhuman) justice claims. Furthermore, basing normative benchmarks on resemblances of this kind conjures the moral hazards of ethical narcissism. Those claiming to be the true interpreters of how nonhuman law resembles human law can succumb to such narcissism.

Acknowledging the Inherent Value of the Nonhuman Other

The third variant of embracing nonhuman law, acknowledging the inherent value of the nonhuman other, indeed abandons the primacy of human law. Here, human law is subject to a more radical reading as the means by which the earth and all living things are put in jeopardy and under threat. Such an ethic of subrogation is, contrary to its self-understanding, often a radical form of self-referencing. The notion that we can rely upon our understanding of what nonhuman law would mandate to the point of obscuring our ethical obligations to others or ourselves becomes a *petitio principii*. The premise is that Nature is *prima facie* ethically inviolable because it is an ethical *a priori*. But this argument stands in for, and takes precisely the same form as, the anthropocentric argument that it seeks to replace: namely, that human beings are the measure of all things and are thus an ethically inviolable *a priori*. While intending the opposite, this embrace of nonhuman law taken to its extreme is deeply anthropocentric. Roberto Esposito, in *Biopolitics and Philosophy*, relies on a radical existentialist ethic, deprivileging any transcendent categories that would give humans standing or dominion over other life forms:

> But how is a life or being there [*esserci*] configured so that it can decide for itself [*su se stessa*], or even that it is such a decision, if not in an intrinsically political modality? What opens the possibility of thinking

> *bíos* and politics within the same conceptual piece is that [first] at no point does authentic being [*poter-essere*] exceed the effective possibility of being there [*dell'esserci*], and second that the self-decision of this being is absolutely immanent to itself. It is from this side, precisely because it is entirely impolitical, which is to say irreducible to any form of political philosophy, that Heidegger's thought emerges in the first half of the twentieth century as the only one able to support the philosophical confrontation with biopolitics (2008, 152).

Esposito's approach runs into the contradiction between the reliance on the alterity of justice as reflected in his use of Heidegger's phenomenology of presence, on the one hand, and any acknowledgment of justice claims of human law on the other. Adorno compares this contradiction to being like rhinoceroses, who "drag their protective armour with them, an ingrown prison which they seem—anthropomorphically, at least—to be trying vainly to shed. The subjective moment is framed, as it were, in the objective one. As a limitation imposed on the subject, it is objective itself" (1973, 180). A justice imaginary predicated on self-overcoming in the service of nonhuman law necessarily abstracts from the antinomical burdens imposed by exoteric claims. This decoupling aligns the entire justice imaginary with the most incidental claims of the individual. Only such incidental claims (e.g., those drawn from one's love of animals) can find their place in the affirmation of nonhuman law.

Thus, the very antinomical capacity that would be necessary to confront and understand the interdependence of claims, as well as any ability to rise to the challenges of justice alterity and indeterminacy, are forfeited in favour of a quasi-emancipatory narrative. Life is to be freed from human law so that it can decide for itself and have its own politics. This third variant can create a significant sense of emancipatory empowerment given the extent to which incidental claims are affirmed. Yet, as such, it is also prone to profound ethical narcissism. The conceit that the exoteric frame—that of the otherness of nonhuman law—can be eclipsed by the embrace of the esoteric frame—that of identifying ourselves with nonhuman law—serves to decontextualize the attendant emancipatory claims and vitiate their capacity to serve justice. Emancipatory claims can only have meaning when their concomitant antinomical burdens are confronted and indeed have resources devoted to redressing them. While the presumption of a shared ontology points toward overcoming the limitations of exoteric law, it nevertheless anchors justice to the overlap between human and nonhuman. The assumed overlap inevitably leads to emancipatory disappointment, since any attempt to qualify its fundamentalist ontology will be disqualified as being contingent. And yet no individual human or nonhuman *is* for itself ever exclusively through the mere fact of being. Thus every step taken beyond this stasis is marked by both failure and legitimacy, irrelevant of its impact on other planes of ethical value.

Affirmation of Transhuman Justice

This leads us to the fourth variant: affirmation of transhuman justice. A critical turn to the immanent alterity within human law as a source of justice imaginary for nonhuman law can produce significant insight into both emancipatory claims and unarticulated justice reserves within human law. Predicating legitimacy on the endlessness of immanent justice alterity theoretically avoids the wilful blindness to our personal limitations within the economy of affirmation. The economy of affirmation is, if you will, the household management of all the affirmations that are available to our existing and reproduced subjectivity. It is what we reproduce ad nauseam without being able to step over its threshold.

Critical thinkers may come to believe that they float free from an economy of affirmation and sometimes they can achieve partial weightlessness. But if, when floating free, we simply affirm an alterity as a new economy of affirmation, we will reproduce antinomical overburdening and emancipatory disappointment. Emancipatory disappointment can be divided into (1) that which cannot change and will not "benefit" from emancipation; (2) that which is experienced as an emancipatory moment (by definition unsustainable); and (3) an *ex post* transformed state, which is both other to the outgoing, legacy subjectivity, but is also other to the emancipatory moment itself. Any emancipatory process needs to resource all of these disappointments to be sustainable.

In Cary Wolfe's affirmation of justice as *immanent* alterity, what is liminal to human law elides into nonhuman law. Wolfe writes:

> Here, then, the biopolitical finds a new vocation, precisely by sustaining and deepening the logic that already constitutes it—a logic that, if pushed far enough, breaks down the stark opposition between the thanatopolitical and the affirmative that has tended to paralyze biopolitical thought: either unconditionally embrace all forms of life as subjects of immunitary protection, or suffer the autoimmune consequences that follow. But what this either/or logic misses is that the performative structure and logic of immunitary indemnification is precisely the condition of possibility for any possible affirmation, thus opening the community to its others—potentially, all its others, wherein reside the inseparable possibilities of both promise and threat (2013, 103).

Imagining justice in this way subjects us to continuous antinomical overburdening, a product of the counter-facticity of the frame, expressed in an infinite regress of emancipatory disappointments. Thus the challenge to the fourth effort to embrace nonhuman law becomes how to devote resources to the externalities of emancipatory failure, including those of making the "right decisions." This problem can betray the project of justice no less than simply reproducing any existing justice imaginary. In fact, it carries with it the danger of a kind of emancipatory self-referentiality, overwhelming other threshold justice considerations, and turning the field over to *realpolitik* while producing a kind of meta-ethical aesthetic.

Nonetheless, proponents of the fourth variant who productively embrace this disappointment can paradoxically exceed the limitations of the second and third variants. The value of the most radical emancipatory claim can lie in its manifest implausibility, provided that implausibility is acknowledged. Doing so prepares for a fiduciary relationship to justice alterity. A fiduciary is by definition one who gives up her interests for the benefit of another. Fiduciary claims go even beyond the embrace of justice alterity by acknowledging the necessity of devoting resources to indeterminacy. A fiduciary is always in some state of failure toward the impossible goal of being entirely without conflict of interest. The fiduciary therefore maintains a relationship to the conflict of laws. In this way, since the effort to overcome the injustices of the conflict between human and nonhuman law involves making emancipatory claims, one comes to sense that understanding the link between resourcing emancipatory justice claims in all their antinomy and the indeterminacy of fiduciary relations produces a threshold signal for the justice aggregate to be produced.

However, achieving a fiduciary turn within the fourth variant is regrettably an unlikely outcome. There is no incentive for emancipatory actors who have embraced transhuman law to sublate the necessary inadequacy of their emancipatory claims, as those claims do paradoxically enable a form of seeming self-abnegation that apparently maps directly on to emancipatory justice. And it is this hypostasis of alterity to a new conventional human subjectivity that forms the basis for the economy of affirmation of such radical communities. Transhuman law generates a human law that is now newly in conflict with nonhuman law.

However, the profound but neglected fiduciary insight is that the leap of faith to radicalism is both a narcissistic failure as well as an invitation to explore what that failure can tell us about the limitations of our justice imaginary. The fourth variant requires such a continuous confrontation with its own inherent inadequacy. And its inadequacy will inherently reside in its production of human norms—unless, of course, it seeks to abandon normativity altogether, which will itself be its human law. In short, the emancipatory moment requires the resourcing of a continuous iterative process before which every actor fails. Failed radicals are not to be confused with radical failure. With adequate social resources, emancipatory failure is part of the feedback we need to work with and through iteratively as we approach justice alterity and indeterminacy. This is arguably the only way we can work through the conflict of human and nonhuman laws.

Conclusion: For a New Conflict of Laws Regime

Even the most promising effort to overcome the dichotomy of human and nonhuman law by positing the transhuman itself unfolds into a new conflict of laws. Of course the term "conflict of laws" is jarring because it invokes overlapping and unresolved claims to jurisdiction. It also stretches our legal imaginary since we have begun to imagine nonhuman subjects of human law but not agents of nonhuman law. Yet the mastery we have achieved of nonhuman law has not simply given us dominion over it. Rather, our extrinsic relationship to the boundary conditions of the biosphere and our intrinsic relationship to the biochemical determinants of our identity can suddenly invert the sovereignty of laws.

The idea of conflict of laws is premised upon the coexistence of sovereigns. It entails that humans discover techniques for recognizing overlapping norms and disentangling their contradictions. As humans reach the boundary conditions of the biosphere, we remain sorely tempted by the effort to extend human norms to it by placing a price upon what we do to approach the boundary. That is how we imagine fashioning an emissions regime, for example. As mentioned, the other kind of temptation to which we can succumb is that of affirming nonhuman law in place of human law. The conflict of laws regime we need is one that can respond iteratively to the inadequate responses of human law to nonhuman law. A form of communication is required. Signals must be sent and received. Fiduciary resources must be deployed.

Acknowledgments

The authors would like to thank Irus Braverman, Mireille Fournier, Caitlin McIntyre, Jean-Christophe Paré, and Andreas Philippopoulos-Mihalopoulos for their helpful comments.

Notes

1 Or at least we can say that the Stratigraphy Commission of the Geological Society of London is in the midst of determining whether to adopt the term "Anthropocene" and to accept formally that we are no longer in the Holocene. The Geological Society of America, for its part, has already declared its acceptance of the term (Zalasiewicz et al. 2008).

2 We are thinking of Schmitt (2003), but also of Derrida (1990). Derrida is far less enthralled by the relationship between law and violence.

3 We cannot here document how the passage of the Enlightenment involved severing our connection to nonhuman laws on the one hand by reconceiving them

as being internal to ourselves as natural law and on the other hand as placing them in the realm of facticity as physical laws. This is traced out in part by Horkheimer and Adorno (2002) and, differently, by Berman (1983).

References

Adorno, Theodor. 1973. *Negative Dialectics.* Trans. E.B. Ashton. New York: Continuum.

Bacon, Francis. 1815 [1620]. *Novum Organum Scientiarum.* In *The Works of Francis Bacon, Vol. 4.* London: M. Jones.

———. 1659 [1627]. *New Atlantis: A Work Unfinished.* London: Tho. Newcomb.

Berman, Harold J. 1983. *Law and Revolution: The Formation of the Western Legal Tradition.* Cambridge: Harvard University Press.

Bergoglio, Jorge Mario (Pope Francis) 2015. *Encyclical Letter Laudato Si' of the Holy Father Francis on Care for our Common Home.* Rome: Vatican.

Christian, David, Cynthia Brown and Craig Benjamin. 2013. *Big History: Between Nothing and Everything.* New York: McGraw-Hill.

Derrida, Jacques. 1990. "Force of Law: The Mystical Foundation of Authority." *Cardozo Law Review* 11 (5–6): 920–1045.

———. 1994. *Specters of Marx: The State of the Debt, the Work of Mourning, and the New International.* Translated by Peggy Kamuf. London: Routledge.

Donaldson, Sue and Will Kymlicka. 2011. *Zoopolis: A Political Theory of Animal Rights.* Oxford: Oxford University Press.

Esposito, Roberto. 2008. *Bíos: Biopolitics and Philosophy.* Translated by Timothy Campbell. Minneapolis: University of Minnesota Press.

Foucault, Michel. 2003. *Society Must Be Defended: Lectures at the College de France 1975–1976.* Translated by David Macey. New York: Picador.

Francione, Gary. 2008. *Animals as Persons: Essays on the Abolition of Animal Exploitation.* New York: Columbia University Press.

Hawking, Stephen and Leonard Mlodinow. 2010. *The Grand Design.* New York: Bantam Books.

Holt, Emily and Scott Miller. 2010. "Bioindicators: Using Organisms to Measure Environmental Impacts." *Nature Education Knowledge* 3 (10): 8.

Horkheimer, Max and Theodor Adorno. 2002. *Dialectic of Enlightenment.* Translated by Edmund Jephcott. Stanford: Stanford University Press.

Latour, Bruno. 1993. *We Have Never Been Modern.* Translated by Catherine Porter. Cambridge: Harvard University Press.

———. 2013a. *An Inquiry into Modes of Existence: An Anthropology of the Moderns.* Translated by Catherine Porter. Cambridge: Harvard University Press.

———. 2013b. *Gifford Lectures, Facing Gaia: A New Inquiry into Natural Religion.* http://www.ed.ac.uk/about/video/lecture-series/gifford-lectures.

———. 2014. "Agency at the Time of the Anthropocene." *New Literary History* 45 (1): 1–18.

Lehun, Richard. 2014. *The Emancipatory Justice Claim.* D.C.L. Thesis, Montreal: McGill University.

Massey, Doreen. 2004. "Geographies of Responsibility", *Geografiska Annaler, Series B, Human Geography, Special Issue: The Political Challenge of Relational Space* 86(1): 5–18.

Merchant, Carolyn. 1980. *The Death of Nature: Women Ecology and the Scientific Revolution.* San Francisco: Harper & Row.

Rockström, Johan, Will Steffen, Kevin Noone, Åsa Persson et al. 2009. "A Safe Operating Space for Humanity." *Nature* 461: 472–5.

Schmitt, Carl. 2003. *Nomos of the Earth in the International Law of the Jus Publicum Europaeum.* Translated by Gary L. Ulmen. New York: Telos.

Swartz, Norman. 1985. *The Concept of Physical Law.* Cambridge: Cambridge University Press.

United States Environmental Protection Agency (USEPA). 2006. "Life Cycle Assessment: Inventory Guidelines and Principles" (EPA/600/R-92/245). http://www.epa.gov/nrmrl/std/lca/lca.html.

Weisman, Alan. 2007. *The World Without Us.* New York: Picador.

Wolfe, Cary. 2012. *Before the Law: Humans and Other Animals in a Biopolitical Frame.* Chicago: University of Chicago Press.

Zalasiewicz, Jan, Mark Williams, Alan Smith, Tiffany Barry et al. 2008. "Are We Now Living in the Anthropocene?" *GSA Today* 18 (2): 4–8.

Chapter 10

Lively Agency: Life and Law in the Anthropocene

Andreas Philippopoulos-Mihalopoulos

Across the Continuum

To be lively is to be singular. In its turn, to be singular is to be connected. And to be connected is to be withdrawn. These are the premises of the present text. Let me explain briefly. Liveliness is a paradox. While it points to life in the sense of animate being, it must not be conceptualized as another tool for legitimation of animate versus inanimate hierarchies, and then for further internal, anthropocentric hierarchies amongst the animate. I am interested in expanding the concept of life to the inanimate, while not circumventing the animate. For this reason, I am linking liveliness to singularity, namely the absolute difference of each individual body. This absolute difference emerges under paradoxical conditions: each body, namely each singularity, is both "withdrawn" and gathered in itself (for how else would it be singular), and at the same time connected to other singularities (for how else could it carry on).

Unlike the rest of the chapters in this collection, I connect liveliness to every body, animate or inanimate. In this I follow the Spinozan/Deleuzian understanding of a body: "a body can be anything: it can be an animal, a body of sounds, a mind or idea; it can be a linguistic corpus, a social body, a collectivity" (Deleuze 1988, 127). As I show below, anything that connects in assemblages with other bodies, provided, I would add, that it withdraws simultaneously, is a lively body. I conceptualize liveliness as a cut across human and animal, temporality and spatiality, actual and virtual, and animate and inanimate. Lively is not alive, is not animistic, is not even vitalist. Lively is singularity in the midst of an ontological continuum, where distinctions are not made on the basis of predetermined categories (such as human/nonhuman or animate/inanimate) that feed into existing

Rupture in geological formation, Eilat Mountains, Israel. Photo by Irus Braverman, June 2015.

hierarchies; rather, distinctions *rupture* the continuum, emerging each time anew depending on the particular combination of bodies participating in it.

From the above, the concept and practice of agency emerges. In thinking about lively agency, I am drawing on discussions in postfeminism, material and spatial ontologies, and posthuman thinking, and linking them to a Deleuzian understanding of life. I am defining lively agency by stripping it down to its bare essential: *the ability of bodies (animate and inanimate) to withdraw in their singularity while connecting to other bodies.* Agency is not only a site of privilege but also of responsibility, which in what follows I define from a spatial–juridical perspective. Responsibility emerges in the space of law, which in its turn is folded with the way bodies arrange themselves in relation to other bodies. Lively agency, in other words, is the vessel through which the law emerges, since each body is responsible for its position in relation to the wider assemblage.

This is not an espousal of neoliberal individualism. Quite the contrary, it is a collectivization of responsibility that includes the various bodies participating in the particular conditions under which responsibility emerges. Humans are only one participant but also, as the Anthropocene has taught us, *always* a participant, always situated within the ecological conditions of our planet. For this reason I refer to a *situated* responsibility that a body bears as part of its liveliness. As Elizabeth R. Johnson writes in this volume, the Anthropocene points toward a *spatialization* of human presence and human responsibility. This new space reveals the paradox of the situation: humans find themselves both at the center of geologic change, and exposed to it. Human omnipotence is fragile. The law, in the form of channeling of responsibility toward facing the particular situations in which it emerges, offers part of the answer to the question of what life is. Thus, if the Anthropocene obliges us to situate ourselves in relation to our responsibility, the law's responsibility is to situate itself in relation to other bodies and their laws, whether human or nonhuman, as Richard Janda and Richard Lehun show in their chapter.[1]

In what follows, I map a continuum that consists of singularities. This continuum cuts across human and nonhuman, as well as animate and inanimate, bodies. Its main characteristic is its immanence—namely, that it has no outside. The continuum is not, however, uniform. It is continuously ruptured, thus allowing the emergence of singularities. Rupture and continuum are the main tools through which the notions of agency and responsibility are played out. The second part of my chapter draws on Deleuze's notion of a life, Spinozan ethics, and current postfeminist and posthuman material ontologies to explore what lively singularities are. Briefly put, lively singularities are bodies that are both connected to other bodies and withdrawn ontologically. This is the characteristic of the absolute difference of *a* life, namely the singularity of each life that cannot be compared to another life. From this, the concept of lively agency emerges, which is the focus of the third part of my chapter. Lively agency is characterized by the singularity of life in the above sense, yet its agency is not conferred by law, politics, or even society. Rather, it emerges from the very operation of a life, that is, once again, the paradox of connection and withdrawal. I define agency not as the *ability to act*, but rather as the *ability to be acted upon* by a life. It follows that an agent is never individual but always embedded in a collective, material and immaterial, animate and inanimate, assemblage. In the fourth and final section, I consider the juridical responsibility of the human in the face of the Anthropocene. In this context, responsibility is connected to the Deleuzian wound from which singularity surges, and refers to the indistinguishability between the bodies that populate the continuum. The principal aim of my contribution is to construct an ontological continuum onto which the positions of the various agents can be conceptualized, both connected and withdrawn, both indistinguishable from other bodies and singular. On this continuum, law emerges to regulate body positions vis-à-vis other bodies.

Lively Singularities

A life is a singularity. As a singularity, a life is absolute. It cannot be compared to other singularities. It is pure incommensurable difference, complete and self-enclosed: it is pure *immanence*. This means that there is nothing outside a life, no possibility of transcending a life onto something other, further, better, more just. This is not an objection to the usual theological constructions. Theological immanence is tight: for some religions this world and the next are in an immanent continuum. Buy now, pay later. Or act now, reap later. There is always some causality that brings this and that world together in an inescapable immanence. But here we are talking about a different immanence that has no gradations and cannot be attributed to individual deeds.

Gilles Deleuze has dedicated a short essay (and, incidentally, a lifework) to showing how a life is singularity. Written shortly before the end of his life, *Pure Immanence: Essays on A Life* (2001) understands pure immanence as unanchored to a subject, a being, or even a supreme being. Pure immanence cannot be understood through empirical connections between subjects or between subject and object, although one necessarily begins with them. But these need to be left behind in order to pass on to a life co-extensive with pure immanence: "The life of the individual gives way to an impersonal and yet singular life that releases a pure event freed from the accidents of internal and external life, that is, from the subjectivity and objectivity of what happens" (Deleuze 2001, 28). This is the passage from *the* life to *a* life, from *individuation* to *singularization*: "a man who no longer has a name, though he can be mistaken for no other. A singular essence, *a* life" (29).

A life has some unique characteristics. It is spatially everywhere, actualized in subjects and objects yet exceeding them. It is also temporally everywhere, but not continuously. Its everywhere-ness is ruptured and sharded in *entre-moments* ("between-times"). It is connected to *the* life in a parallel way: there is correspondence and coexistence but no connection in the traditional sense of causality or anticipation. *A* life is virtual, namely real but not actualized. It is pure potentiality, febrile future, pulsating present. Its virtualities become actualized through the bodies and objects of *the* life, but *a* life itself remains purely virtual, an event and a singularity. Finally, *a* life is preceded by a wound, which, as I show below, is neither an *a priori* nor an origin or a higher actuality.

I build on the idea of a life by Deleuze in order to contextualize liveliness in what I call the *continuum.* I have elsewhere (2014) defined the continuum as the surface that cuts across animate and inanimate objects, bodies, discourses and so on. This continuum is not equivalent to a flat ontology, nor to the vastness of the plane of immanence (Deleuze and Guattari 1988). Rather, it is a tilted, power-structured surface, on which bodies move, rest and position themselves, affecting the tilt while being affected by it. The continuum is influenced by Foucauldian biopolitics because its sovereignty is diffused and embodied in each participating body. It differs from the biopolitical, however, because it is characterized by the persistent erection of boundaries in the form of ruptures without predetermined ethical value. Ruptures can be both positive differences that encourage identity, as well as exclusions or hierarchies that discourage specific kinds of identity; they can be conflicts (necessary or engineered) as well as ontological 'gatherings' as I show below. Whatever they are, ruptures remain part of the continuum. Rather than annulling it, ruptures nourish the continuum, which can be thought of as a (continuous) series of ruptures. Finally, the continuum is entirely immanent, closed upon itself and without an outside.

In this ruptured continuum, a life's omnipresence runs through singularities and flushes them out. A life is what makes a singularity lively, as it were. Every singularity is a rupture of the continuum of immanence, without however rupturing immanence itself. There can only be immanent singularities, on the same plane as other singularities, sharing in a continuous becoming. Rosi Braidotti (2012; 2013), who has developed Deleuze and Guattari's ideas in a vitalist direction, understands life as a process of self-preservation. Braidotti goes beyond the classic distinction between *bios,* reserved for humans of a certain type only that tends to be the glorified cudgel of Enlightenment humanism; and *zoë,* which encompasses animal and nonhuman life (for the distinction, see Elan Abrell in this volume). It is indeed important to resist this distinction, not because it is not real but because it has been co-opted and instrumentalized in order to produce and legitimize further distinctions that lie in the core of exploitation of nonhuman species by humans: *zoë* in the service of *bios*, nonhumans in the service of the good human life.

For this reason, I revisit and criticize the distinction between animate and inanimate. The inclusion of the inanimate is where this chapter differs in relation to the rest of the volume. The contrast between *bios* and *zoë* is indicative not merely of anthropocentrism but of an omnipresent, movable, fractal boundary between hierarchically positioned (animate and inanimate) bodies, organized in some enlightenment-infused fantasy of harmoniously centralized imperium, where Man (masculine and capitalised) in the center dominates and determines all distinctions. *A* life is actualized in *bios* and *zoë*, but finds itself in a relation of continuum/rupture to them. *A* life cannot unfold through the distinction but through the unity of the distinction. A life is given to any body that, in its turn, is given to a life. It can blossom in an insect, a marine environment, a stone, or a planet. By attempting to redress the distinction between human and nonhuman, discussions on liveliness often bypass the distinction between animate and inanimate. Undoubtedly important, the former distinction is only a symptom of the latter. Treating the symptom is necessary. Treating the condition, however, is the task I have set myself.[2] While a discussion on this eschews the limits of the present text, it is important to clarify this: the use of the term *lively* in the present context relies on the understanding of *a* life that trammels every singularity. A life is not about consciousness, perception, or even a body, but about a *process* that occurs spatiotemporally and allows a singularity to emerge. A life is the operation of singularity that emerges along the only constituent element of the continuum: its rupture. A life, in other words, is the ruptured continuum brought forth in every singularity: the condition of simultaneous connection and withdrawal.

I would describe the focus of this collection as the quest for a life; all chapters share this preoccupation and struggle to determine it. I understand the focus on the animate as a necessary further rupture of the quest for *a* life, itself folding out in numerous ruptures, one of which is also the animate/inanimate. In its turn, even the animate becomes ruptured in classifications and lists, which, as Irus Braverman shows in this volume, also need to be questioned. In other words, every battle is worth fighting, since every one of them fractally affects the assemblage of battles around it.

The issue of withdrawal is one of the points of difference between what I propose here and current understandings of assemblage thinking, be they Latourian networks, vitalist flows, or other new material ontologies. Unlike Bruno Latour (2005), my understanding of withdrawal is a quality that does not contradict but rather enables assemblage formation. Just as the continuum is made of ruptures, and just as ruptures are continuous, in the same way withdrawal and assemblage clustering are not dialectically opposed values. There is no difference, only parallel folding of one into the other. Every singularity assembles itself in larger bodies while at the same time withdrawing from the ontology of the assemblage. Withdrawal has been referred to by Deleuze and Guattari (1988) in the context of their discussion on Nietzsche, where the movement was linked to the schizophrenic and her revolutionary potential. This is a *strategic* understanding of withdrawal, in the sense of a machine that goes against issues of identity, origin, causality, and other enlightenment cudgels. But there is also another, complementary way of thinking about withdrawal. In his work on Leibniz, Deleuze (2006) refers to the famous formula of the monad as "no windows." There is no opening in Leibniz's monad. A monad is "an inside without outside" (Deleuze 2006, 31). Every body is a closure that withdraws from full openness, connectivity or exteriority, and into a monadic singularity that is gathered around its need for perpetuating this singularity. Its openness rests on its closure. Assemblage rests on withdrawal.

In his work on Latour, Graham Harman positions himself in similar terms by writing that "objects are not defined by their relations: instead they are what enter into relations in the first place. Objects enter relations but withdraw from them as well; objects are built of components but exceed those components. Things exist, not in relations but in a strange sort of vacuum from which they only partly emerge into relation" (Harman 2009, 132). The above shows that objects (here: bodies) withdraw not just from each other but also from themselves. This is the crux of the foundational unknowability of bodies: a body never fully presents itself to itself. In that sense, withdrawal is ontological. The world is what each body makes of it. But this is not relativism or subjectivism. The world withdraws as much as the body withdraws. "Nothing 'points' toward anything else or bleeds into anything else. Everything withdraws into itself" (Harman 2009, 113).

I have so far set the basis for the ontological continuum onto which the concept of agency emerges. To sum up: first, the continuum is continuously ruptured, separating bodies from other bodies, allowing them to withdraw to their own absolute difference. Second, the above paradox is embodied in each body that constitutes the continuum (therefore, *every* body, since the continuum is immanent). A body, therefore, is by definition part of *a* life, namely the process of connection and simultaneous separation, regardless of whether it is animate or inanimate, material or immaterial. On the basis of these two propositions, the following section attempts to sketch an understanding of lively agency as emergence.

Lively Agency

The original term that Deleuze and Guattari employ for assemblages is *agencements*. This gives a clearer idea of the kind of role envisaged for the gathering of singularities. As the editors of *New Materialisms* Diana Coole and Samantha Frost write, we have moved away from an epoch where

> agents are exclusively humans who possess the cognitive abilities, intentionality, and freedom to make autonomous decisions and the corollary presumption that humans have the right or ability to master nature. Instead, the human species is being relocated within a natural environment whose material forces themselves manifest certain agentic capacities and in which the domain of unintended or unanticipated effects is considerably broadened (2010, 10).

One can take this further: there can no longer be a pre-given boundary between a body and its environment. The whole point of assemblages is that they are bodies themselves (perhaps larger and more complex but still bodies) that necessarily include their "environment," whether "natural" or otherwise. A body is an assemblage of various conditions and materialities. Eben Kirksey's multispecies families in this volume is an example of such an assemblage containing human and animal bodies, discursive bodies of economics, politics and law, conservation agencies, wildlife experts, government agents and hobbyists, the spatiality of Florida, affects from gentleness to aggression, and so on. The total sum of these connections constitutes a body that is internally ruptured in an infinity of modalities (Morton 2013). Rigid separation between bodies is an epistemological construct, perhaps even a necessity, according to the foundational fantasy of distinction between self and environment, as Teresa Brennan (2004) writes. And, yet, as we have seen, every body withdraws.

Agency emerges when, at an *entre-moment* between connection and withdrawal, a life becomes singled out. Agency is grabbed from the vast immanence of a life and donned by a singularity at the height of this singularity's withdrawal. *An agent is not someone who acts, but someone who is acted upon by a life.* Agency emerges from within, at the moment where singularity gathers itself to produce itself. At that moment, a body becomes infinite in its withdrawing isolation, so infinite that it includes the vastness of a life. This is the paradox of distance and immersion, of withdrawal and connectivity, of singularity and assemblage. An agent is a body withdrawn and at the same time assembled in infinite connectivity.

Karen Barad (2006, 175) has introduced the term "agential separability" to signal the need for boundaries between bodies. These boundaries are not placed as fixed constructions between subject and object, human and animal, or indeed animate and inanimate. Rather, they emerge in order to produce meaning relative to the continuum on which the boundary appears. I understand this as the rupture of withdrawal that brings agency forth without flattening it to an all-connected ontology. It is significant that these boundaries are not conceptualized as either prior or immutable: they are drawn every time as part of the emergence of agency. This is the foundational paradox: bodies are singular because they withdraw from the assemblage, and they can only be part of an assemblage because of their withdrawing.

Both assemblaging and withdrawing come from *conatus*, the Spinozan term (in turn inspired by Hobbes) for the striving to affirm and maintain oneself. Moira Gatens and Genevieve Lloyd put it thus: "the endeavour or struggle to persist in being" (Gatens and Lloyd 1999, 26). The term *conatus* has been used and developed extensively and in a juridical way by Deleuze:

> the *conatus* defines the *right* of the existing mode. All that I am determined *to do* in order to continue existing (destroy what doesn't agree with me, what harms me, preserve what is useful to me or suits me) . . . all this is my natural right. This right is strictly identical with my power and is independent of any other ends, of any consideration of duties, since the *conatus* is the first foundation, the *primum movens*, the efficient and not the final cause (1988, 102).

By building on Spinoza's understanding of power as the affect between bodies that become stronger or weaker as a result of encountering each other, Deleuze brings down *conatus* to a juridical–ontological category, a body's *right*. Deleuze adds another decisive aspect in his reading of *conatus*, and this is the immeasurable and excessive *conatus*. The conative excess is the reason for which every body withdraws. The vastness of the conative machine, always overflowing the body itself and affecting all others, renders a body immeasurable. Immeasurability is at the core of ontological withdrawal: no body ever presents itself fully ontologically. Even *conatus* exceeds itself. In other words, conative striving and withdrawal are one and the same. The *conatus* is a tool of a life, itself excessive and immeasurable, beyond prescription yet instrumental in the emergence of agency. It follows that to be an agent is an ontological condition, a body's *right*, a condition of a life. This is why we can talk about *lively agency*.

To repeat, lively agency is not an effect of an agency-giving social system (such as the law or politics or the state) but an emergence from within an assemblage (Lenco 2012) that includes law or politics or other social institutions in its assembled body. The body does not have a pregiven agentic outline. Deleuze (2013) writes: "the limit of something is the limit of its action and not the outline of its figure." Agency is an open emergence, each time differently positioned in relation to its constituent elements. Karen Barad (2012, 54) puts it clearly: "Agency is not held, it is not a property of persons or things . . . is not about choice in any liberal humanist sense; rather, it is about the possibilities and accountability entailed in reconfiguring material-discursive apparatuses of bodily production, including the boundary articulations and exclusions that are marked by those practices." Agency, in other words, unfolds in the continuum, taking up forms that are co-determined with this very continuum while rupturing it.

To summarize, lively agency is an always already emergence that does not depend on an agency-giving institution. It emerges between connection and withdrawal of each body (which means, each assemblage, each collectivity) as the *right* of the particular body to perpetuate its *conatus*, namely to carry on existing. In that sense, agency is an ontological condition. Not merely a privilege, but a responsibility, as I show below.

Responsibility in the Anthropocene

The emergence of law in an assemblage, at least at first instance, renders an agent legal. This is the way one can think of agency in terms of Bruno Latour whereby agency can be attributed to any object (actant) in a network of relations. Simply put, if an actant has an effect on another, then agency is established. In that sense, agency is merely the ability to act, or actancy (Latour 2005; Law 2009). To describe an agent as legal denotes nothing more than a "legal" network of actants operating in what can be constructed as a legal environment. Despite this initial openness, in his work on the French Conseil d'Etat (2009) Latour found a rather limited legal agency, embodied in files, courtrooms, and so on, but not so much in terms of the broader life of the law. This tendency to return to a standard, text-based materiality of the law has encountered resistance from legal materialists (Pottage 2012; Philippopoulos-Mihalopoulos 2014b). Let me therefore broaden the conceptualization of legal agency in order to include the more "hidden," less "institutionally vouched-for," legalities.

I will start with a rather simple hypothesis: if an agent orients itself in a way that its assemblage includes legal positions (from basic claiming of rights to adhering to legal obligations, to going through a legal procedure, to intentionally disobeying the law), then the legality of the agent would seem to become predominant, and one could talk about a *legal* agency. However, this is only partly true. First, in terms of temporality since nothing remains settled for long in an assemblage: bodies move around and assume different positions, velocities, and directions. Second, in terms of unitary characterization: law is simply one of these positions, directions, and bodies, part of an assemblage, that may or may not pull or push an assemblage in a certain, more obviously legal direction. A house whose ownership is disputed at a court case will not stop being a building, a home, a nest for birds, an economic unit, an outlet of electric energy and so on while the court case is carried out. This means that it will *also* be a legal agent, while retaining other sorts of agency. But the real question is this: can an agent ever *not* be legal? Is the above, standard understanding of the law-in-court or law-as-statute the only space of law?

To put this even more radically, is there a space without the law, inhabited by a body that is not related in some way or other to the law? This is an extensive and well-rehearsed discussion, captured by the ambiguous but catchy "the law is all over" articulated by Austin Sarat (1990). I have discussed the omnipresence of the law elsewhere (2014a), and I have also sketched out the basics of legal material agency (2014b); so here I will limit myself, somehow axiomatically, to two points (but see the discussion in Adam Reed's chapter, this volume). First, there can be no agency that is not legal. In this sense, the law is not linked to humans but to the material positioning of various bodies in relation to others. This is the *lawscape*, namely the ontological tautology between matter and law (Philippopoulos-Mihalopoulos 2014a). This is not some sort of legal supremacist point but, rather, a point of legal banalization. Just as any other body, the law crops up in assemblages alongside other bodies, and informs the way bodies position themselves. The same can be said about economy, politics, science, religion, and so on. But this does not amount to an eradication of the other bodies that partake in the assemblage.

Second, an agent becomes *predominantly* legal, meaning that it is immediately recognized by other bodies as first and foremost of the legal system, when the emergence of the law within the assemblage is connected to a life. Let me recall the final characteristic of a life, which is the wound: "A wound is incarnated or actualized in a state of things or of life; but it is itself a pure virtuality on the plane of immanence that leads us into *a* life. My wound existed before me: not a transcendence of the wound as higher actuality, but its immanence as a virtuality always within a milieu (plane or field)" (Deleuze 2001, 31).

The wound is the juridical moment of a life. It is inseparable from the body, yet belongs to the virtual pure immanence of *a* life. It emerges at the gashing *entre-moment* of *the* life of the body in a mundane, everyday way as a rupture; but points to the vastness of the continuum that trammels everything. The wound needs to be embodied to be understood, but its embodiment does not exhaust it. In *What is Philosophy*, Deleuze and Guattari write: "my wound existed before me; I was born to embody it" (Deleuze and Guattari 1994, 159). This is neither fatalistic, nor transcendental. It emerges from the body itself. This is the law: the wound at the beginning, the arch-rupture. This wound makes a body cry for the law. The body nurtures its own actualized and embodied wound, its very own rupture, in the form of a life whose actuality is dealt by the law (and, as often, also inflicted by the law).

At the same time, however, the body reaches out toward the pure virtuality of the wound. "I was born to embody [the wound] as event because I was able to disembody it as a state of affairs or lived situation" (159). This disembodiment is the reaching out for the virtuality of the law: the call for justice. Interestingly, this is also the kind of justice sought by Barry, an animal welfare charity's officer, who is the focus of Adam Reed's chapter in this volume. Reed places justice outside the law because the desire for it is driven by moral outrage and compassion, in turn feeding legal strategies. Its placement outside the law follows Barry's own positioning as affected by his understandable mistrust toward the law. However, to seek justice outside the law is to succumb to the old semantics of a justice that exceeds the parameters of the assemblage in which it emerges. To talk about justice in a transcendental or even universal way does little more than re-embodying the wound as *impossibility* of justice. Law might indeed be "an ass," in Barry's words (this volume, 111); but it is the common wound of a life and, as such, it is the only law we have. It is only through this law that justice can be sought, not outside it. Although pure virtuality, this is a non-transcendental justice. Rather, it is an immanent justice, namely a justice determined by the conditions of the particular assemblage in which it emergences. Justice can only come about through law.

The wound is already here, embodied by every body like an original sin. Its name is the Anthropocene, the geological epoch determined by the (over)presence of a single species on earth: the human. The term was coined by Crutzen and Stoermer in 2000, and has become the source of a cross-disciplinary debate on the repercussions of both the name and the idea of a separate geological era. The wound is being inflicted by humans on the surface of the earth, but also embodied by humans and the whole earth—for, as mentioned earlier, there is no meaningful boundary between humans and environment, and the Anthropocene is the living proof. While waiting for the 2016 International Geological Congress to decide on whether we are in a new epoch, and whether it can indeed be called the Anthropocene, an authoritative cluster of 14 geologists led by Jan Zalasiewicz have announced that "some types of anthropogenic changes may now be compared with those of 'the great forces of Nature'" (Zalasiewicz et al. 2011, 1037). The surface of the earth has changed, both lithostratigraphically (i.e., geologically proper) and biostratigraphically (i.e., the strata produced by animate beings):

> Anthropogenic modification of sedimentary patterns comprises both modifications to natural sedimentary environments (such as the damming or straightening of rivers and coastal reclamation) and the creation of novel sedimentary environments and structures (such as the construction of cities and anthropogenic deposits); these are not entirely separate categories, but are to some extent inter-gradational. In detail, they are diachronous, reflecting the spread of human activity across the Earth (ibid., 1038).

The only position left to assume is that of responsibility. No longer able to hide behind a benevolent anthropocentrism or a well-wishing ecocentrism, the human is de facto placed in the center of the wound. But how to redescribe things in a way that neither absolves a body from the responsibility of situating itself, nor inebriates this body with the illusion of control of the assemblage, or indeed the whole world if we are talking about human-centered bodies? The question of the *anthropocenic* responsibility is this: how to take advantage of the human omnipresence and not be fooled by the superficial impression that to be *everywhere* equates to being *central* to everything (Chandler 2013). It is clear that responsibility now becomes *situational*: it is the juridical responsibility of situating one's body within an assemblage. Responsibility needs to be thought of as *extended*, namely both material and unrestricted by the immediate or the local. Doreen Massey (2004, 9) puts this as "the Russian Dolls issue of care and responsibility: we always begin with the proximate, home, and then move outwards. But care diminishes as we move out." We might think we try to be "responsible" about our presence in a locality, even a locality that "thinks globally," as the motto goes. But the problem is much vaster. Timothy Morton (2013, 140) writes: "the problem goes beyond how to dispose of human-sized things, like the stuff that gets flushed down a toilet. What should we do about substances on whose inside we find ourselves?"

This gives rise to what I would call the *responsibility of indistinction*, which refers to the ontological indistinguishability between bodies. Before I explain this, one clarification: indistinguishability is not annulled by the rupture of singularity. Ruptures do not disband the ontological continuum, nor however do they fix it in immutable hierarchies. They are not Foucauldian "caesuras within the biological continuum addressed by biopower" (Foucault 2003, 255). Ruptures can be organized politically to serve different masters, but are inherently amoral. Their ontology is one with the continuum: every body emerges into a life, quickens into a lively agency, assumes its situated juridical responsibility. The ontology of indistinction is translated juridically as the inability to distinguish. This is the source of a responsibility that extends spatially and temporally across bodies: future generations but also fossilized past, as Kathryn Yussof writes in her work on fossils in the Anthropocene:

> The assumption is often that something of one (mineral) passes to the other (life), but that this crossing is a one-way street until death fossilises life, returning it to mineral. . . But what if the relationship has other paths in which the geologic criss-crosses corporeality not only to make fossils per se, but also to mobilise specific modalities of geologic life? (Yussof 2013, 786).

This criss-crossing is only one of the avenues in which Yussof questions existing conceptualizations and hierarchies of life. Her deep inquiry into the forms of life accepted as "lively" that include what would be considered inanimate (such as fossils), are invariably connected to "forms of responsibility and inheritance (in a genealogy of concepts of the human and the propagation of these forms into the future)" (2013, 786). This is both a material and a discursive responsibility and refers to the way a body (material, immaterial, of discourse) situates itself in relation to the assemblage.

Yussof's concept of responsibility goes further than Latour's argument that everything can be an actant/agent, because it refers to specific responsibilities linked to the *situational* emplacement of each body. Karen Barad (2006, 393) writes: "we (but not only 'we humans') are always already responsible to the others with whom or which we are entangled, not through conscious intent but through the various ontological entanglements that materiality entails." We are all responsible because we are all situated in a continuum of indistinction. Yet, human responsibility must be heightened: being indistinguishable does not mean being the same in terms of power. Assemblages are bodies, and each body, individually or collectively, has some power (and responsibility) to move the assemblage in specific directions. Some bodies have more power than others—and this applies to human bodies in relation to nonhuman or inanimate bodies (and then some human bodies in relation to other human bodies). This is emphatically not a neoliberal discourse. It is not about one's individual, or even collective, freedom to decide one's own fate. If there is freedom in it, it is a Spinozan freedom, namely the *necessity* of self-actualization of each body, rather than an expression of free will. Since every body is part of the continuum, freedom is the actualization of one's situatedness within that continuum, as mediated by that continuum. This is a distinctly *collective* freedom (Braidotti 2013) that operates as the enabling bondage of the responsibility of being situated with regards to other bodies. Freedom is a responsibility, and the responsibility of freedom is to unveil the illusion of freedom (in the sense of free will) and allow this to inform our knowledge of the causes for which bodies move the way they do. No body decides its own fate, not because there is a teleology that determines it, but because a body is part of a continuum (Spinoza 2000, Part IV).

In the legal context, there are prejudices that count more than formal law. There is formal law in the service of corporations. Some bodies weigh more, whether they are a corporation, a billionaire, a religion or a tsunami. This means that not every body is equally able to act and react. This, however, also means that the old categories between "the powerful" and "the weak" are just that: old categories in the service of existing structures. When we eternally recycle these categories (and others, such as private/public, us/them, north/south, formal/informal), we remain with the problem. Of course there are inequalities. But it is much more complex than this. To retain distinctions of this sort (such as the ones who decide as opposed to the ones whose fate is decided) is an abstraction in the service of the distinction itself. All bodies are part of an assemblage, and while one is always determined by the structures, one is also able to move this assemblage, including the structures.

This is not always a peaceful process. Kathryn Gillespie in this volume eloquently shows how animal resistance is a spontaneous affect that differs from the equivalent human affect, and pushes the assemblage of property relations in such a way that can inform the human reaction to it, in turn altering the positioning of the various bodies in the assemblage. It is true that some bodies manage to move assemblages more efficiently than others. This does not necessarily happen because they are more powerful, but because the rest of the assemblage allows them to move in such a way. A body is not necessarily able to change the assemblage just because it is an individual agent or even a multitude (Hardt and Negri 2001). But a body can organize itself in relation to the rest of the assemblage, in turn in relation to the world, and in turn in relation to a future.

Will this be a future or *a* future? Claire Colebrook (2014, 30) writes: "the anthropocene thought experiment also alters the modality of geological reading, not just to refer to the past as it is for us, but also to our present as it will be without us. We imagine a viewing or reading in the absence of viewers or readers, and we do this through images in the present that extinguish the dominance of the present." Human extinction is a possibility ontologically included in the Anthropocene, and epistemologically required. Jean-François Lyotard (1993, 11) spoke about the *inhuman* already in the 1980s: "Human death is included in the life of human mind. Solar death implies an irreparably exclusive disjunction between death and thought: if there's death, then there's no thought. Negation without remainder. No self to make sense of it. Pure event. Disaster. All the events and disasters we're familiar with and try to think of will end up as no more than pale simulacra."

Solar death is one way, death by human is another. Whatever it is, the Anthropocene asks of us to consider the earth without us. In order to do this, we need to reach for *a* future, from where we can glimpse at our *inhumanity*. In other words, the responsibility in the epoch of the Anthropocene is one of *withdrawal*: withdrawing from the present in order to read it as inhuman future; withdrawing from centrality while retaining omnipresence; withdrawing from ourselves in order to read our traces. In withdrawing, human bodies learn to situate themselves in a position of responsibility, "embedded in geologic temporalities (rather than just as authors of them) . . . beyond the narrow confines of 'our' humanism and historicity into inhuman beginnings, and beyond biological materialism into thinking better with different geologic materialisms" (Yussof 2013, 785).

Admittedly, this is not an obvious place to conclude. The challenge of imagining new ways of assuming that responsibility, as well as fleshing out the existing ways in which this responsibility is already embodied, is considerable. But it is an interesting precipice, at which point the rest of this collection can enter and populate the horizon. For, in a way, this is precisely what the collection offers. The perspectives here trace *a* life that is both absolutely singular and connected to other bodies. Many of the chapters refer to specific animals, often by name, acknowledging the way lively agency springs up in the *entre-moment* between singularity and connectivity (from life-threatening moments as Gillespie, Abrell, and Reed show, to moments of quotidian repetition in the case of Braverman, Kirksey, and Bear), and finally solidifying this to embodied gestures of juridical responsibility, whether seen from the narrow understanding of textual legality, as Abrell has shown in terms of administrative law; the broader legal understanding of governance, as Johnson has done in the context of jellyfish; or the vastness of nonhuman legality in the case of Janda and Lehun.

What I have attempted to show in this chapter is simply this: that every body is fleshed out by the singularity of a life and, as such, flourishes into the position of a lively agent, whether animate or inanimate. The immediate consequence of this is that no body is exempted from the juridical responsibility that comes with being part of the continuum. This responsibility, which originates in the indistinguishability between bodies, weighs heavier on human shoulders because of the privileged position on the otherwise tilted, power-determined flat ontology of the continuum.

Acknowledgments

My thanks to all the participants of the *More-than-Human Legalities* workshop at the Baldy Center for Law & Social Policy, Buffalo, New York, for the many valuable discussions. Special thanks to Elan Abrell for his careful critique of my previous draft; very special thanks to Irus Braverman for her immaculate organization, meticulous editing, and generally for being herself.

Notes

1 However, I respectfully disagree with their notion of nonhuman law as transcendent. As I try to show, nothing transcends the immanence of the juridical responsibility of a body.

2 This task has been attempted by Jane Bennett's (2010) vibrant materiality for example, which only to some extent kept a distance from vitalism. The focus of her book *Vibrant Matter* is greatly on animate matter (with exceptions, such as the grid of objects, which is, however, still intimately connected to the animate).

References

Agamben, Giorgio. 1998. *Homo Sacer: Sovereign Power and Bare Life*. Translated by Daniel Heller-Roazen. Stanford: Stanford University Press.

Barad, Karen. 2006. *Meeting the Universe Halfway: Quantum Physics and the Entanglement of Matter and Meaning*. Durham: Duke University Press.

———. 2012. "Matter Feels, Converses, Suffers, Desires, Yearns and Remembers: Interview with Karen Barad." In *New Materialism: Interviews and Cartographies.* Edited by Rick Dophijn and Iris van der Tui, 48–70. Ann Arbor: Open Humanities Press.

———. 2014. Invertebrate Visions: Diffractions of the Brittlestar." In *The Multispecies Salon.* Edited by E. Kirksey, 221–241. Durham: Duke University Press.

Bennett, Jane. 2010. *Vibrant Matter: A Political Ecology of Things.* Durham: Duke University Press.

Braidotti, Rosi. 2012. *Nomadic Theory.* New York: Columbia University Press.

———. 2013. *The Posthuman.* Cambridge: Polity Press.

Brennan, Teresa. 2004. *The Transmission of Affect.* Ithaca and London: Cornell University Press.

Chandler, David. 2013. "The World of Attachment? The Post-Humanist Challenge to Freedom and Necessity." *Millennium: Journal of International Studies* 41: 516–35.

Colebrook, Claire. 2014. *Death of the PostHuman: Essays on Extinction, Vol. 1.* Ann Arbor: Open Humanities Press.

Coole, Diane and Samantha Frost. 2010. *New Materialisms: Ontology, Agency and Politics.* Durham: Duke University Press.

Deleuze, Gilles. 1988. *Spinoza: Practical Philosophy.* Translated by Robert Hurley. San Francisco: City Light Books.

———. 2001. *Pure Immanence: Essays on A Life.* Translated by Anne Boyman. New York: Zone Books.

———. 2006. *The Fold: Leibniz and the Baroque.* Translated by Tom Conley. London: Continuum.

———. 2013. "Cours Vincennes: Sur Spinoza, 17.02.1981." Translated by Leopold Lambert. In *The Funambulist Pamphlets 01: Spinoza.* Edited by Leopold Lambert, 73–5. Brooklyn, NY: Punctum Books.

Deleuze, Gilles and Felix Guattari. 1988. *A Thousand Plateaus: Capitalism and Schizophrenia.* Translated by Brian Massumi. London: Athlone Press.

———. 1994. *What is Philosophy?* Translated by Hugh Tomlinson and Graham Burchell. New York: Columbia University Press.

Foucault, Michel. 2003. *Society Must Be Defended: Lectures at the College de France 1975–1976.* Translated by David Macey. New York: Picador.

Gatens, Moira. 1996. *Imaginary Bodies: Ethics, Power and Corporeality.* London: Routledge.

Gatens, Moira and Genevieve Lloyd. 1999. *Collective Imaginings: Spinoza, Past and Present.* London: Routledge.

Harman, Graham. 2009. *Prince of Networks: Bruno Latour and Metaphysics.* Melbourne: re.press.

Hardt, Michael and Antonio Negri. 2001. *Empire.* Cambridge, MA: Harvard University Press.

Latour, Bruno. 2005. *Reassembling the Social: An Introduction to Actor-Network-Theory.* Oxford: Oxford University Press.

———. 2009. *The Making of Law: An Ethnography of the Conseil D'Etat.* Cambridge: Polity Press.

Law, John. 2009. "Practising Nature and Culture: An Essay for Ted Benton." In *Nature, Social Relations and Human Needs: Essays in Honour of Ted Benton.* Edited by Sandra Moog and Rob Stones, 65–82. Basingstoke: Palgrave Macmillan.

Lenco, Peter. 2012. *Deleuze and World Politics.* London: Routledge.

Lorimer, Jamie. 2012. "Multinatural Geographies for the Anthropocene." *Progress in Human Geography* 36 (5): 593–612.

Lyotard, Jean-Francois. 1993. *The Inhuman.* Cambridge: Polity Press.

Massey, Doreen. 2004. "Geographies of Responsibility." *Geografiska Annaler, Series B, Human Geography, Special Issue: The Political Challenge of Relational Space* 86 (1): 5–18.

Merleau-Ponty, Maurice. 1995. *Phenomenology of Perception.* Translated by Colin Smith. London: Routledge.

Morton, Timothy. 2013. *Hyperobjects: Philosophy and Ecology after the End of the World.* Minneapolis: University of Minnesota Press.

Philippopoulos-Mihalopoulos, Andreas. 2014a. *Spatial Justice: Body Lawscape Atmosphere.* London: Routledge.

———. 2014b. "Critical Autopoiesis and the Materiality of Law." *International Journal of Semiotics of Law* 27 (2): 165–77.

Pottage, Alain. 2012. "The Materiality of What?" *Journal of Law and Society* 39 (1): 167–83.

Sarat, Austin. 1990. "'. . . The Law is All Over': Power, Resistance and the Legal Consciousness of the Welfare Poor." *Yale Journal of Law and Humanities* 2 (2): 343–80.

Spinoza, Baruch. 2000. *Ethics.* Translated by George Henry Radcliffe Parkinson. Oxford: Oxford University Press.

Yussof, Kathryn. 2013. "Geologic Life: Prehistory, Climate, Futures in the Anthropocene." *Environment and Planning D: Society and Space* 31 (5): 779–95.

Zalasiewicz, Jan, Mark Williams, Richard Fortey, Alan Smith, et al. 2011. "Stratigraphy of the Anthropocene." *Philosophical Transactions of the Royal Society A: Mathematical, Physical and Engineering Sciences* 369: 1036–55.

Afterword

Lively Ever After: Beyond the Cult of Immateriality

David Delaney

> Men should stop fighting among themselves and start fighting insects.
>
> —Luther Burbank

> If all mankind were to disappear, the world would regenerate back to the rich state of equilibrium that existed ten thousand years ago. If insects were to vanish, the environment would collapse into chaos.
>
> —Edward O. Wilson

As the chapters of *Lively Legalities* demonstrate, there are multiple ways of looking at the interrelations between law and life. One way assumes that what we call law, no matter how capacious our definition, is—like poetry, religion, and science—an endeavor that is solely within the domain of human practice. The laws of nature, as Janda and Lehun discuss in their chapter, were so named based on analogy. But I would differ from Janda and Lehun in suggesting that natural or nonhuman laws are more than homonyms; they are elements of a two-way metaphor. To those who borrowed the term it must have appeared as though the physical world were indeed "governed" by "rules" that could be stated propositionally and to which obedience is perfect. One might speculate that having become conventionalized subsequent jurists borrowed it back so as to capture the aspirations of certainty, systematicity, and perfect obedience that underpinned the desire for a genuine legal science.

But, borrowing aside, the two legalities are not at all the same. Human law, henceforth "law," is a historical, cultural phenomenon. It is made and continually re-made. It is a means for attempting to accomplish distinctively human desires and to forestall distinctively human fears. The vast and

A fly. Photo by Richard Bartz, licensed under CC BY-SA 2.5 via Wikimedia Commons, https://commons.wikimedia.org/wiki/File:Schwarze_Habichtsfliege_Dioctria_atricapilla.jpg#/media/File:Schwarze_Habichtsfliege_Dioctria_atricapilla.jpg.

divergent ways of constructing legalities: Roman, Chagga, Diné, medieval Japanese, Soviet, liberal–neoliberal, and so forth, offer evidence of the enormous range of desires and fears that may find distinctively legal expression. They also suggest something of the plasticity of law and its involvement in *homo sapiens*' continuous world-making projects. Much of what is most commonly thought of as law is propositional: it is seemingly made out of language—with *its* own discoverable laws and rules. And even as its discursivity may account for its seemingly infinite mutability, law sees only what language permits it to see and is blind to what language occludes. As a discursive phenomenon it is intrinsically communicative—namely, it is made by and for human beings and its propositions are directed at other human beings for their comprehension and compliance. Many of law's propositions are thus concerned with how human beings should engage with each other with respect to other-than-human forms of life.

As a distinctively human creation, law—and more specifically, modern law, "our" law, the only kind of law under discussion in this volume—has its own peculiar dispositions and conceits. Among these is a strong tendency to valorize the imagined immaterialities associated with particular conceptions of mind and mindedness. It is this conceptualization of immateriality, essentially the repurposed soul, that metaphysical dualists have relied upon to construct the hundred hierarchies that purport to diagram modern truths: mind/body, human/animal, human/nature, subject/object and their many permutations. In accordance with these hierarchies, circuits of power have been instituted and activated and worlds have been assembled, disassembled, and re-assembled. I'll call this the cult of immateriality.

By the cult of immateriality, I do not simply mean merely the belief in non-material entities such as mind, thought, soul, or spirit. These are unexceptional elements of all cultural formations. Rather, I mean the default assumptions that: 1) only self-named *homo sapiens* and gods (et cetera) have access to the immaterial; 2) exclusive access is sufficient to secure the absolute primacy of humans in the earthly realm; and 3) this primacy justifies domination over those excluded as well as their reduction to instruments of will or to the status of resources. Further, it pre-supposes, without argument, that knowing and reasoning are the "highest" mental faculties, that only humans are capable of knowing, and that all of what is real is, in principle, knowable and expressible in human language, including mathematics. The cult of immateriality is a cult in so far as it is based on unassailable fundamentalist assumptions that are, of course, unknowable. They are articles of faith. Could this system of belief, when coupled with the technological capabilities associated with the present era, have resulted in anything other than the Anthropocene? The cult of immateriality finds clear expression throughout law. Law is both its catechism and one of its primary means of dissemination and indoctrination.

Many of the chapters of *Lively Legalities* trace the effects of the cult of immateriality on, in, and through the material world. We can and perhaps should think of law as a complex and dynamic human artefact through which the cult of immateriality conditions *how homo sapiens* configure relations of power amongst themselves and thereby *how* they engage with and transform the material world, especially those entities who live. So much depends upon these "hows." Within the conventions of modern law, and of language and culture more broadly, other-than-human entities, living or not, may be *topics* of legal utterances—but no more than that. The cult of immateriality disqualifies them as anything other than objects.

But our time, the time of the Anthropocene, is also shaping up to be something of a golden age of anti-dualism. The same circumstances that have given rise to this proposed re-periodization of (un)natural history have also inspired the arrival of this golden age. The chapters gathered together in this volume may be part of a broader cultural shift that could be as significant in its way as is the Anthropocene itself. Humans are re-thinking themselves in the most fundamental ways with the most profound *potential* consequences. As we do so, we are required to re-think the legal and what law could be. The task is nothing less than to imagine how it should work should it become "de-programmed" out of the cult of immateriality. Many of us have become acutely and urgently aware that thought, forms of consciousness, ideologies, those manifestations of human social being called culture, and even the grammatical structures of language itself—have all contributed to the epoch-defining cataclysm called the Anthropocene. At the same time, this awareness brings with it the inescapable recognition that thought and language are *also* the *only* means available for mitigating if not reversing the future consequences of the catastrophe. This is not a paradox.

The chapters of *Lively Legalities* exhibit a wide diversity in topics, foci, and style. As a whole, the volume offers different and possibly incommensurable conceptions of life, of law, and of the interconnections between the two. Some are less concerned with legalities, while others take the legal as their primary focus of attention. This is the result, in part, of the novelty and openness of the task assigned, but also of disparate commitments, areas of expertise, and styles of inquiry. Each chapter emerged out of the life of its creator; this is part of what makes the collection *lively*. All the chapters are provocative and insightful. Taken as a whole, the volume presents the reader with a wide array of interpretive resources to advance the necessary re-thinking of what law and life have to do with each other and of how, as humans, we can think the life of law differently. Many of the chapters describe how law *now* conditions the ways in which differently situated humans (although all inhabiting liberal legal regimes) engage with nonhuman forms of animate life and the consequences of these engagements for other-than-human lives.

Not surprisingly, many chapters attend to the mysteries of liberal "property": their deployment in the service of the reduction of nonhuman modes of life to thinghood and the resultant legitimated subordination of these lives to the desires and fears of particular possessive subjects also referred to as "owners." Tony the tiger, Myrtle the macaw, Yvonne the cow, the bludgeoned crows in Scotland: each, though differently, is fixed or figured in relation to property. Property, like kinship, is a cultural meaning system. It is a grid of distinctively legal intelligibility, consisting of a field of signifiers that blankets the world. Liberal property connects objects to subjects through the ascription of rights and no-rights. But this type of property is not only about how subjects and objects are related, nor is it about how subjects relate to each other with respect to objects. Liberal property is constituted by the state, which both allocates power through the allocation of rights and also obligates itself to protect and enforce these rights against threats to the subject's desires. Furthermore, the state assumes a default position of normative neutrality with respect to the owner's intentions and desires. Concerning units of living property—you may torture them or kiss them as you desire; law is largely indifferent to *how* life is subordinated through property to the will of the minded legal subject. Each reduction of life is another mundane sacrifice to the cult of immateriality. Even the project of re-wilding or de-domesticating requires the accomplishment of "un-owning." As Lorimer demonstrates, the conceptual and practical constraints of property make these projects more difficult and ambiguous than a simple relinquishing of rights might suggest. And even so, these projects are *also* acts of will facilitated by legal means in the furtherance of human desire.

The contradictions of de-propertization, or "un-owning," and the decoupling of animal life from the whims of individual humans reveal the effects of another fundamental sense-making binary of liberal thought: the property/sovereignty distinction. When un-tethered to the will of the "owner," most forms of other-than-human life will be positioned within the net of legal signifiers and practices associated with the sovereign prerogatives of management and regulation. Of course, living property is subject to regulation; there are limits on what owners can do to or with other life forms. But, as both Abrell and Kirksey show, these limits are often little more than nominal. And so it is that the super-proliferation of life in the form of swarming jellyfish, a situation linked to the cascade of human-induced ecological destabilizations, becomes a management problem, and the condition of indiscriminately defecating seagulls becomes the occasion for heightened monitoring, measurement, and warning. These events register as problems of too much of the wrong kind of life or of the undesirable consequences of the fact that to live is to shit.

Braverman's chapter examines the technologies of life-management at a general level. She convincingly argues for the importance of the regulatory device that is the list. Generic forms of life are made meaningful and interpretable through the complex practices of listing. Nearly all kinds of animals, she writes, are, "relegated to the realm of biological life—namely, that which is killable" (this volume, 20). The Red List re-positions some, few, as no longer killable because already killed more than enough. Forms of life that are acknowledged as threatened or endangered with existential erasure by the antecedent operations of law become worthy of concern. In other words, these concerns become authorized, sovereign concerns. Those listed become worthy of state expenditure and protection. De-listing, of course, changes their legal meaning and re-positions them within webs of power that re-render them killable.

Lively Legalities shows, then, how the ontological grid of human/other-than-human combines with the distinctively legal grids of property/sovereignty and private/public so as to situate forms of life within authorized vectors of power. As a result of these operations, manifestations of these forms of life appear (to humans) to be the bearers of legal signifiers. Human agents assign and interpret these signs and act in relation to each other with respect to these forms of life (appropriately or not). But this view of law is still underwritten by the cult of immateriality. These forms of life may be more than extra-legal things upon which legal signifiers are projected and made meaningful.

Another way of thinking about law asks us to consider that such "things" are not simply objects *about* which law has something to say. Renouncing the cult of immateriality facilitates a fuller appreciation of the materiality of law itself. Law not only gives expression and support *to* the cult of immateriality, it is commonly imagined as *instantiating* its virtues. One says, "There ought to be a law!" One speaks of "the letter and spirit of the law." The fundamental truths of law are revealed by reason. "Real" law, positive law, is commonly understood primarily as interpretable text, as constellations of propositions, categories, syllogisms, rules, as linguistic expressions of thought. Even notions such as legal ideology and legal consciousness position law as primarily within the metaphysical domain of the immaterial.

The boundaries of what counts as "law" are essentially contested. The shift from formalist legal science to sociological jurisprudence and the expansion from law as text (law on the books) to law as behavior (law in action) was a reworking of the boundaries of law that had been secured by the distinction between the legal and the social. In our time the boundary between the immaterial and material dimensions of law is likewise being dissolved. We can come to recognize that other-than-human bodies, their enactments (flying, shitting, swarming, floating, scurrying, kicking, panting, kissing) and their distinctive modes of living in their worlds are material elements *of* the legal *as such*. Each bit (molecule, cell, organism, habitat, biome, etc.) and the ways in which they combine and change through the processes we call "life" are not, after all, other-than law. They are the manifestations of law. Law is what it is and does what it does as a result of precisely *how* it is materially manifested in the world. The materiality of the legal is most easily apprehended with respect to distinctively "legal things" such as bullets, seals, documents, barbed wire, courtrooms. Law can no more be what it is without its distinctive assemblages of things than can music or science or medicine without their things. Music, for example, is not only the sequence of sounds in the composer's imagination nor is it the remembered melody in the minds of those who heard it. It requires strings, reeds and membranes to vibrate in order to become manifest in the sensual world. So too, law is not only idea, principle, syllogism. It requires materialities in order to manifest as a presence in the world.

But here law *is* different from, say, science or music, because *every* "thing" is always potentially a legal thing in so far as it is positionable within the signifying grids of property and sovereignty. The body is a legal thing, the uterus is a legal thing, the city is a legal thing, the ocean is a legal thing. Through the incorporation of things into the dynamic networks of social relations of power law could be understood as animating the inanimate. Certainly, those owned things that are commodities or the components of commodities or the resources from which commodities are derived are put into motion through the circulatory effects of markets. However, as *Lively Legalities* demonstrates, *living* things are also incorporated into the webs and circuits of law. As they are, then perhaps law is, in a real sense, re-animated. Living legal things participate in the life of law. Human and other-than human forms of life are the bearers of law's sensory, and not only symbolic, manifestation in the world.

Among the possibilities raised by the chapters of *Lively Legalities* is that the *world* is now a legal thing, that *life as such* has become a legal thing. It is certainly the case with respect to cows, pigs and dogs; to tigers, rhinoceroses, rats, and Karner blue butterflies, and to the countless forms of life, animate, and sessile, to which zoologists, botanists, and mycologists have yet to assign names. The idea of the Anthropocene has powerfully focused attention on the irreversible entanglements of human, desire-driven processes with the processes associated with the atmo-, bio-, hydro- and litho-spheres. But the argument can be made that the term Anthropocene is imprecise, and perhaps even misleading. Not all members of "anthros" are equally responsible for the conditions the term seeks to capture. Likewise, it is generally recognized that these conditions arose with the peculiar, contingent and metastatic social processes associated with the emergence of modernity and capitalism. One might, with greater accuracy and precision, refer to it as the Capitalocene, the Modernocene, and even the Liberalocene. Likewise, *had* law been significantly different during these last few (from the perspective of life, extraordinarily brief) centuries or decades, then the world and its life dynamics would *also* be profoundly otherwise than they are. As legal scholars, then, we could, with justification, refer to the dawning epoch as the "Nomocene." The conditions of irreversible entanglement are not only a function of technological capacity but also of the particular allocation of social relational power as given expression in the notions of rights and no-rights, duties and no-duties, privileges and immunities. It is not only a matter of *can* (be physically capable) but of *may* (be allowed, encouraged, protected). The pesticides developed, marketed, applied; the fossil fuels extracted, marketed, burned; the coastal zones developed; the habitats eliminated, the ocean floors scraped; the junk disposed of—were all underwritten by how law has been done these last few generations. Now, some of this is regulated and some is prohibited. This is important. But the distinctively legal entanglements are irreversible. Every scrap of trash in the North Pacific garbage patch, every molecule of atrazine in the soil and atom of mercury in the clouds, every grain of sand pumped into fracking wells was once an owned thing. This, per Philippopolous-Mihalopolous, is what it means to say that the law is all over.

But if, under conditions of modernity, the world has become a legal thing, this thing is indeed a *lively* thing. As a result of these processes, law has become a worldly thing in ways that are qualitatively and quantitatively different than what had been the case before modernity had the potential to invade every cell and molecule. In the Nomocene, there is very little of life-as-singularity that is not affected by what we call law. The legal and the lively seem to be irreversibly entwined. The normative issue that animates many of the chapters of *Lively Legalities* may be framed by the questions: can that human-made (and human-making) phenomenon we call law be re-made in such a way as to be more respectful of the millions of other-than-human forms of life? If the cult of immateriality fosters thoughtless thinking, can its renunciation promote more mindful ways of being minded—even if ours are not the only minds that matter?

Notes on Contributors

Elan Abrell

Elan Abrell is a PhD candidate in Anthropology at the CUNY Graduate Center and holds a JD from UC Berkeley School of Law. His dissertation, "Saving Animals: Everyday Practices of Care and Rescue in the US Animal Sanctuary Movement," is based on ethnographic fieldwork conducted at several US animal sanctuaries.

Christopher Bear

Christopher Bear is Senior Lecturer in Human Geography in Cardiff University's School of Planning and Geography. Through studies of fisheries and dairy farming, his research examines relations between humans, animals and technologies. He has published in journals including *Environment and Planning D*, *Cultural Geographies*, and *Journal of Rural Studies*.

Irus Braverman

Irus Braverman is Professor at SUNY Buffalo Law School. She is the author of *Planted Flags: Trees, Land, and Law in Israel/Palestine* (2009), *Zooland: The Institution of Captivity* (2012), and *Wild Life: The Institution of Nature* (2015), and co-editor of *The Expanding Spaces of Law: A Timely Legal Geography* (2014).

David Delaney

David Delaney teaches in the department of Law, Jurisprudence and Social Thought at Amherst College. He is the author of a number of books, including *Law and Nature* (2003) and *The Spatial, the Legal and the Pragmatics of World-Making: Nomospheric Investigations* (2010) and a co-editor of *The Expanding Spaces of Law: A Timely Legal Geography* (2014).

Kathryn Gillespie

Kathryn Gillespie is a geographer at the University of Washington dedicated to interrogating structures of power and privilege related to nonhuman animal lives, bodies and deaths. Her forthcoming book, *The Cow with Ear Tag #1389*, is about the lives and labors of cows in the US dairy industry.

Richard Janda

Richard Janda is an Associate Professor in the Faculty of Law, McGill University in Montreal, Canada. He teaches environmental law, sustainable development, business associations, and administrative law. He is the Project Director for the Myko Social Score Platform, which is producing a real-time impact score for our daily personal and collective choices.

Elizabeth R. Johnson

Elizabeth R. Johnson is a human geographer with the Science Technology and Culture Lab and Department of Geography at the University of Exeter. She writes on life and labor in the making of bio-inspired technologies. She is presently writing a book manuscript entitled *Life's Work: Biomimesis and the Politics of Productivity*.

Eben Kirksey

Since completing his Ph.D. at UC Santa Cruz in 2008, Eben Kirksey has published two monographs: *Freedom in Entangled Worlds* (2012) and *Emergent Ecologies* (2015), and one edited collection: *The Multispecies Salon* (2014). Writing in collaboration with Stefan Helmreich, he coined the phrase "multispecies ethnography."

Richard Lehun

Richard Lehun studied under Jürgen Habermas, and wrote his Magister Artium on Adorno's *Negative Dialectics*. He then completed a BCL / LLB, and a DCL at McGill University, while a Visiting Researcher at Harvard Law School. Lehun's current research is on fiduciary law applied to social transformation.

Jamie Lorimer

Jamie Lorimer is an Associate Professor in the School of Geography and the Environment at the University of Oxford. His research explores the history, politics and geographies of nature conservation. He has conducted field-work in several European locations and in South Asia. In 2015, his book *Wildlife in the Anthropocene: Conservation after Nature* was published by the University of Minnesota Press.

Andreas Philippopoulos-Mihalopoulos

Andreas Philippopoulos-Mihalopoulos is Professor of Law & Theory, and founding director of The Westminster Law & Theory Lab, University of Westminster. He is author of *Spatial Justice: Body, Lawscape, Atmosphere* (2014) and editor of *Law and Ecology: New Environmental Foundations* (2012).

Adam Reed

Adam Reed is a Senior Lecturer in Social Anthropology at the University of St. Andrews. His research includes fieldwork conducted in Papua New Guinea and the United Kingdom, and ranges between legal anthropology, anthropology of ethics, anthropology of the city, and anthropology and literature.

Cary Wolfe

Cary Wolfe's books include *What Is Posthumanism?* (2010) and *Before the Law: Humans and Other Animals in a Biopolitical Frame* (2012). He holds the Bruce and Elizabeth Dunlevie Chair in English at Rice University, where he is Founding Director of 3CT: The Center for Critical and Cultural Theory.

Index

For Product Safety Concerns and Information please contact our EU representative GPSR@taylorandfrancis.com Taylor & Francis Verlag GmbH, Kaufingerstraße 24, 80331 München, Germany